PETER CANNON

THUNDERBOLT

DYNAMITE

"It feels like something new. **Something different.**
And even more, a series with something to say"

– MULTIVERSITY COMICS

"This is a more worthy successor to Watchmen than anything
Watchmen's publisher has attempted"

– COMICBOOK.COM

"One of the smartest books being published.
This is a creative team on fire, making ambitious comics that you'd only dream of seeing."

– ADVENTURES IN POOR TASTE

"It's a miracle that Peter Cannon: Thunderbolt
packs as many ideas as it does into 20 pages and still has space for beats like this"

– NEWSARAMA

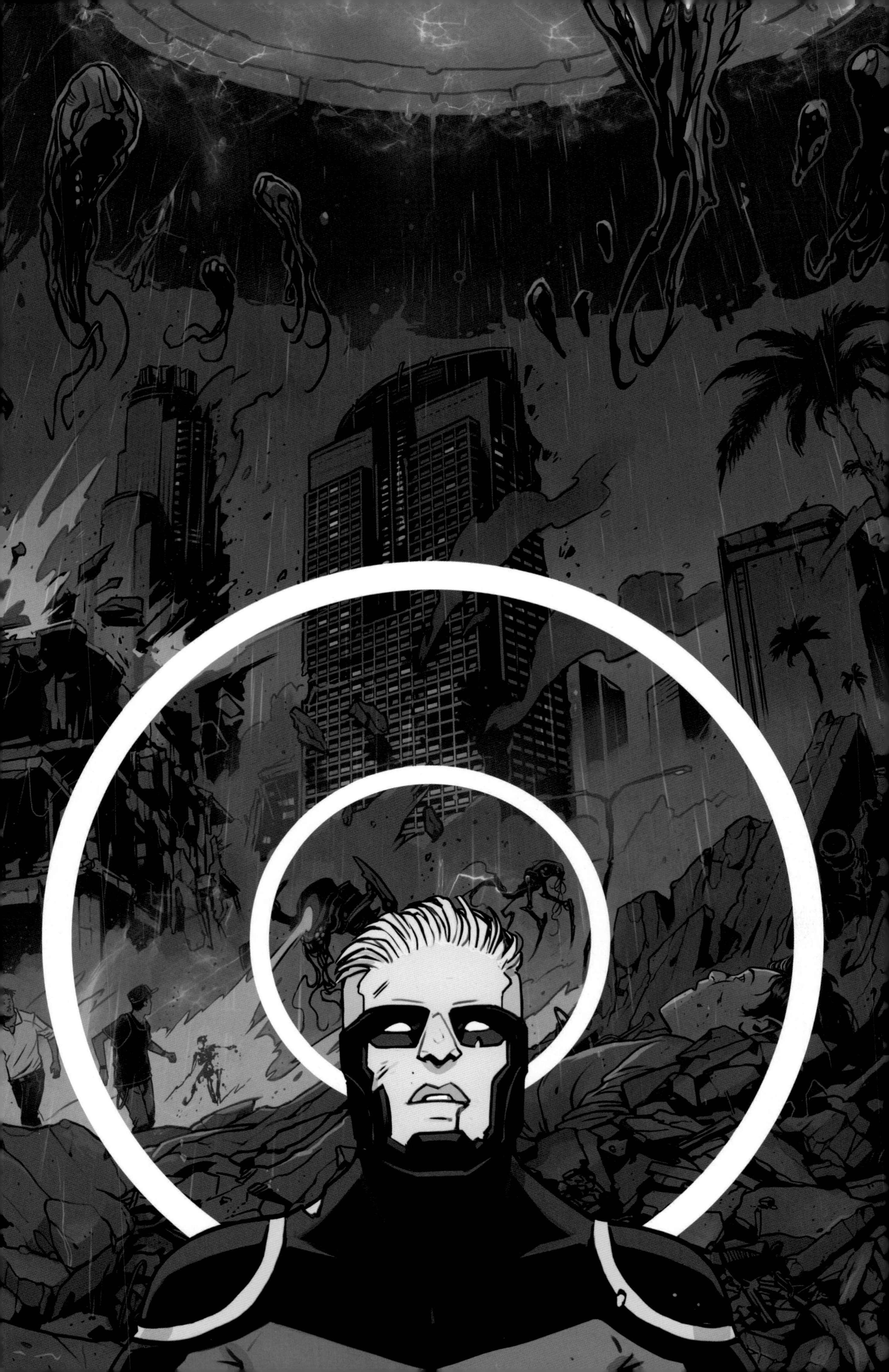

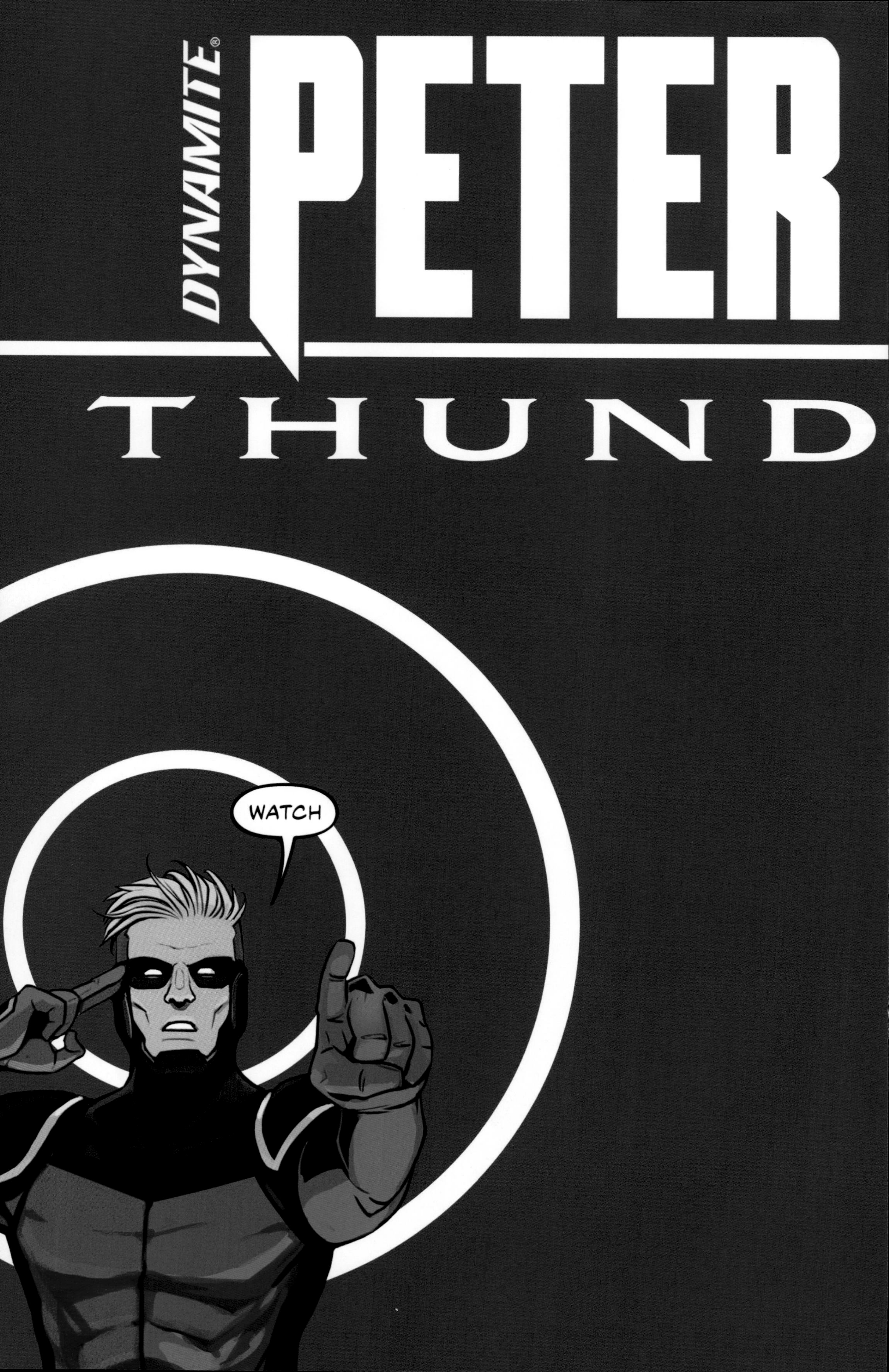
DYNAMITE
PETER
THUND
WATCH

CANNON
~~TH~~UND~~E~~RBOLT

Writer **KIERON GILLEN**

Artist **CASPAR WIJNGAARD**

Colorist **MARY SAFRO**

Letterer **HASSAN OTSMANE-ELHAOU**

Editor **MATT IDELSON**

Associate Editor **KEVIN KETNER**

Creator **PETE MORISI**

Collection Designer **GEOFF HARKINS**

Collection Cover Artist **CASPAR WIJNGAARD**

DYNAMITE®

Nick Barrucci: CEO / Publisher
Juan Collado: President / COO
Brandon Dante Primavera: V.P. of IT and Operations

Joe Rybandt: Executive Editor
Matt Idelson: Senior Editor
Kevin Ketner: Editor

Cathleen Heard: Art Director
Rachel Kilbury: Digital Multimedia Associate
Alexis Persson: Graphic Designer
Katie Hidalgo: Graphic Designer

Alan Payne: V.P. of Sales and Marketing
Rex Wang: Director of Consumer Sales
Pat O'Connell: Sales Manager
Vincent Faust: Marketing Coordinator

Jay Spence: Director of Product Development
Mariano Nicieza: Director of Research & Development

Amy Jackson: Administrative Coordinator

Online at www.DYNAMITE.com
On Facebook /Dynamitecomics
On Instagram /Dynamitecomics
On Twitter @dynamitecomics

Standard ISBN-13: 978-1-5241-1279-0
Signed Edition ISBN: 978-1-5241-1374-2

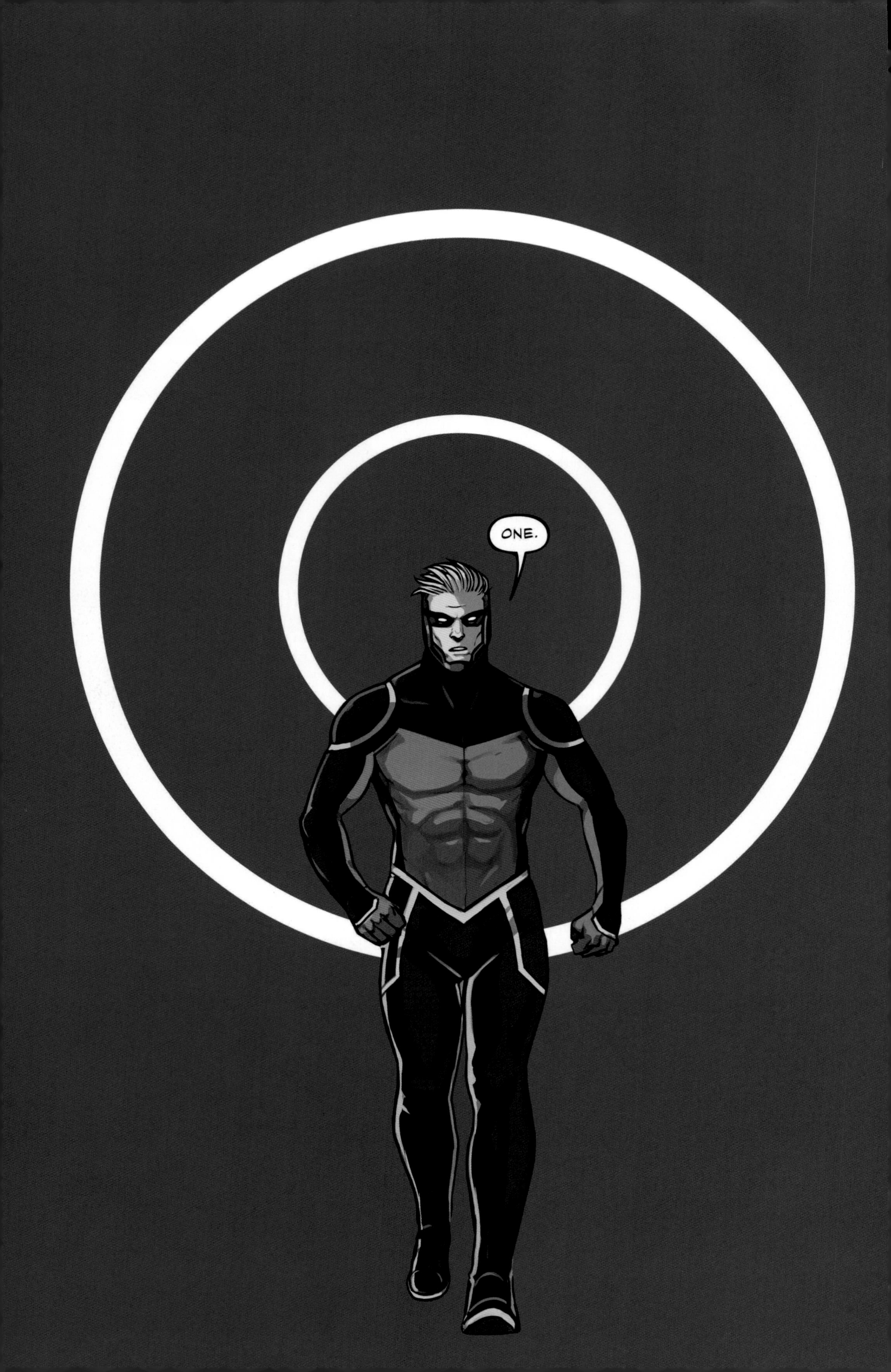
ONE.

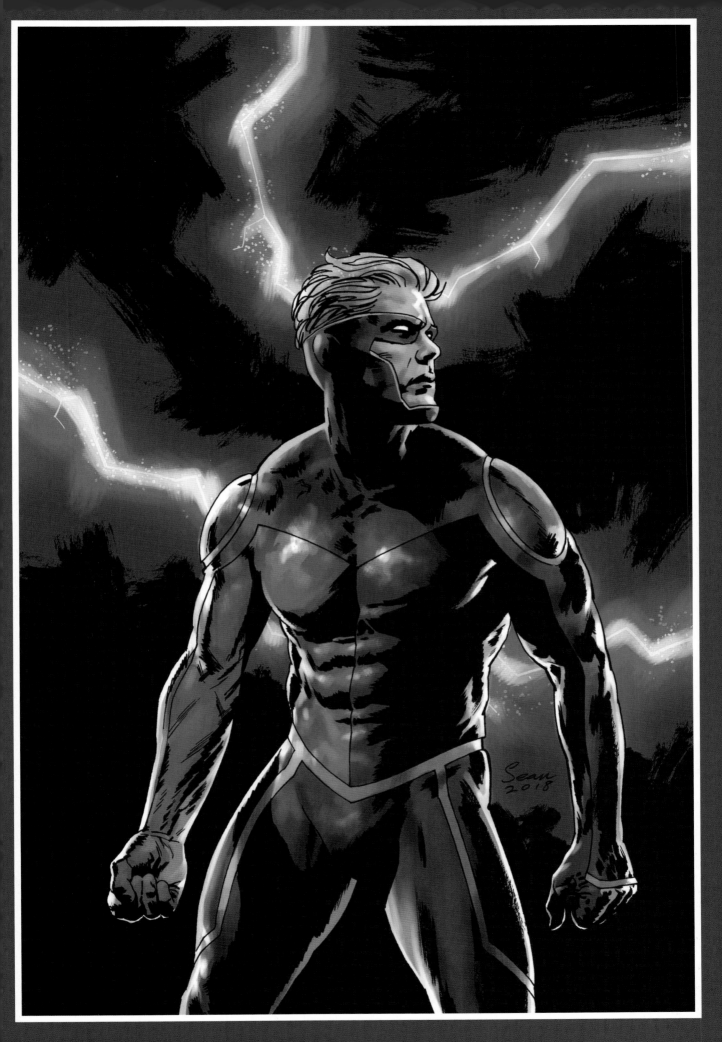

ISSUE ONE COVER BY **SEAN PHILLIPS**

It's 35 minutes into the future.

Relations between nations spiral ever downward.

War, for so long distant, seems possible, even probable.

Our heroes are impotent.

Most people thought it couldn't get worse.

Most people lack imagination.

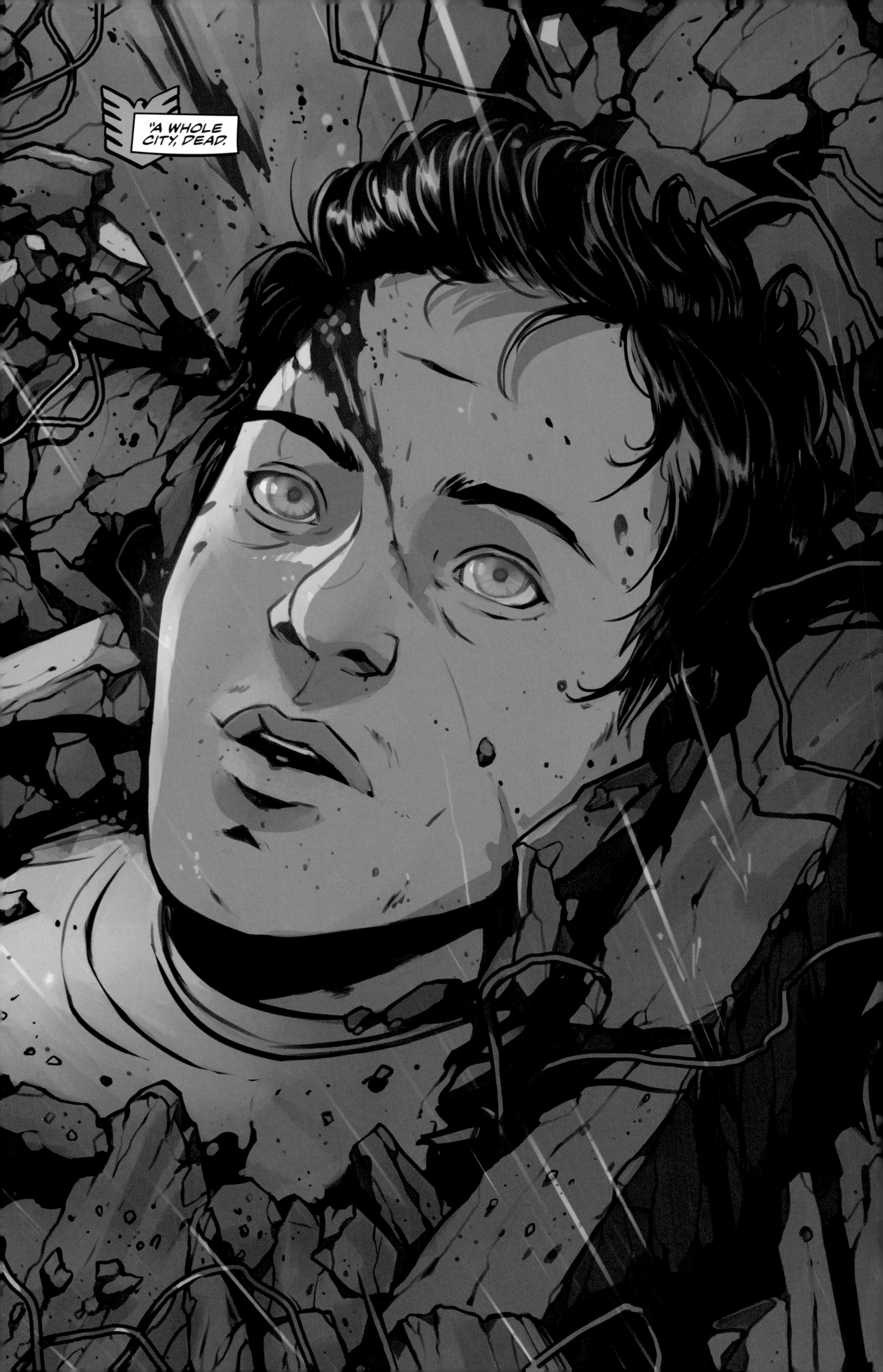
"A WHOLE CITY, DEAD.

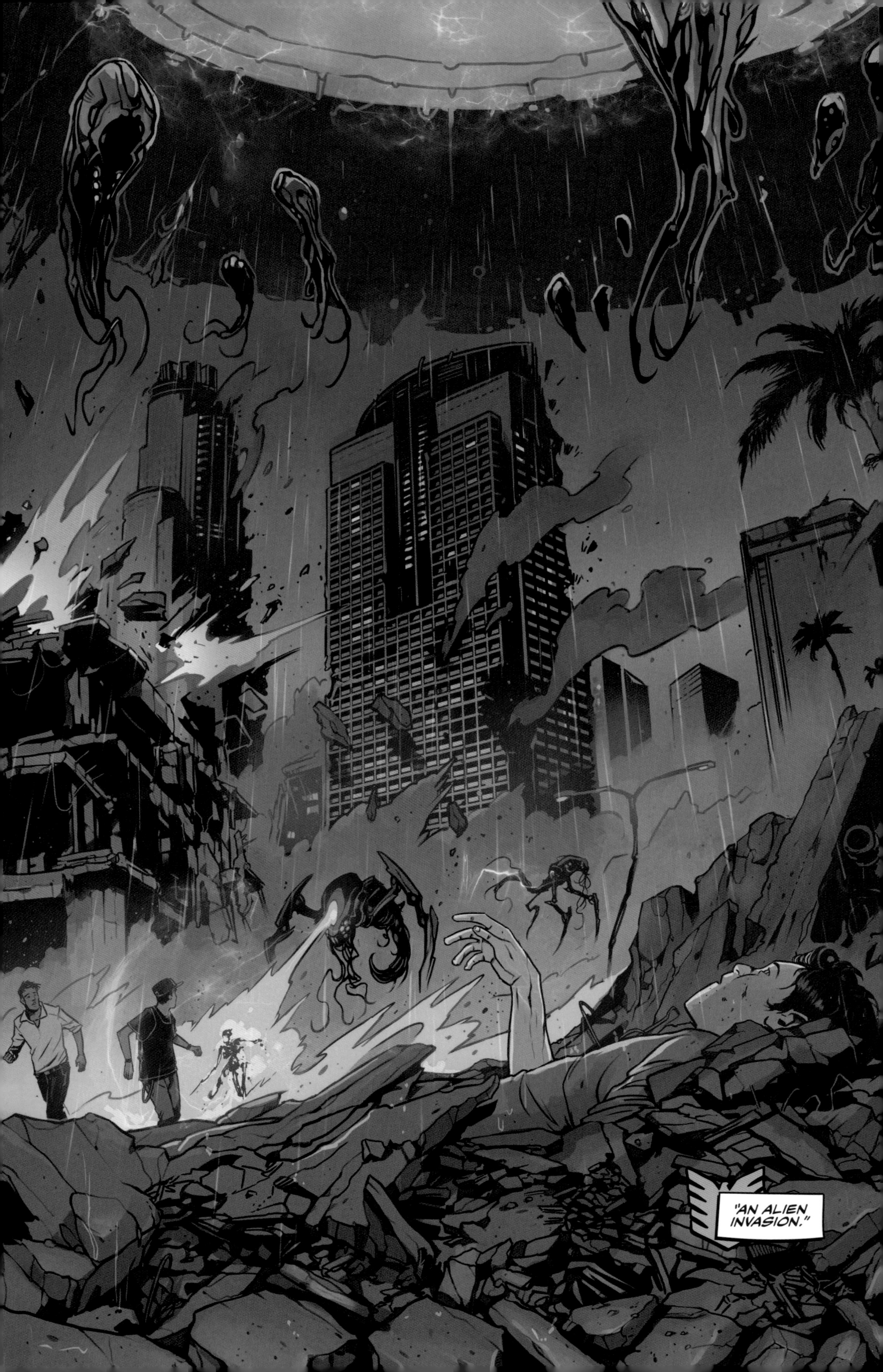
"AN ALIEN INVASION."

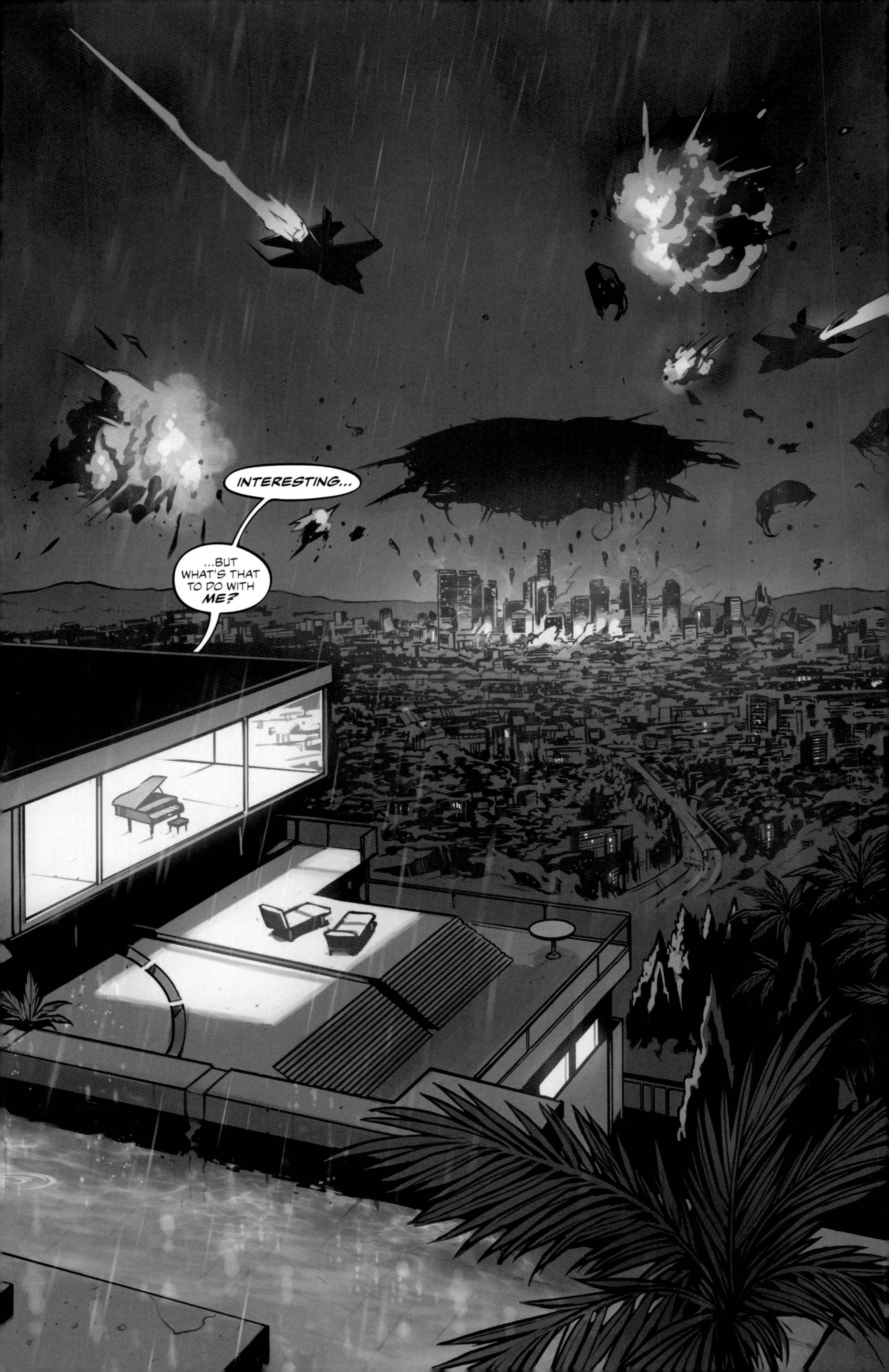
INTERESTING...
...BUT WHAT'S THAT TO DO WITH ME?

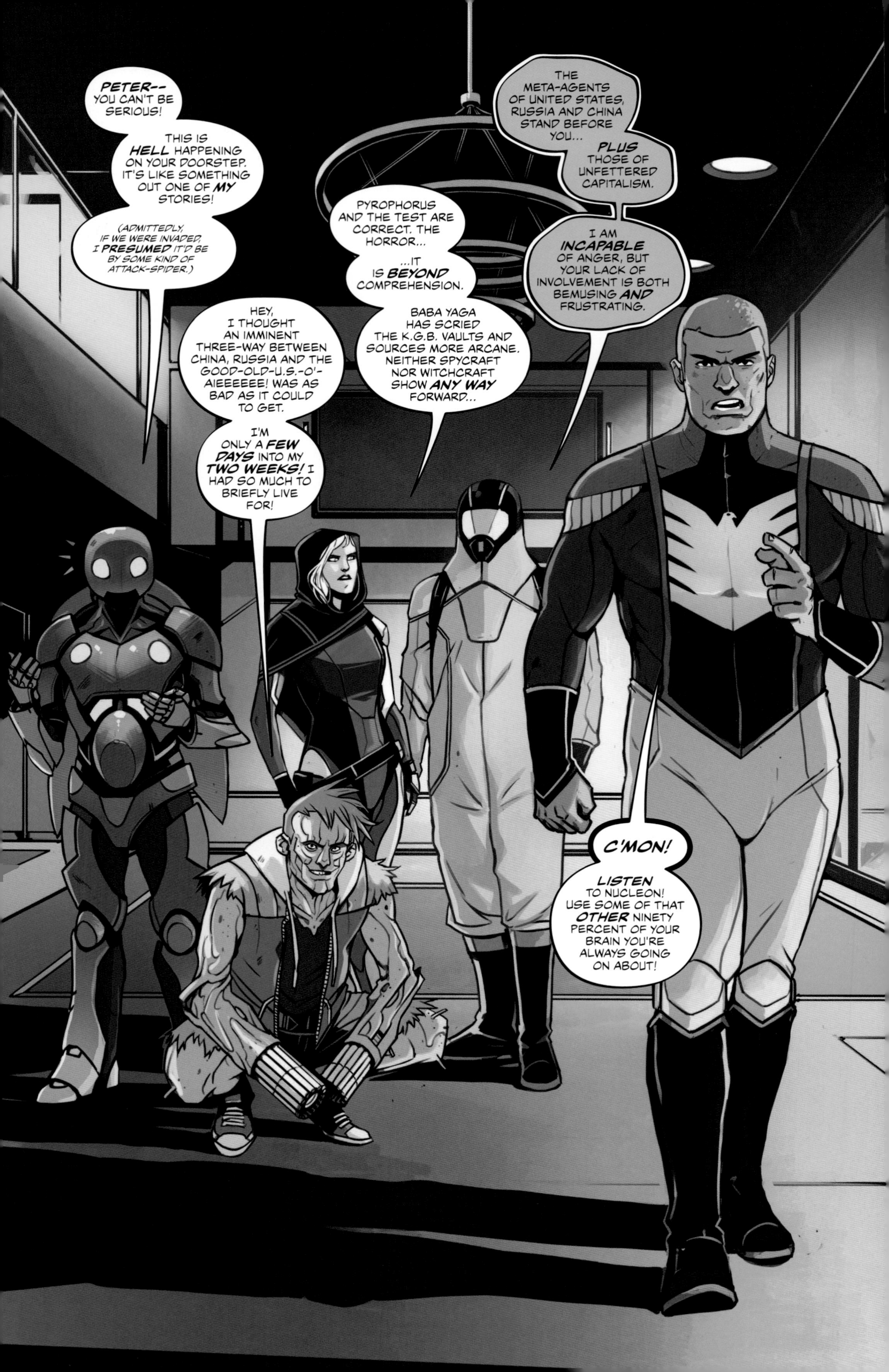
PETER-- YOU CAN'T BE SERIOUS!
THIS IS HELL HAPPENING ON YOUR DOORSTEP. IT'S LIKE SOMETHING OUT ONE OF MY STORIES!
(ADMITTEDLY, IF WE WERE INVADED, I PRESUMED IT'D BE BY SOME KIND OF ATTACK-SPIDER.)
HEY, I THOUGHT AN IMMINENT THREE-WAY BETWEEN CHINA, RUSSIA AND THE GOOD-OLD-U.S.-O'-AIEEEEEE! WAS AS BAD AS IT COULD TO GET.
I'M ONLY A FEW DAYS INTO MY TWO WEEKS! I HAD SO MUCH TO BRIEFLY LIVE FOR!
PYROPHORUS AND THE TEST ARE CORRECT. THE HORROR...
...IT IS BEYOND COMPREHENSION.
BABA YAGA HAS SCRIED THE K.G.B. VAULTS AND SOURCES MORE ARCANE. NEITHER SPYCRAFT NOR WITCHCRAFT SHOW ANY WAY FORWARD...
THE META-AGENTS OF UNITED STATES, RUSSIA AND CHINA STAND BEFORE YOU...
PLUS THOSE OF UNFETTERED CAPITALISM.
I AM INCAPABLE OF ANGER, BUT YOUR LACK OF INVOLVEMENT IS BOTH BEMUSING AND FRUSTRATING.
C'MON!
LISTEN TO NUCLEON! USE SOME OF THAT OTHER NINETY PERCENT OF YOUR BRAIN YOU'RE ALWAYS GOING ON ABOUT!

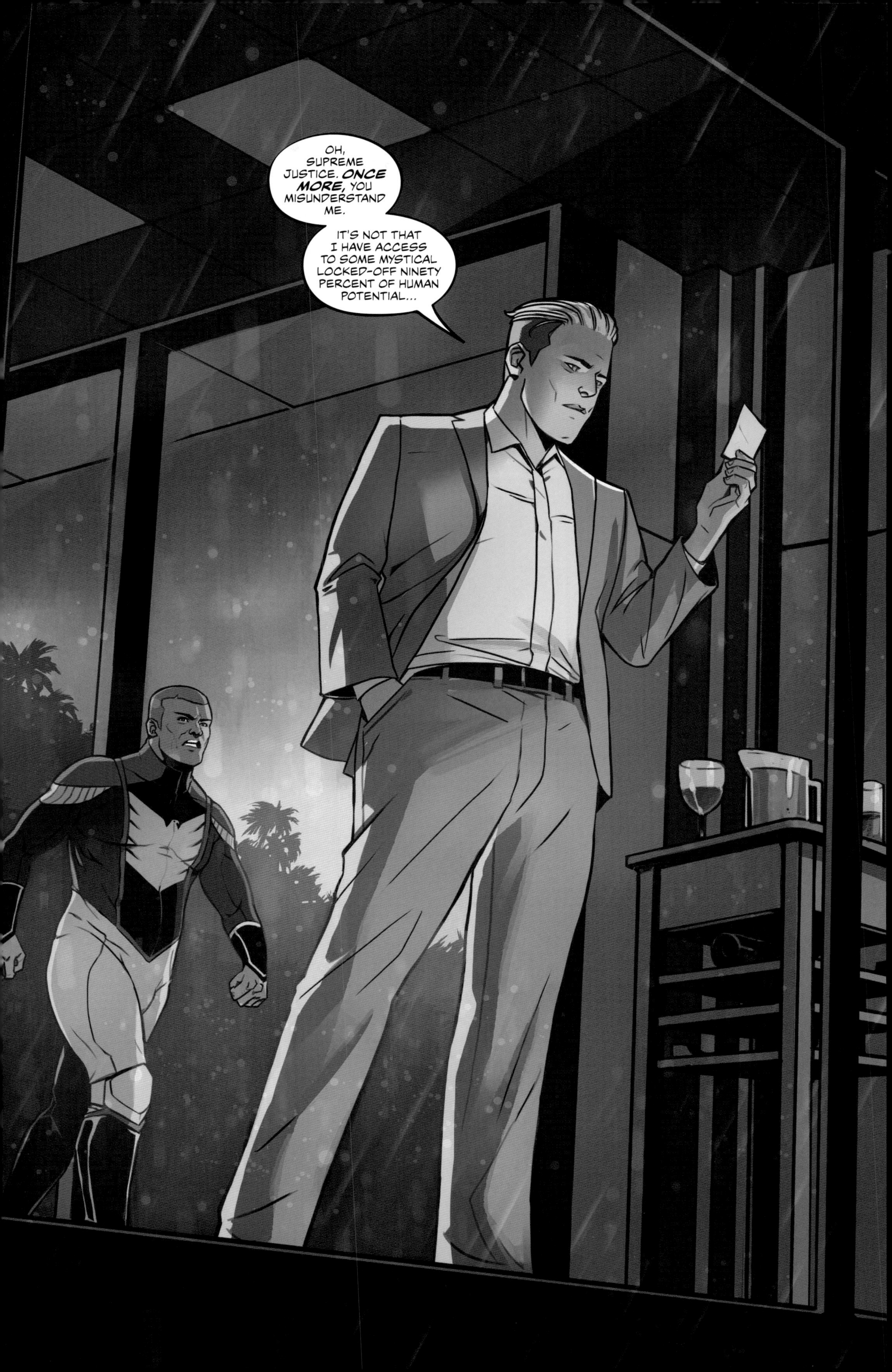
OH, SUPREME JUSTICE. **ONCE MORE,** YOU MISUNDERSTAND ME.
IT'S NOT THAT I HAVE ACCESS TO SOME MYSTICAL LOCKED-OFF NINETY PERCENT OF HUMAN POTENTIAL...

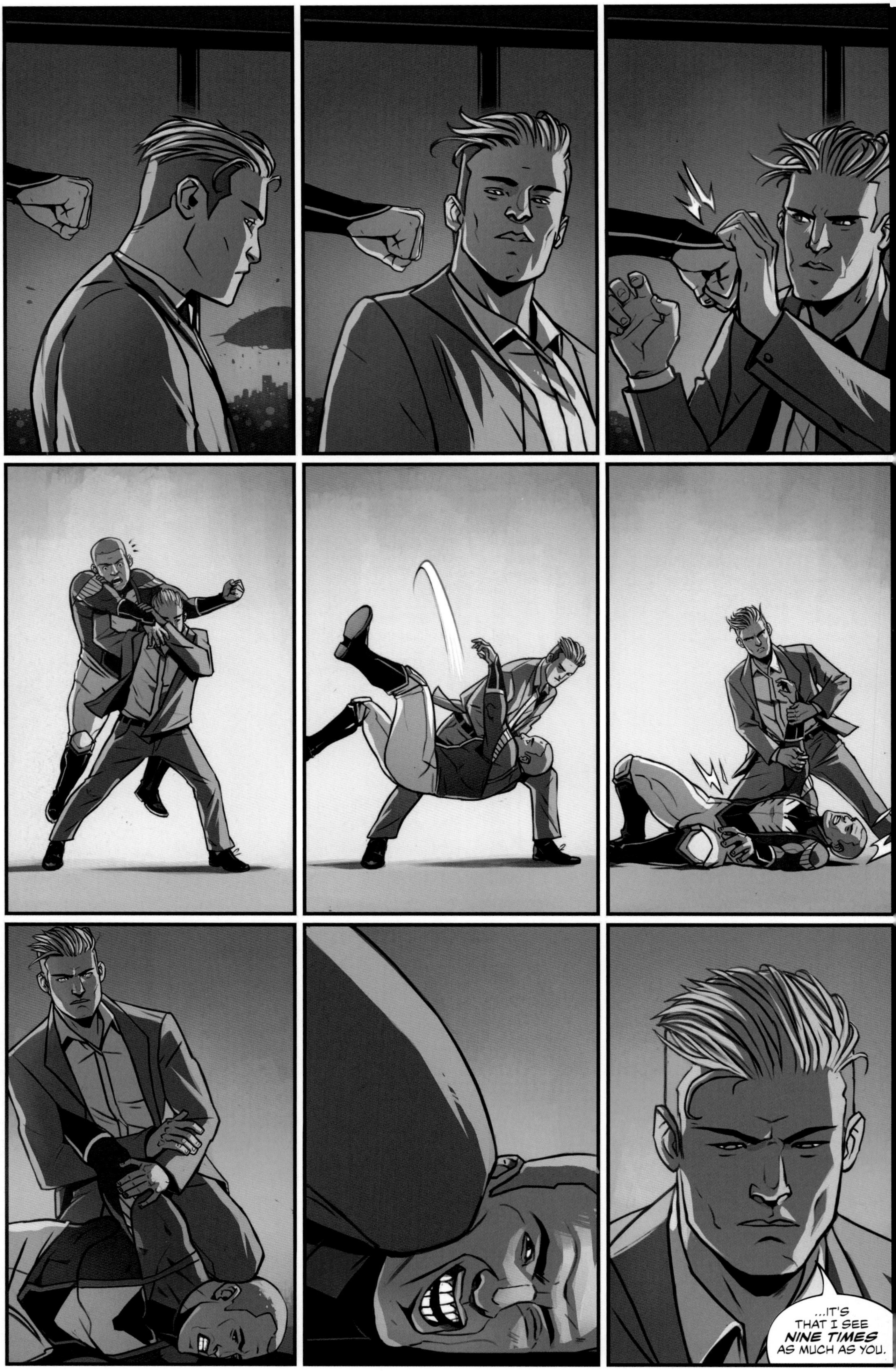
...IT'S THAT I SEE NINE TIMES AS MUCH AS YOU.

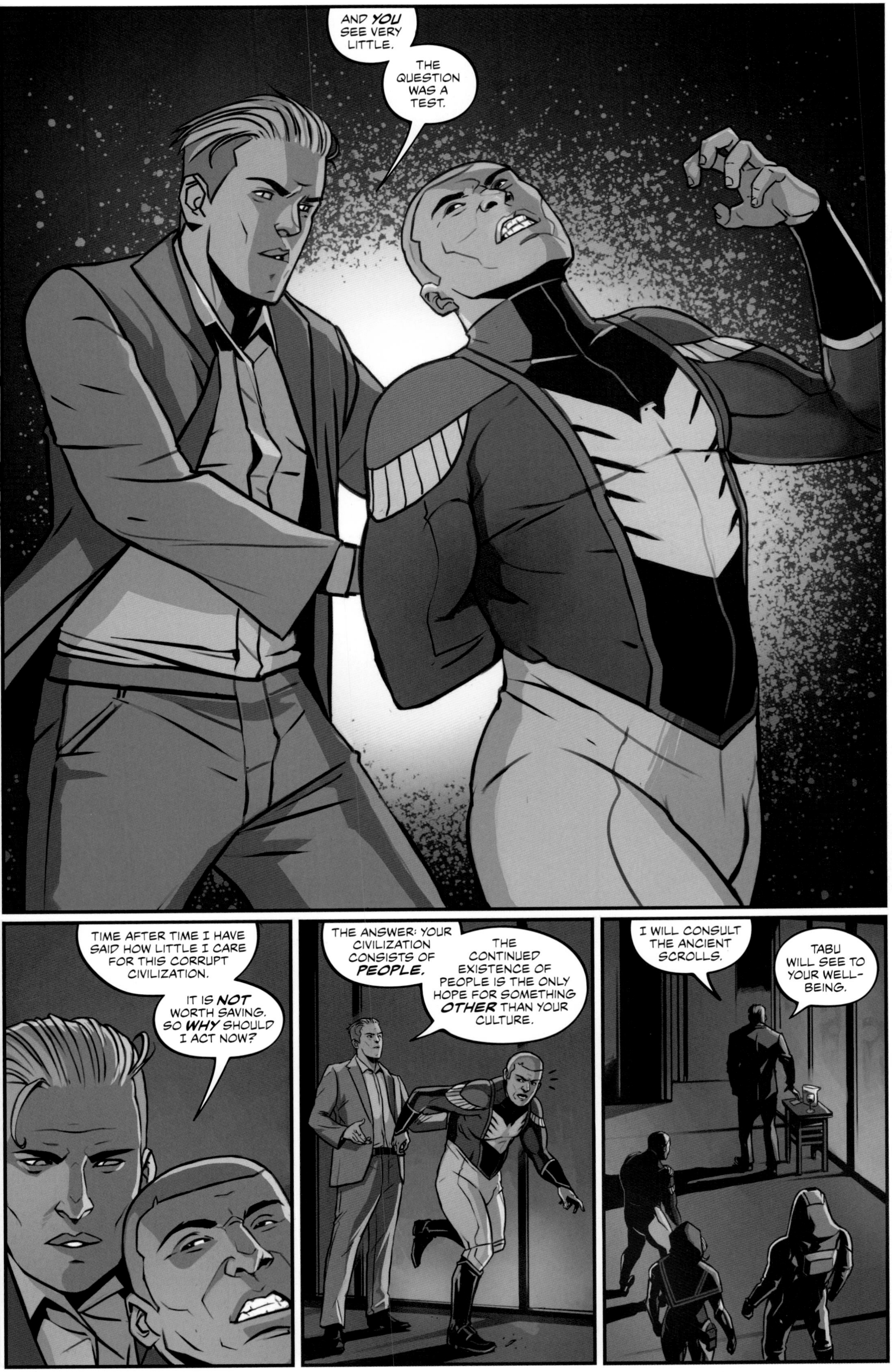
AND YOU SEE VERY LITTLE.
THE QUESTION WAS A TEST.
TIME AFTER TIME I HAVE SAID HOW LITTLE I CARE FOR THIS CORRUPT CIVILIZATION.
IT IS NOT WORTH SAVING. SO WHY SHOULD I ACT NOW?
THE ANSWER: YOUR CIVILIZATION CONSISTS OF PEOPLE.
THE CONTINUED EXISTENCE OF PEOPLE IS THE ONLY HOPE FOR SOMETHING OTHER THAN YOUR CULTURE.
I WILL CONSULT THE ANCIENT SCROLLS.
TABU WILL SEE TO YOUR WELL-BEING.

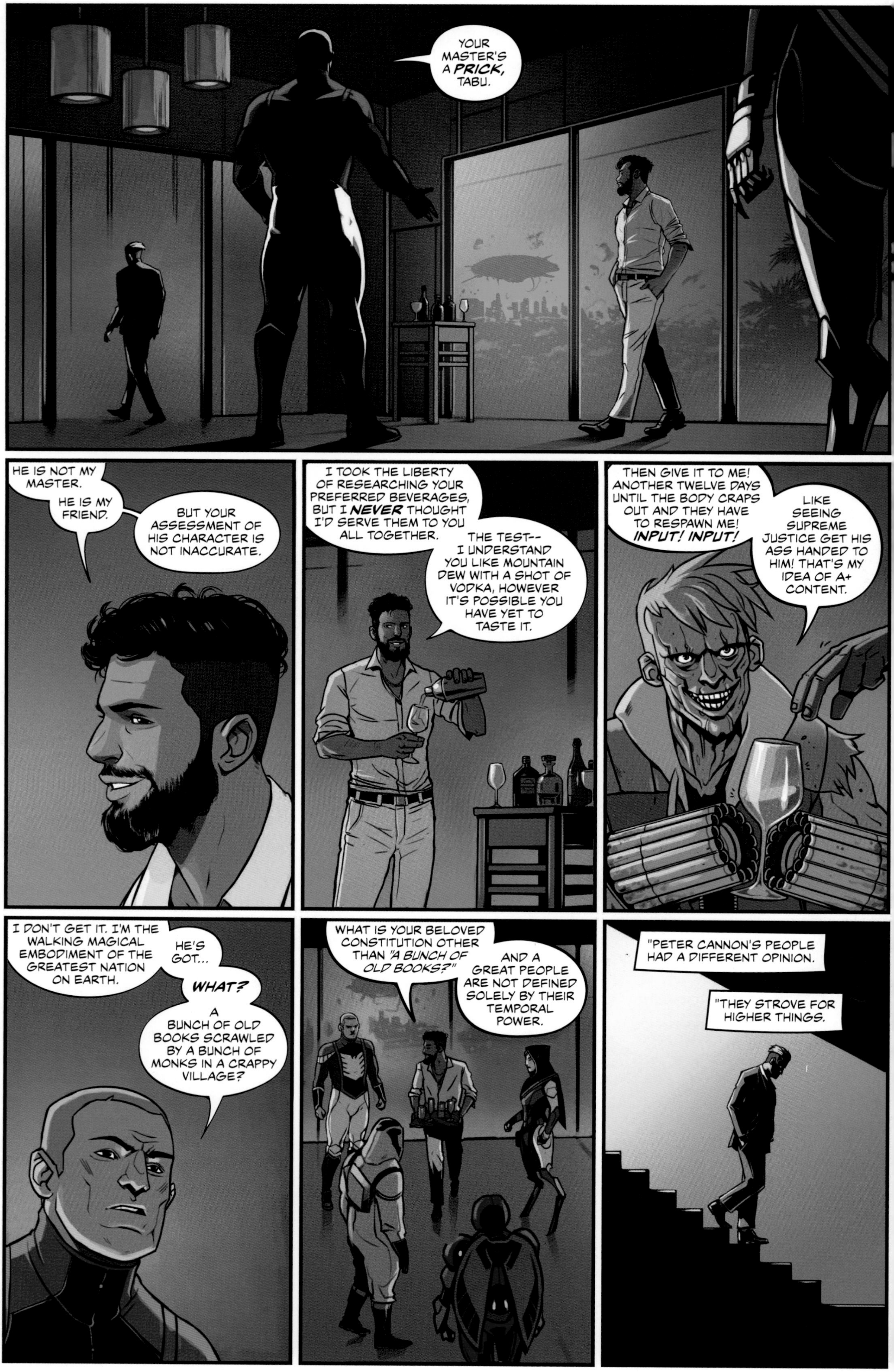
YOUR MASTER'S A PRICK, TABU.
HE IS NOT MY MASTER.
HE IS MY FRIEND.
BUT YOUR ASSESSMENT OF HIS CHARACTER IS NOT INACCURATE.
I TOOK THE LIBERTY OF RESEARCHING YOUR PREFERRED BEVERAGES, BUT I NEVER THOUGHT I'D SERVE THEM TO YOU ALL TOGETHER.
THE TEST-- I UNDERSTAND YOU LIKE MOUNTAIN DEW WITH A SHOT OF VODKA, HOWEVER IT'S POSSIBLE YOU HAVE YET TO TASTE IT.
THEN GIVE IT TO ME! ANOTHER TWELVE DAYS UNTIL THE BODY CRAPS OUT AND THEY HAVE TO RESPAWN ME! INPUT! INPUT!
LIKE SEEING SUPREME JUSTICE GET HIS ASS HANDED TO HIM! THAT'S MY IDEA OF A+ CONTENT.
I DON'T GET IT. I'M THE WALKING MAGICAL EMBODIMENT OF THE GREATEST NATION ON EARTH.
HE'S GOT...
WHAT?
A BUNCH OF OLD BOOKS SCRAWLED BY A BUNCH OF MONKS IN A CRAPPY VILLAGE?
WHAT IS YOUR BELOVED CONSTITUTION OTHER THAN "A BUNCH OF OLD BOOKS?"
AND A GREAT PEOPLE ARE NOT DEFINED SOLELY BY THEIR TEMPORAL POWER.
"PETER CANNON'S PEOPLE HAD A DIFFERENT OPINION.
"THEY STROVE FOR HIGHER THINGS.

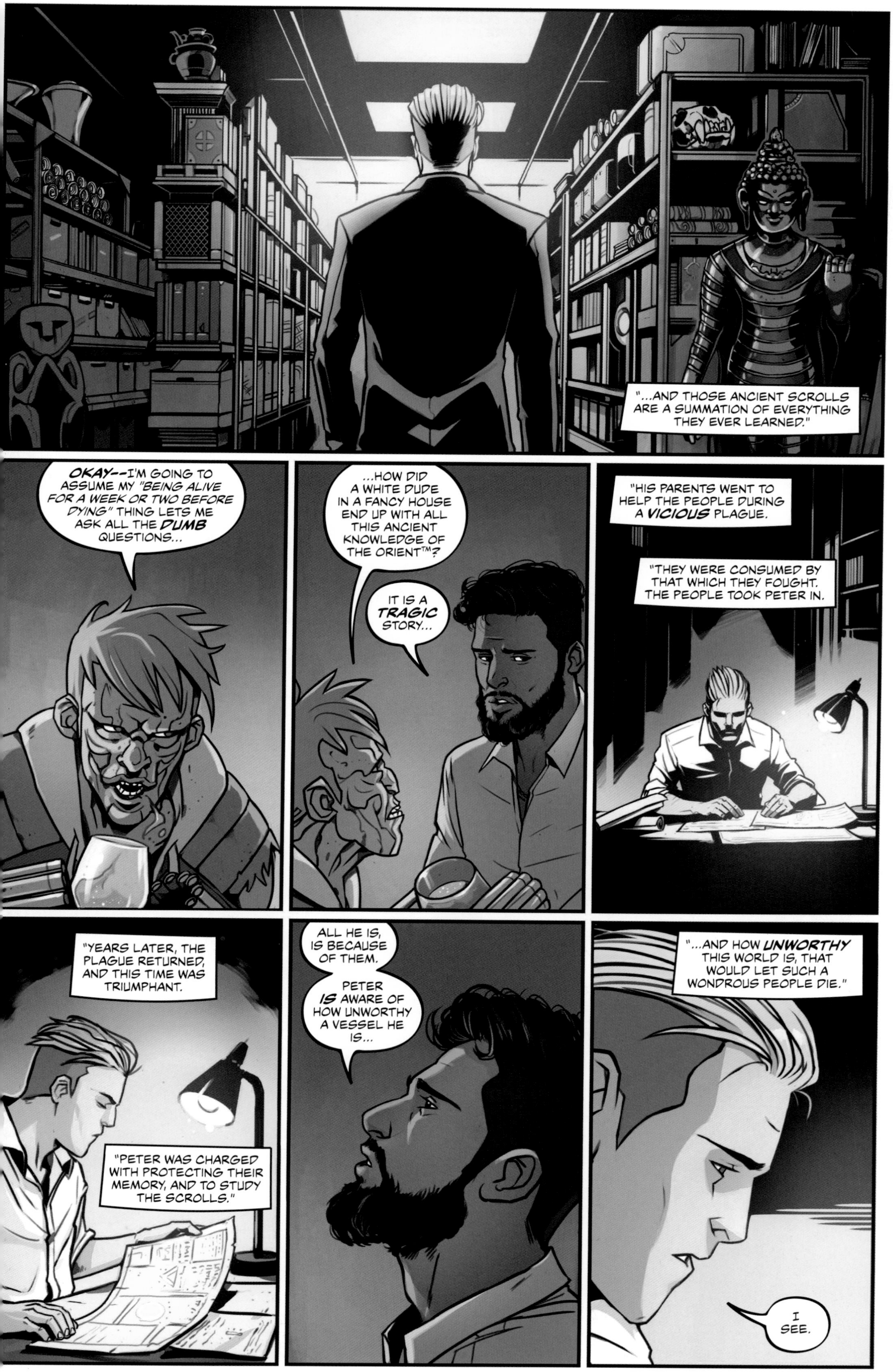
"...AND THOSE ANCIENT SCROLLS ARE A SUMMATION OF EVERYTHING THEY EVER LEARNED."
OKAY--I'M GOING TO ASSUME MY "BEING ALIVE FOR A WEEK OR TWO BEFORE DYING" THING LETS ME ASK ALL THE DUMB QUESTIONS...
...HOW DID A WHITE DUDE IN A FANCY HOUSE END UP WITH ALL THIS ANCIENT KNOWLEDGE OF THE ORIENT™?
IT IS A TRAGIC STORY...
"HIS PARENTS WENT TO HELP THE PEOPLE DURING A VICIOUS PLAGUE.
"THEY WERE CONSUMED BY THAT WHICH THEY FOUGHT. THE PEOPLE TOOK PETER IN.
"YEARS LATER, THE PLAGUE RETURNED, AND THIS TIME WAS TRIUMPHANT.
"PETER WAS CHARGED WITH PROTECTING THEIR MEMORY, AND TO STUDY THE SCROLLS."
ALL HE IS, IS BECAUSE OF THEM.
PETER IS AWARE OF HOW UNWORTHY A VESSEL HE IS...
"...AND HOW UNWORTHY THIS WORLD IS, THAT WOULD LET SUCH A WONDROUS PEOPLE DIE."
I SEE.

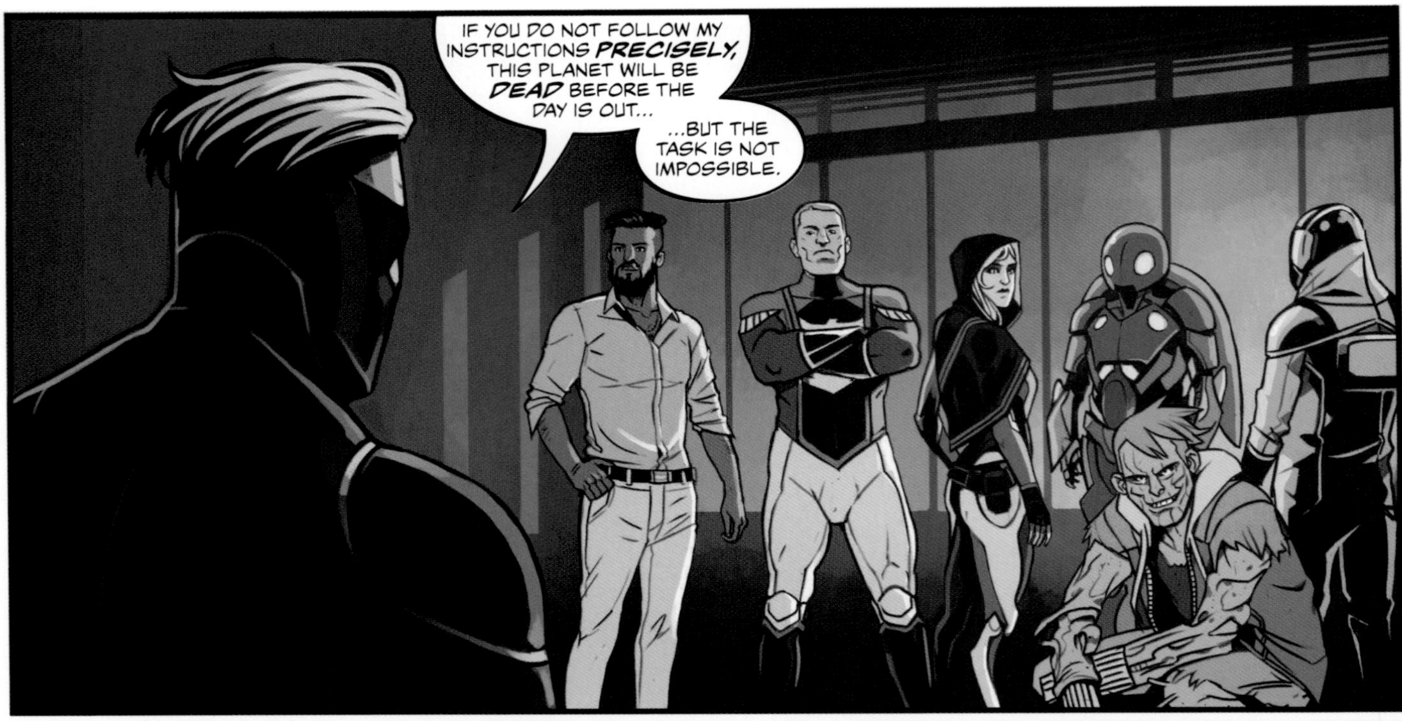
IF YOU DO NOT FOLLOW MY INSTRUCTIONS PRECISELY, THIS PLANET WILL BE DEAD BEFORE THE DAY IS OUT...
...BUT THE TASK IS NOT IMPOSSIBLE.

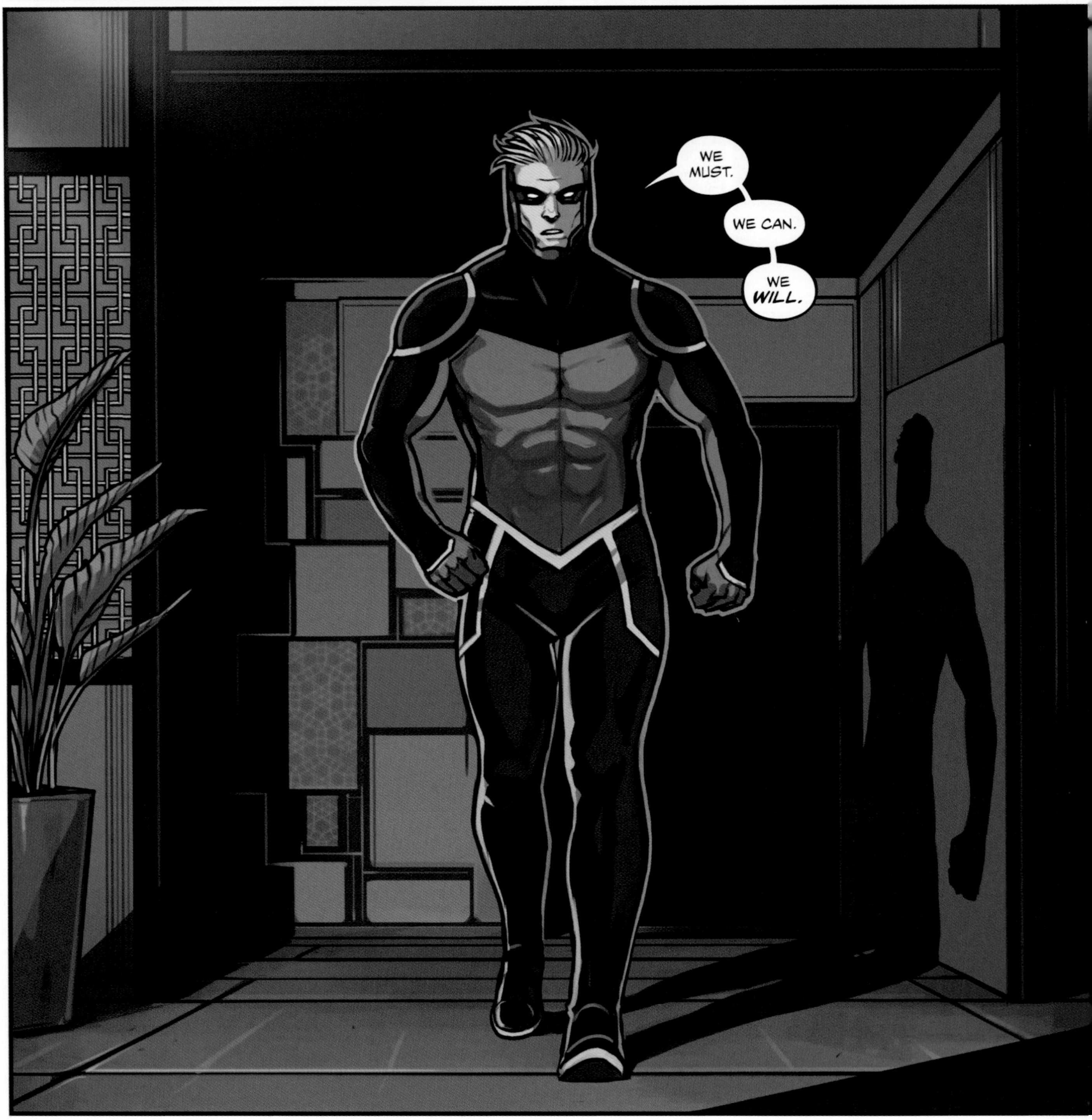
WE MUST.
WE CAN.
WE WILL.

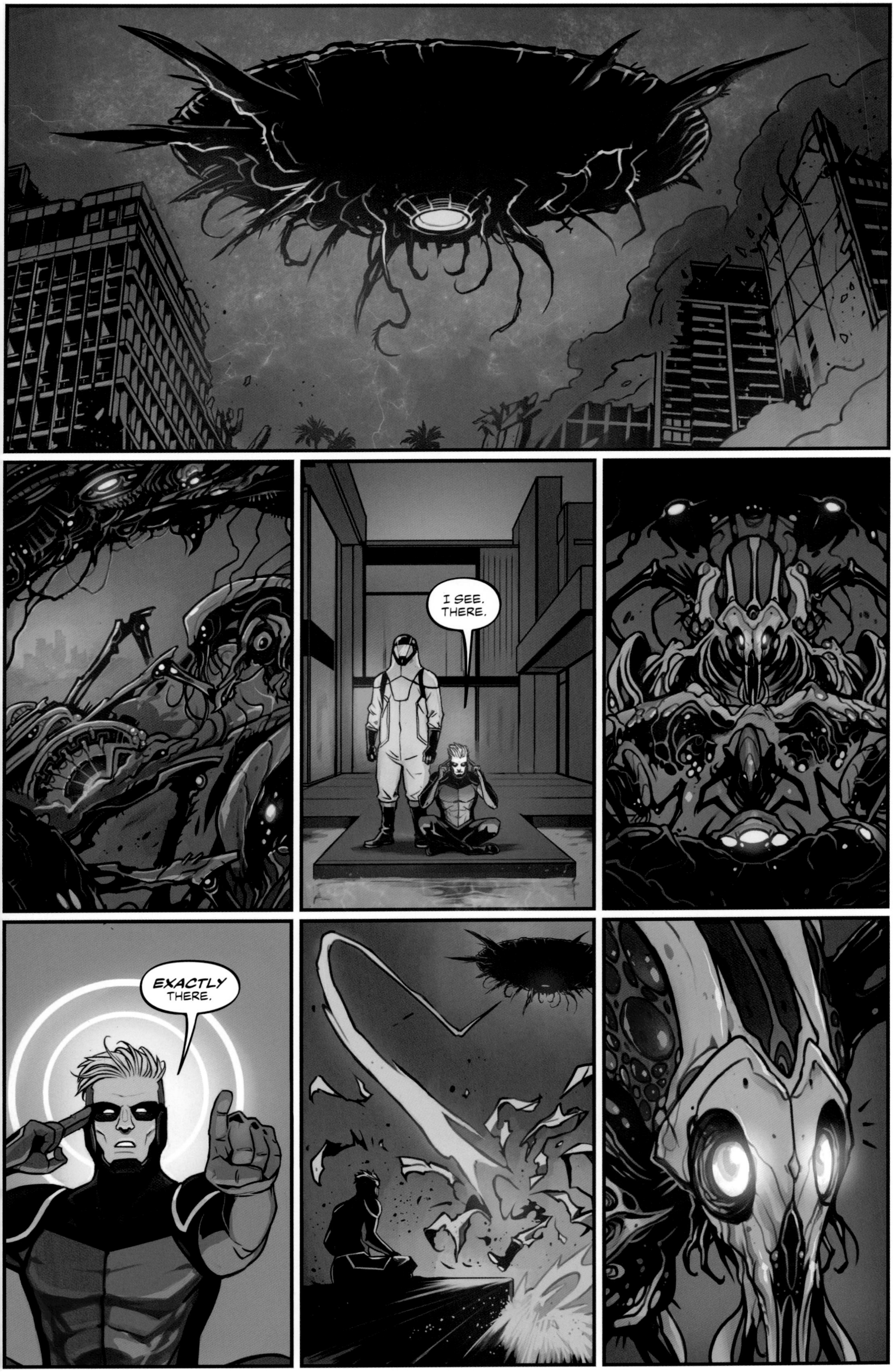
I SEE. THERE.
EXACTLY THERE.

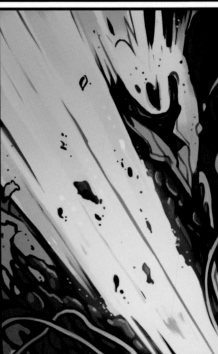

THE EXPERIMENT IS A COMPLETE SUCCESS. THE ALIEN LEADER IS VULNERABLE TO BOTH KINETIC FORCE AND RADIOACTIVE ENERGIES.

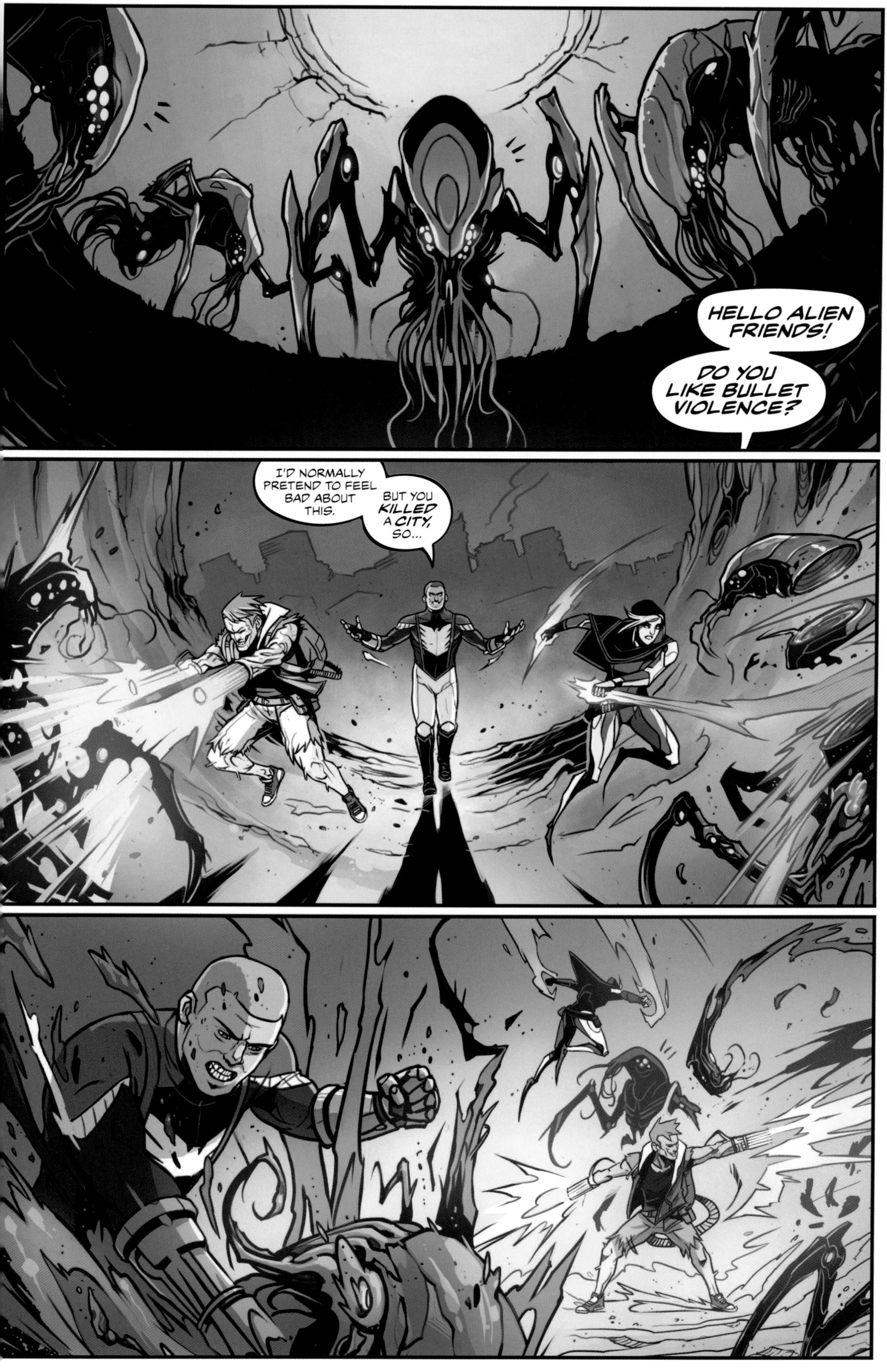
HELLO ALIEN FRIENDS!
DO YOU LIKE BULLET VIOLENCE?
I'D NORMALLY PRETEND TO FEEL BAD ABOUT THIS.
BUT YOU KILLED A CITY, SO...

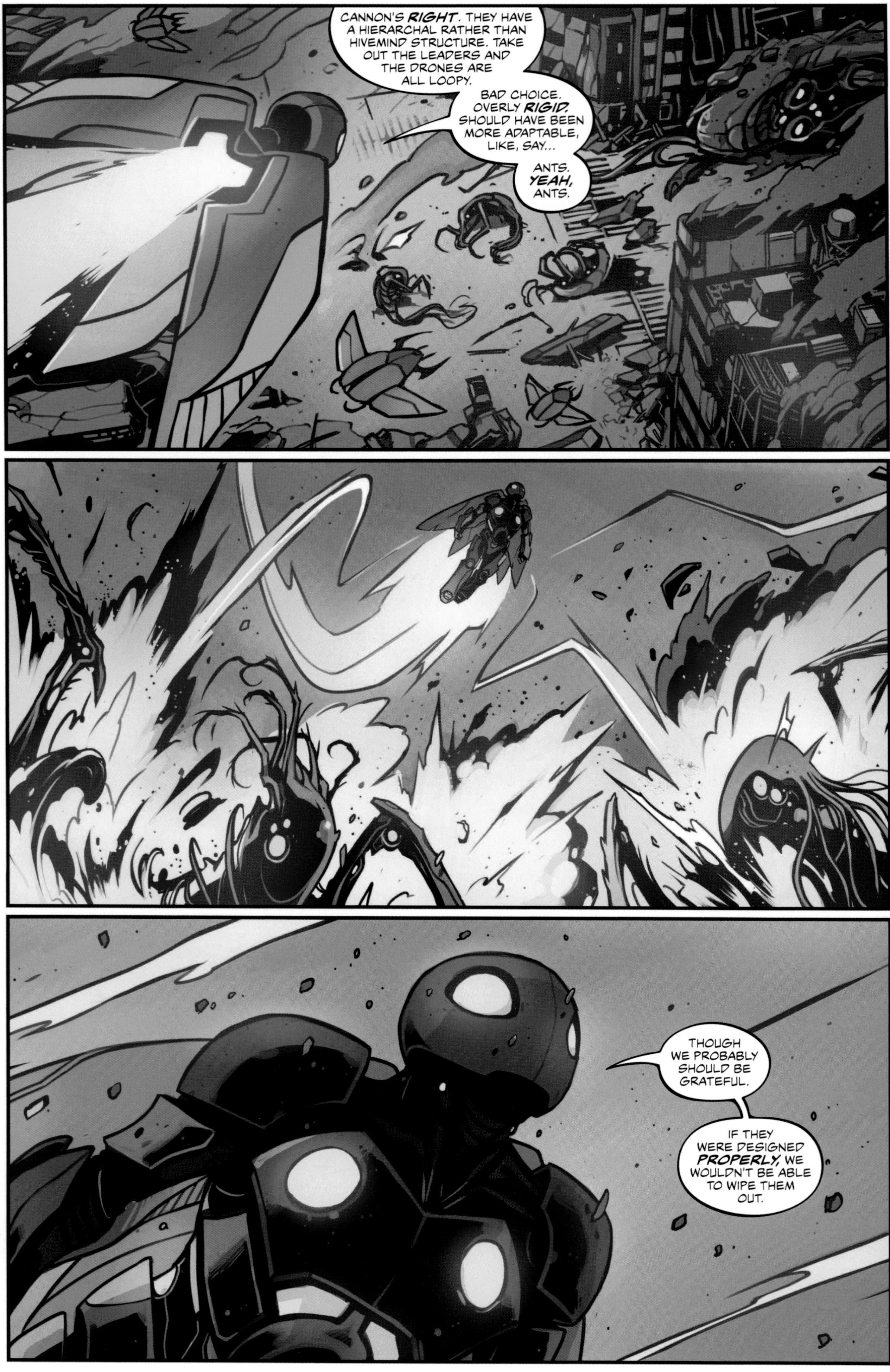
CANNON'S RIGHT. THEY HAVE A HIERARCHAL RATHER THAN HIVEMIND STRUCTURE. TAKE OUT THE LEADERS AND THE DRONES ARE ALL LOOPY.
BAD CHOICE. OVERLY RIGID. SHOULD HAVE BEEN MORE ADAPTABLE, LIKE, SAY...
ANTS. YEAH, ANTS.
THOUGH WE PROBABLY SHOULD BE GRATEFUL.
IF THEY WERE DESIGNED PROPERLY, WE WOULDN'T BE ABLE TO WIPE THEM OUT.

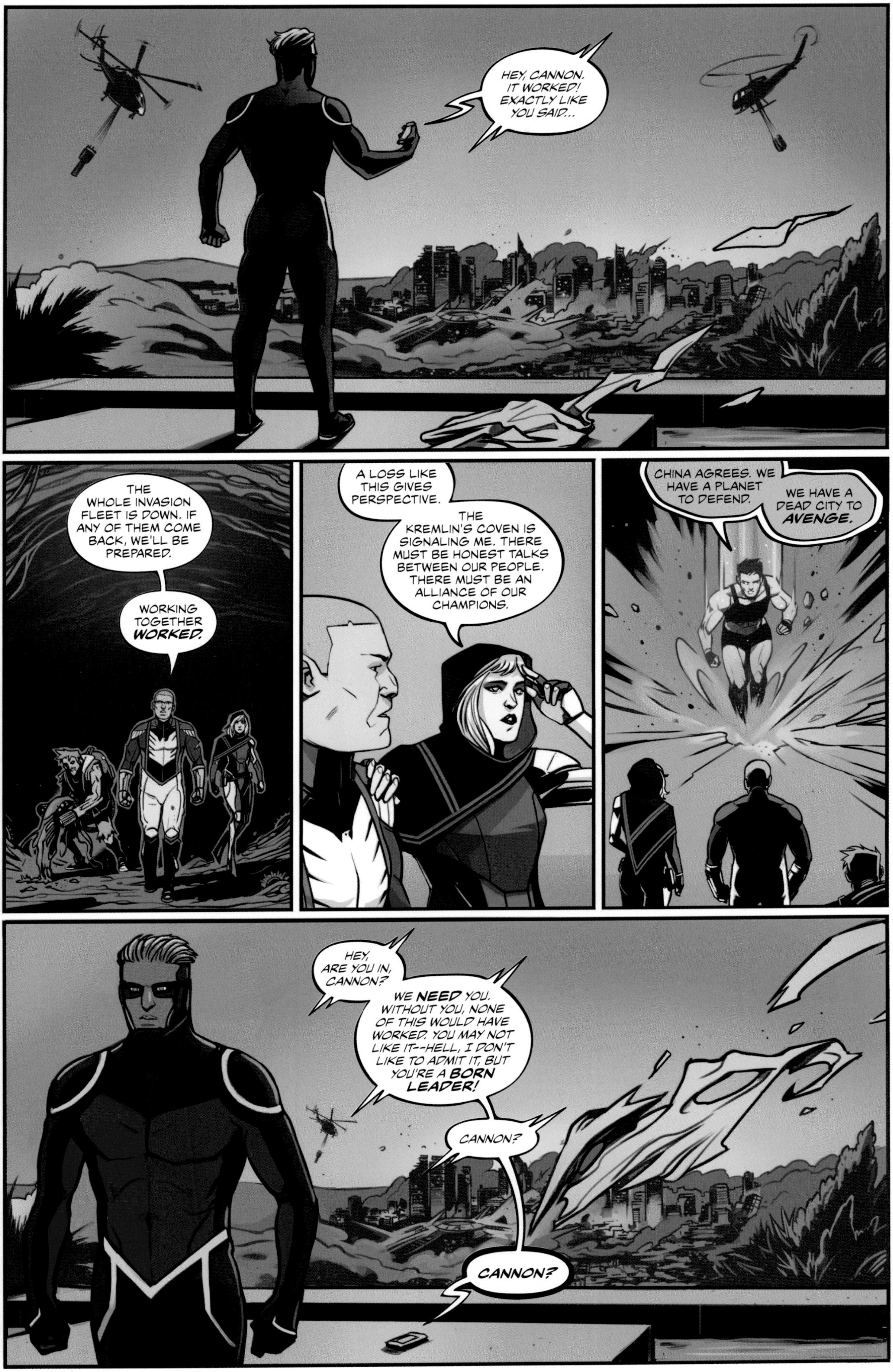
HEY, CANNON. IT WORKED! EXACTLY LIKE YOU SAID...
THE WHOLE INVASION FLEET IS DOWN. IF ANY OF THEM COME BACK, WE'LL BE PREPARED.
WORKING TOGETHER WORKED.
A LOSS LIKE THIS GIVES PERSPECTIVE.
THE KREMLIN'S COVEN IS SIGNALING ME. THERE MUST BE HONEST TALKS BETWEEN OUR PEOPLE. THERE MUST BE AN ALLIANCE OF OUR CHAMPIONS.
CHINA AGREES. WE HAVE A PLANET TO DEFEND.
WE HAVE A DEAD CITY TO AVENGE.
HEY, ARE YOU IN, CANNON?
WE NEED YOU. WITHOUT YOU, NONE OF THIS WOULD HAVE WORKED. YOU MAY NOT LIKE IT--HELL, I DON'T LIKE TO ADMIT IT, BUT YOU'RE A BORN LEADER!
CANNON?
CANNON?

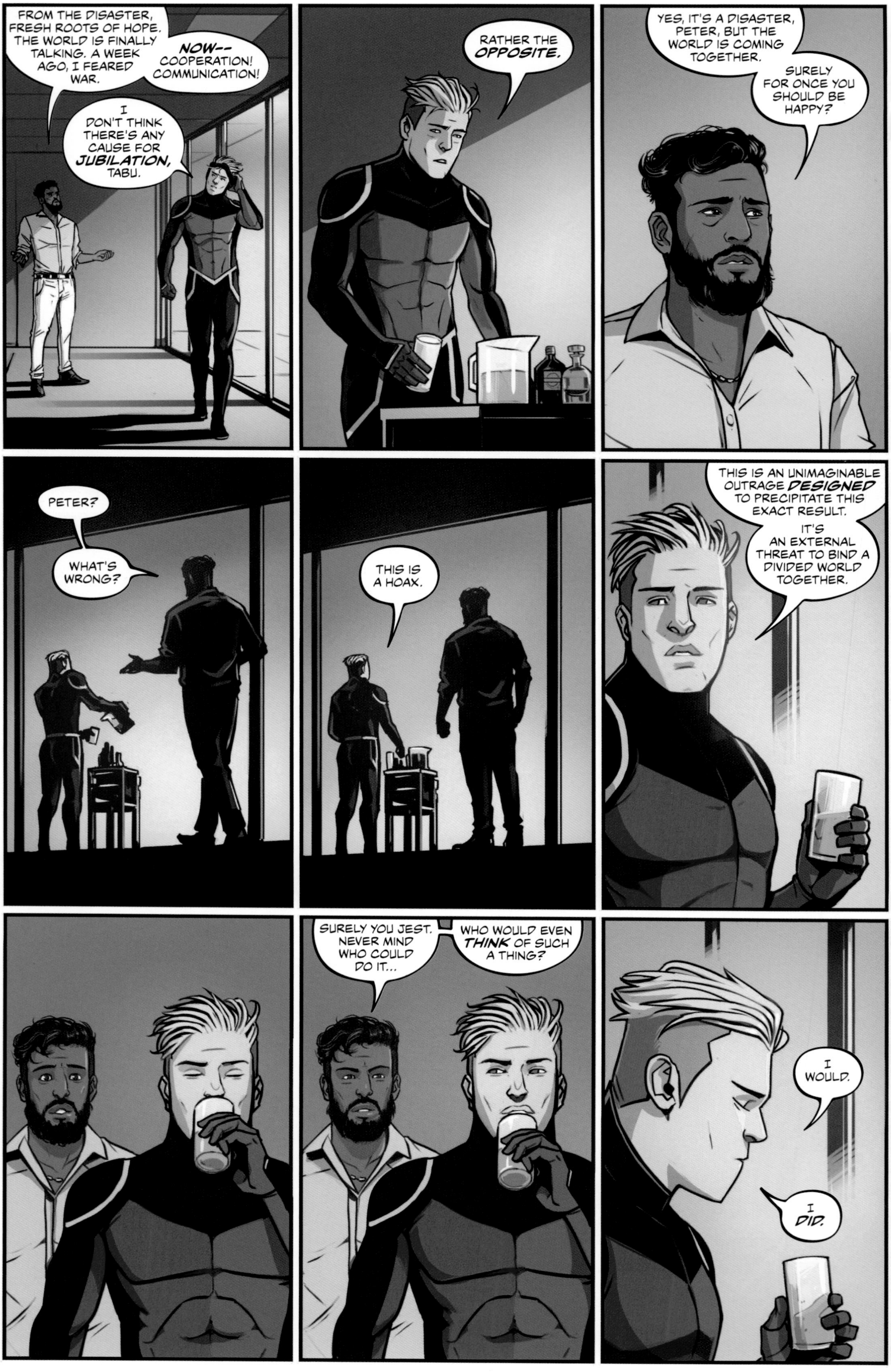
FROM THE DISASTER, FRESH ROOTS OF HOPE. THE WORLD IS FINALLY TALKING. A WEEK AGO, I FEARED WAR.
NOW-- COOPERATION! COMMUNICATION!
I DON'T THINK THERE'S ANY CAUSE FOR JUBILATION, TABU.
RATHER THE OPPOSITE.
YES, IT'S A DISASTER, PETER, BUT THE WORLD IS COMING TOGETHER.
SURELY FOR ONCE YOU SHOULD BE HAPPY?
PETER?
WHAT'S WRONG?
THIS IS A HOAX.
THIS IS AN UNIMAGINABLE OUTRAGE DESIGNED TO PRECIPITATE THIS EXACT RESULT.
IT'S AN EXTERNAL THREAT TO BIND A DIVIDED WORLD TOGETHER.
SURELY YOU JEST. NEVER MIND WHO COULD DO IT...
WHO WOULD EVEN THINK OF SUCH A THING?
I WOULD.
I DID.

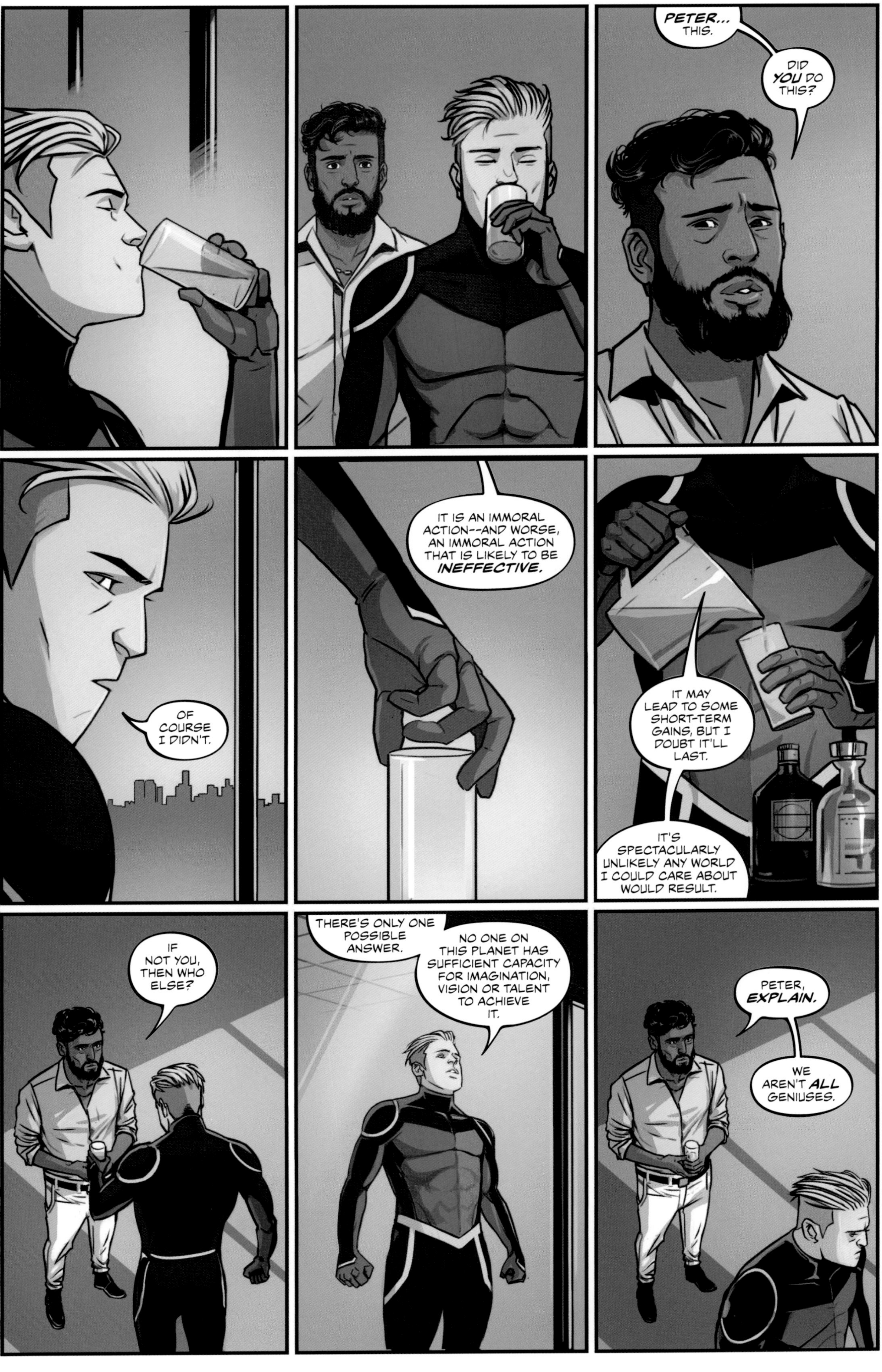
PETER... THIS.
DID YOU DO THIS?
OF COURSE I DIDN'T.
IT IS AN IMMORAL ACTION--AND WORSE, AN IMMORAL ACTION THAT IS LIKELY TO BE INEFFECTIVE.
IT MAY LEAD TO SOME SHORT-TERM GAINS, BUT I DOUBT IT'LL LAST.
IT'S SPECTACULARLY UNLIKELY ANY WORLD I COULD CARE ABOUT WOULD RESULT.
IF NOT YOU, THEN WHO ELSE?
THERE'S ONLY ONE POSSIBLE ANSWER.
NO ONE ON THIS PLANET HAS SUFFICIENT CAPACITY FOR IMAGINATION, VISION OR TALENT TO ACHIEVE IT.
PETER, EXPLAIN.
WE AREN'T ALL GENIUSES.

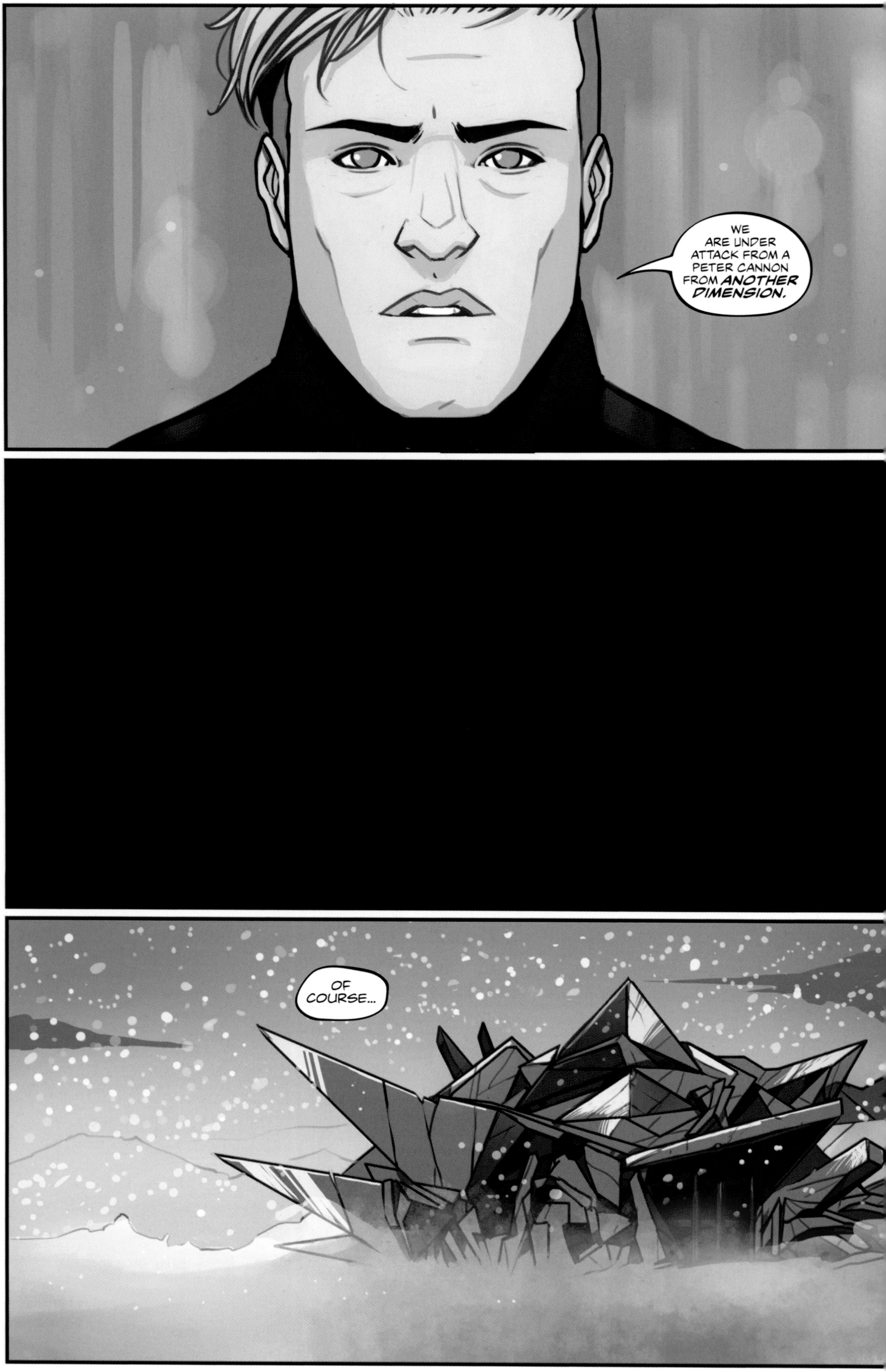
WE ARE UNDER ATTACK FROM A PETER CANNON FROM ANOTHER DIMENSION.
OF COURSE...

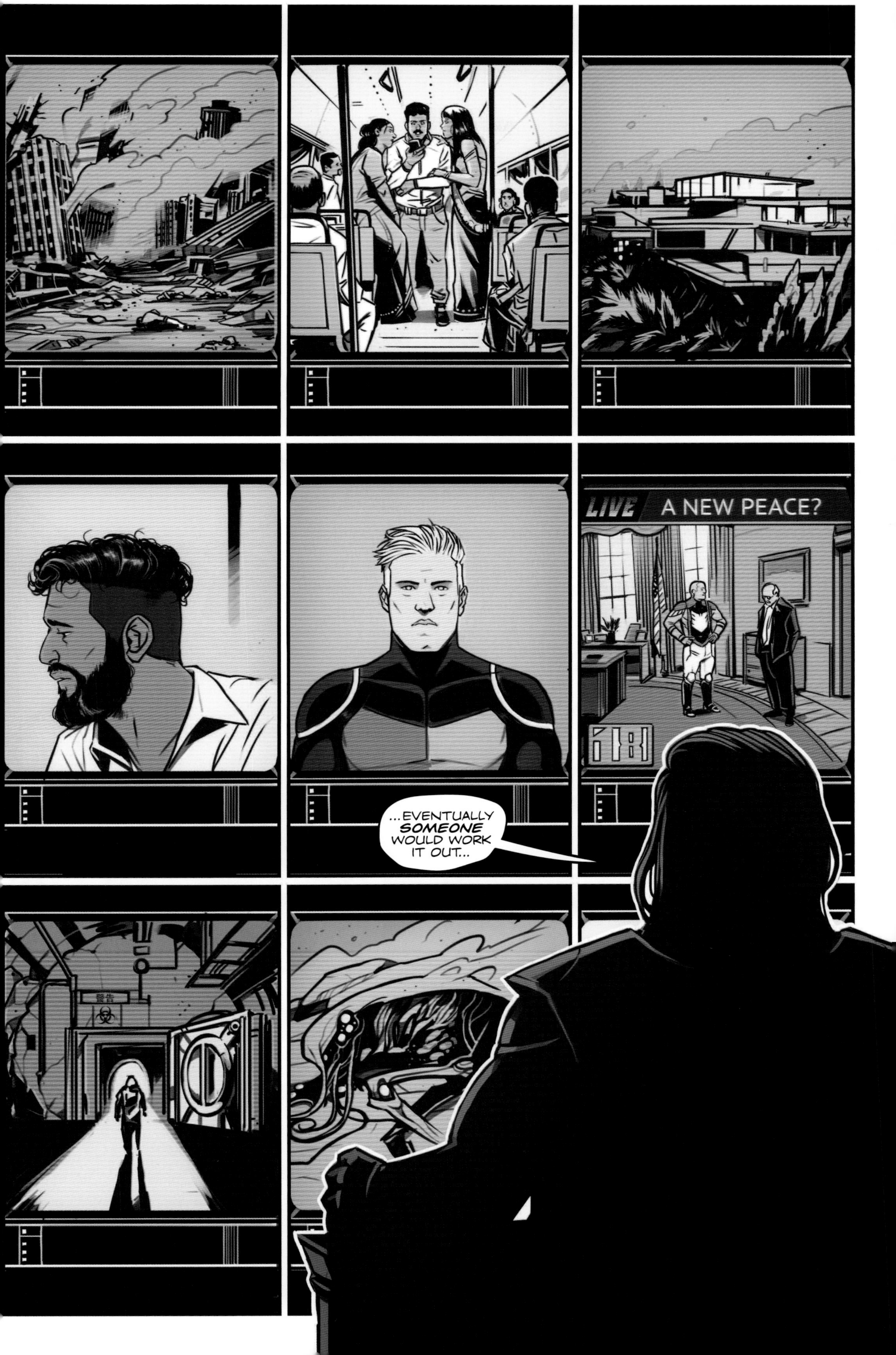
LIVE
A NEW PEACE?
...EVENTUALLY SOMEONE WOULD WORK IT OUT...

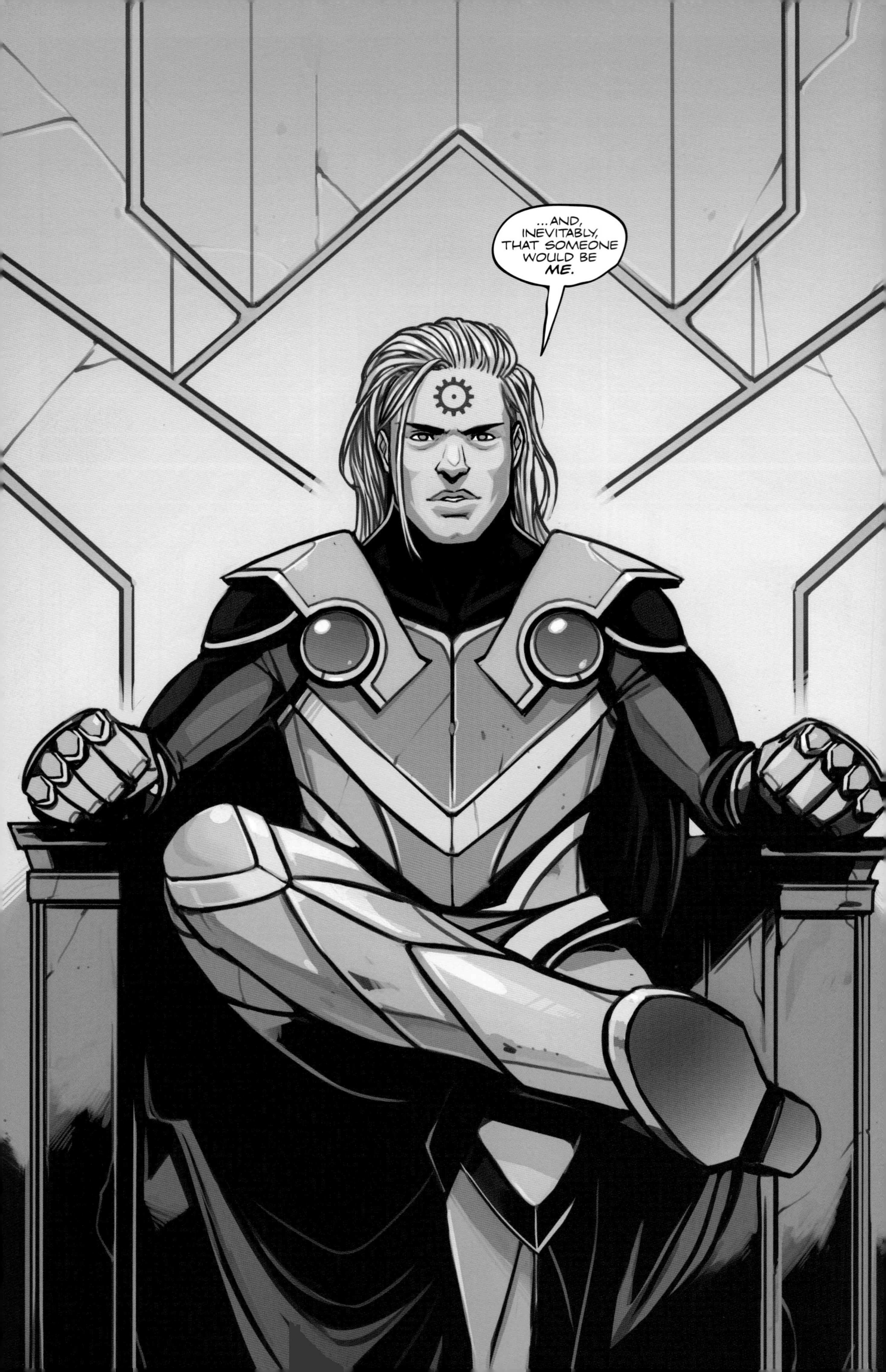
...AND, INEVITABLY, THAT SOMEONE WOULD BE ME.

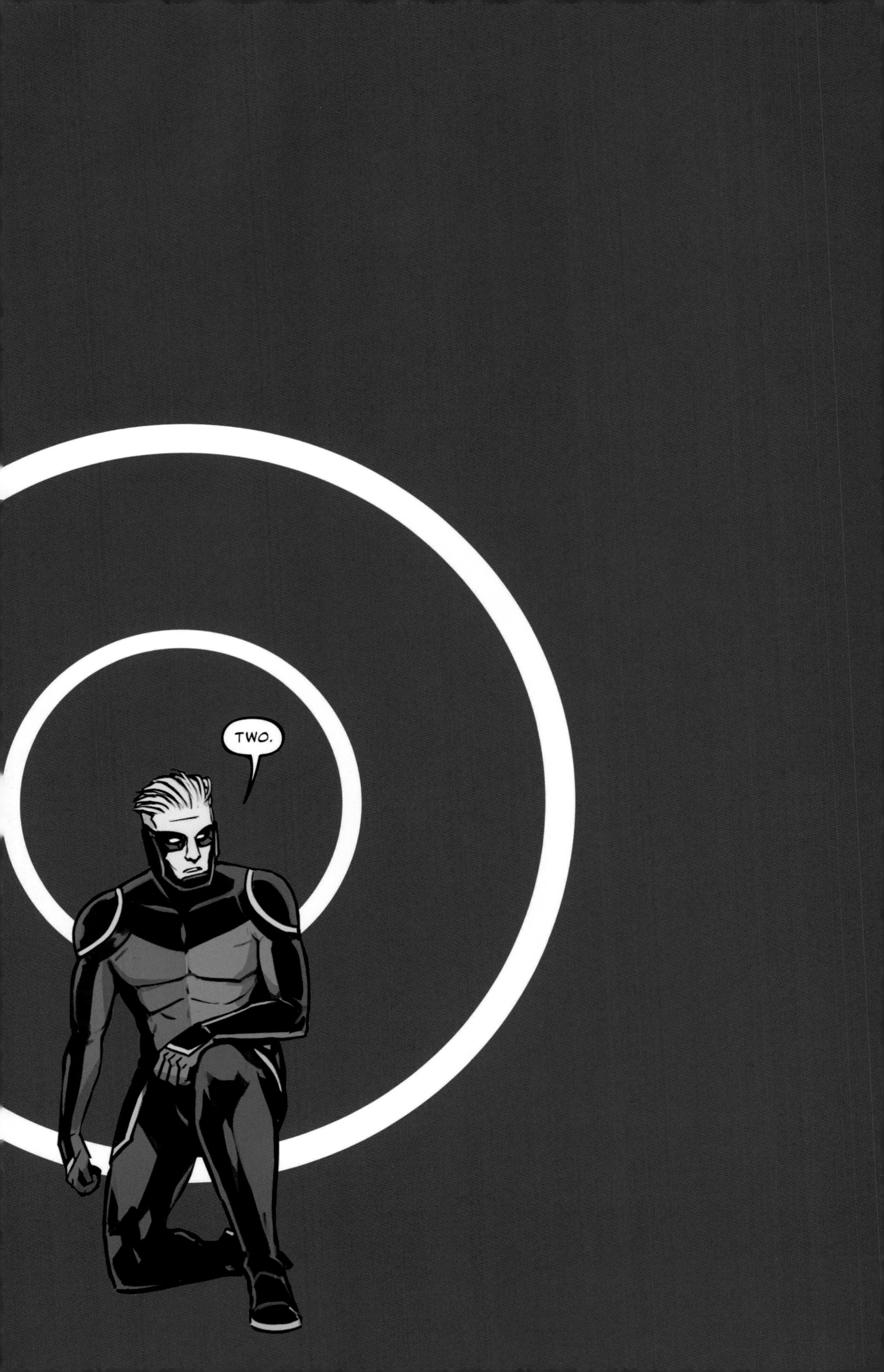
TWO.

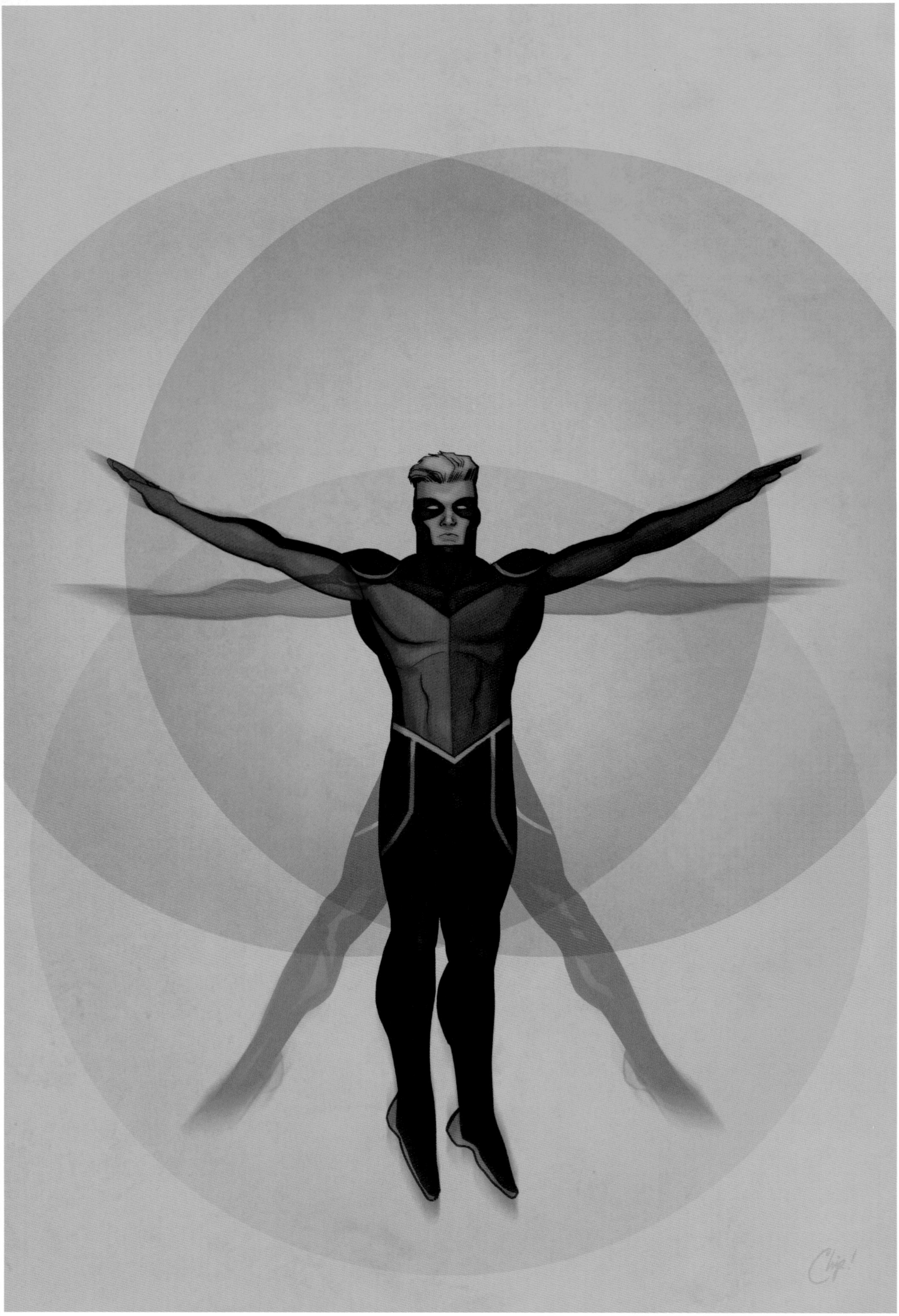

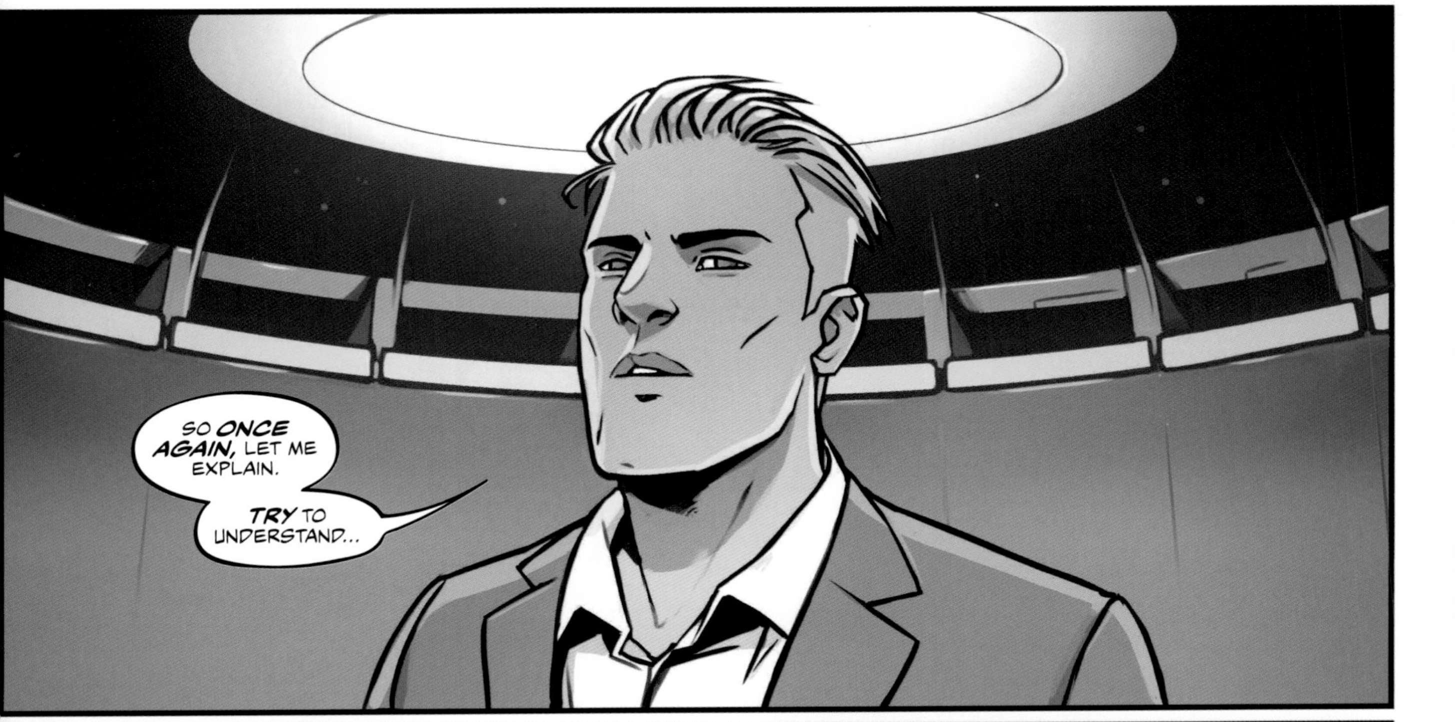
SO ONCE AGAIN, LET ME EXPLAIN.
TRY TO UNDERSTAND...

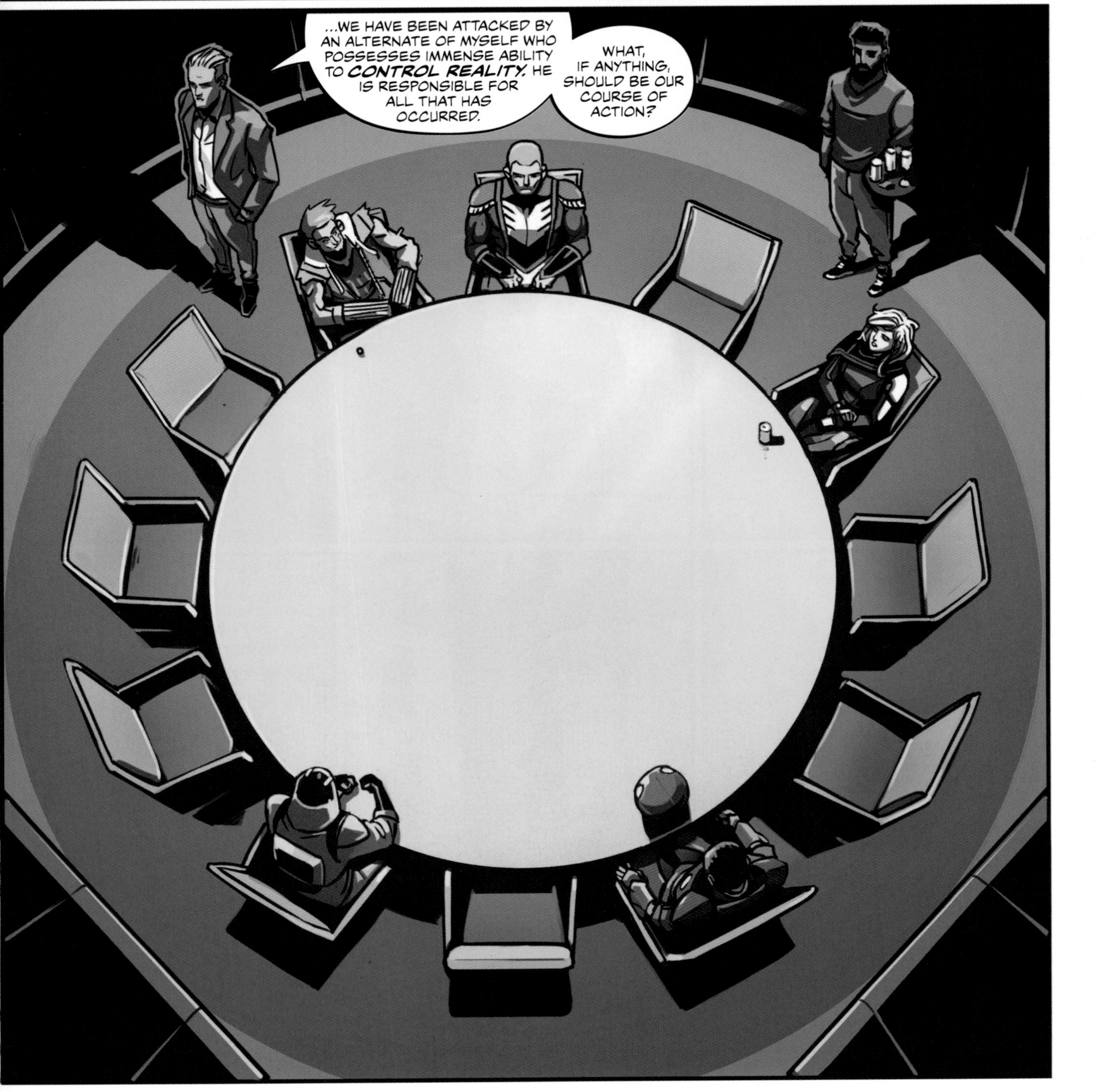
...WE HAVE BEEN ATTACKED BY AN ALTERNATE OF MYSELF WHO POSSESSES IMMENSE ABILITY TO CONTROL REALITY. HE IS RESPONSIBLE FOR ALL THAT HAS OCCURRED.
WHAT, IF ANYTHING, SHOULD BE OUR COURSE OF ACTION?

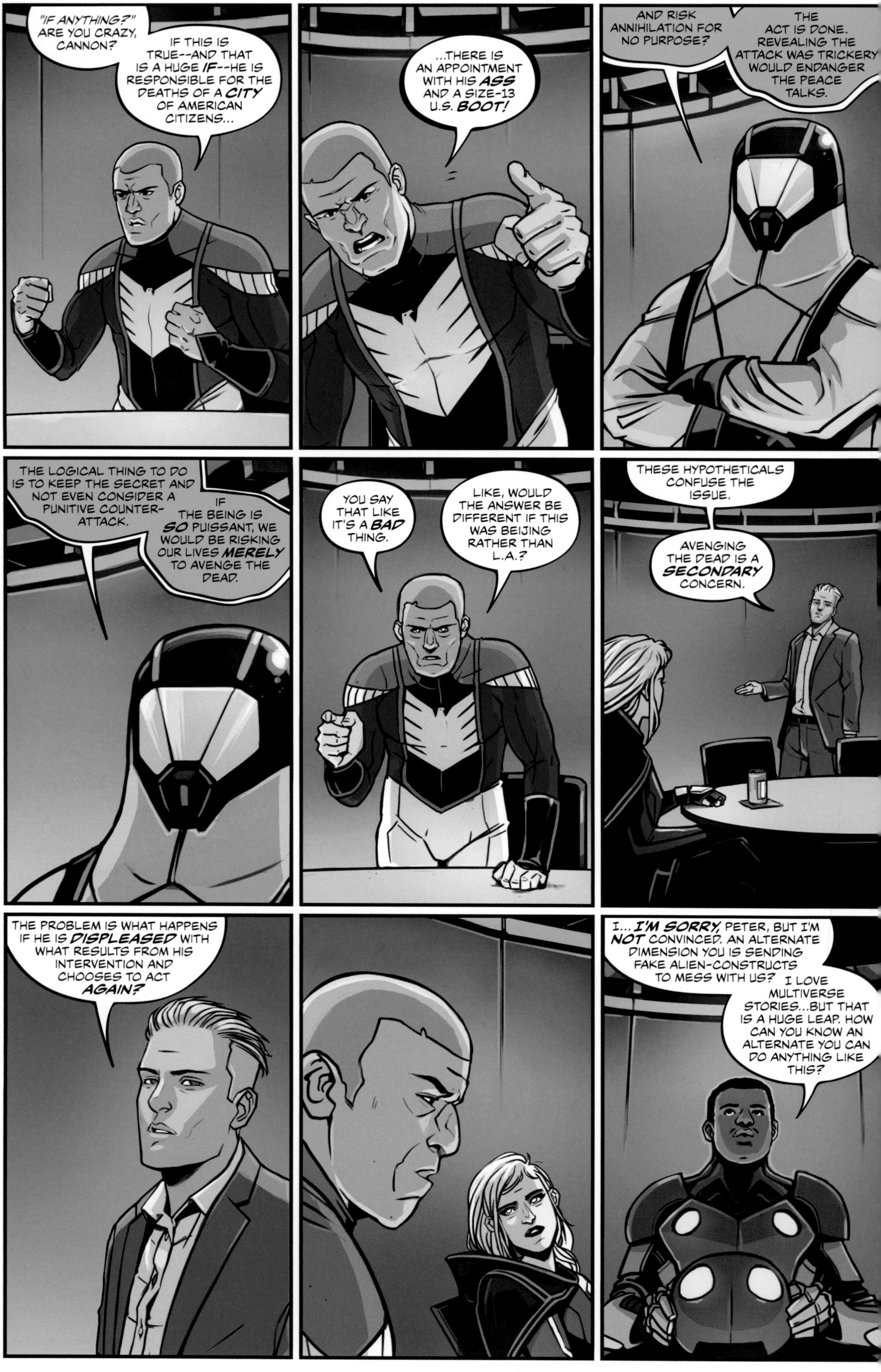
"IF ANYTHING?" ARE YOU CRAZY, CANNON?
IF THIS IS TRUE--AND THAT IS A HUGE IF--HE IS RESPONSIBLE FOR THE DEATHS OF A CITY OF AMERICAN CITIZENS...
...THERE IS AN APPOINTMENT WITH HIS ASS AND A SIZE-13 U.S. BOOT!
AND RISK ANNIHILATION FOR NO PURPOSE?
THE ACT IS DONE. REVEALING THE ATTACK WAS TRICKERY WOULD ENDANGER THE PEACE TALKS.
THE LOGICAL THING TO DO IS TO KEEP THE SECRET AND NOT EVEN CONSIDER A PUNITIVE COUNTER-ATTACK.
IF THE BEING IS SO PUISSANT, WE WOULD BE RISKING OUR LIVES MERELY TO AVENGE THE DEAD.
YOU SAY THAT LIKE IT'S A BAD THING.
LIKE, WOULD THE ANSWER BE DIFFERENT IF THIS WAS BEIJING RATHER THAN L.A.?
THESE HYPOTHETICALS CONFUSE THE ISSUE.
AVENGING THE DEAD IS A SECONDARY CONCERN.
THE PROBLEM IS WHAT HAPPENS IF HE IS DISPLEASED WITH WHAT RESULTS FROM HIS INTERVENTION AND CHOOSES TO ACT AGAIN?
I... I'M SORRY, PETER, BUT I'M NOT CONVINCED. AN ALTERNATE DIMENSION YOU IS SENDING FAKE ALIEN-CONSTRUCTS TO MESS WITH US?
I LOVE MULTIVERSE STORIES...BUT THAT IS A HUGE LEAP. HOW CAN YOU KNOW AN ALTERNATE YOU CAN DO ANYTHING LIKE THIS?

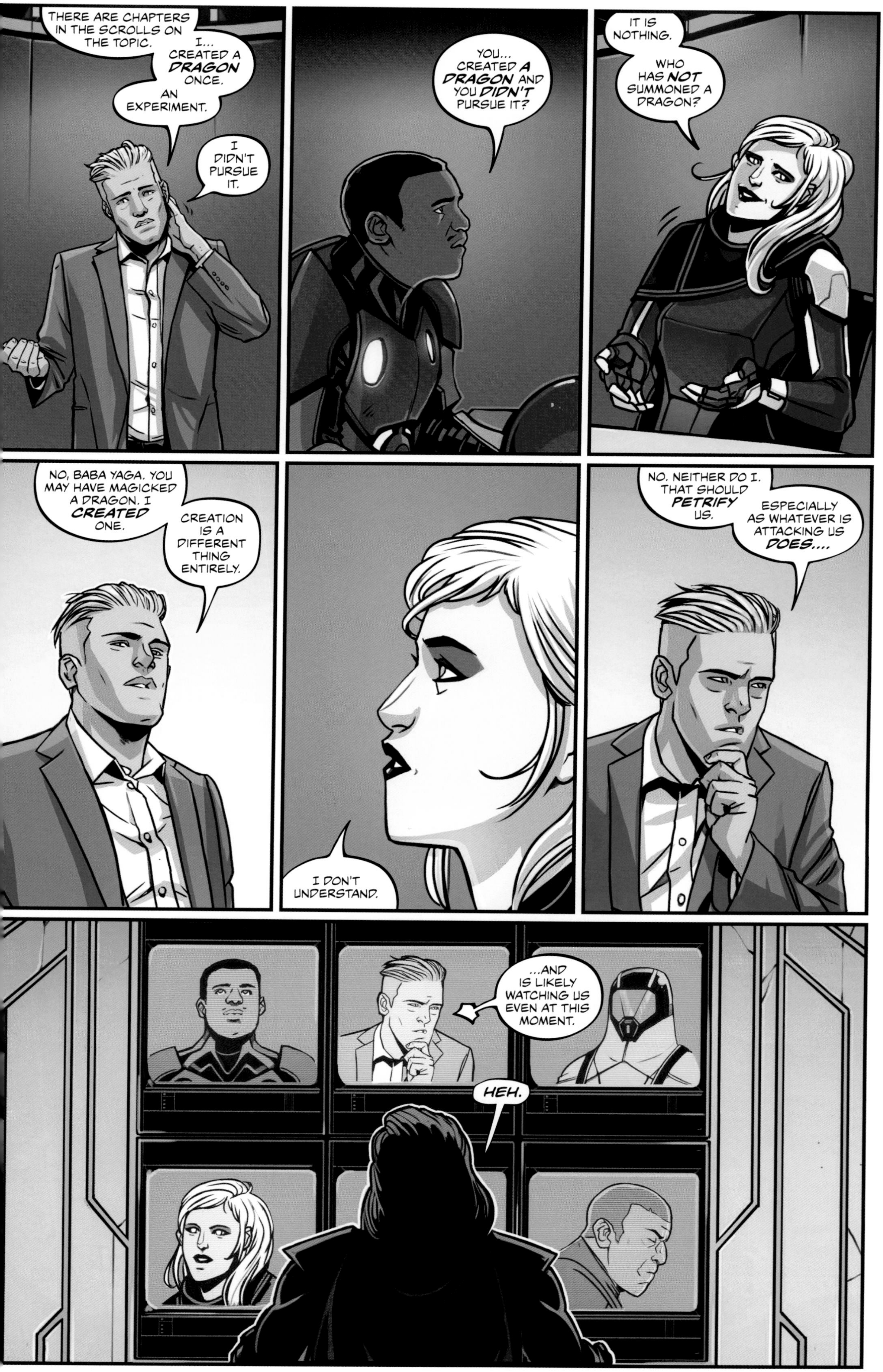
THERE ARE CHAPTERS IN THE SCROLLS ON THE TOPIC.
I... CREATED A DRAGON ONCE.
AN EXPERIMENT.
I DIDN'T PURSUE IT.
YOU... CREATED A DRAGON AND YOU DIDN'T PURSUE IT?
IT IS NOTHING.
WHO HAS NOT SUMMONED A DRAGON?
NO, BABA YAGA. YOU MAY HAVE MAGICKED A DRAGON. I CREATED ONE.
CREATION IS A DIFFERENT THING ENTIRELY.
I DON'T UNDERSTAND.
NO. NEITHER DO I. THAT SHOULD PETRIFY US.
ESPECIALLY AS WHATEVER IS ATTACKING US DOES....
...AND IS LIKELY WATCHING US EVEN AT THIS MOMENT.
HEH.

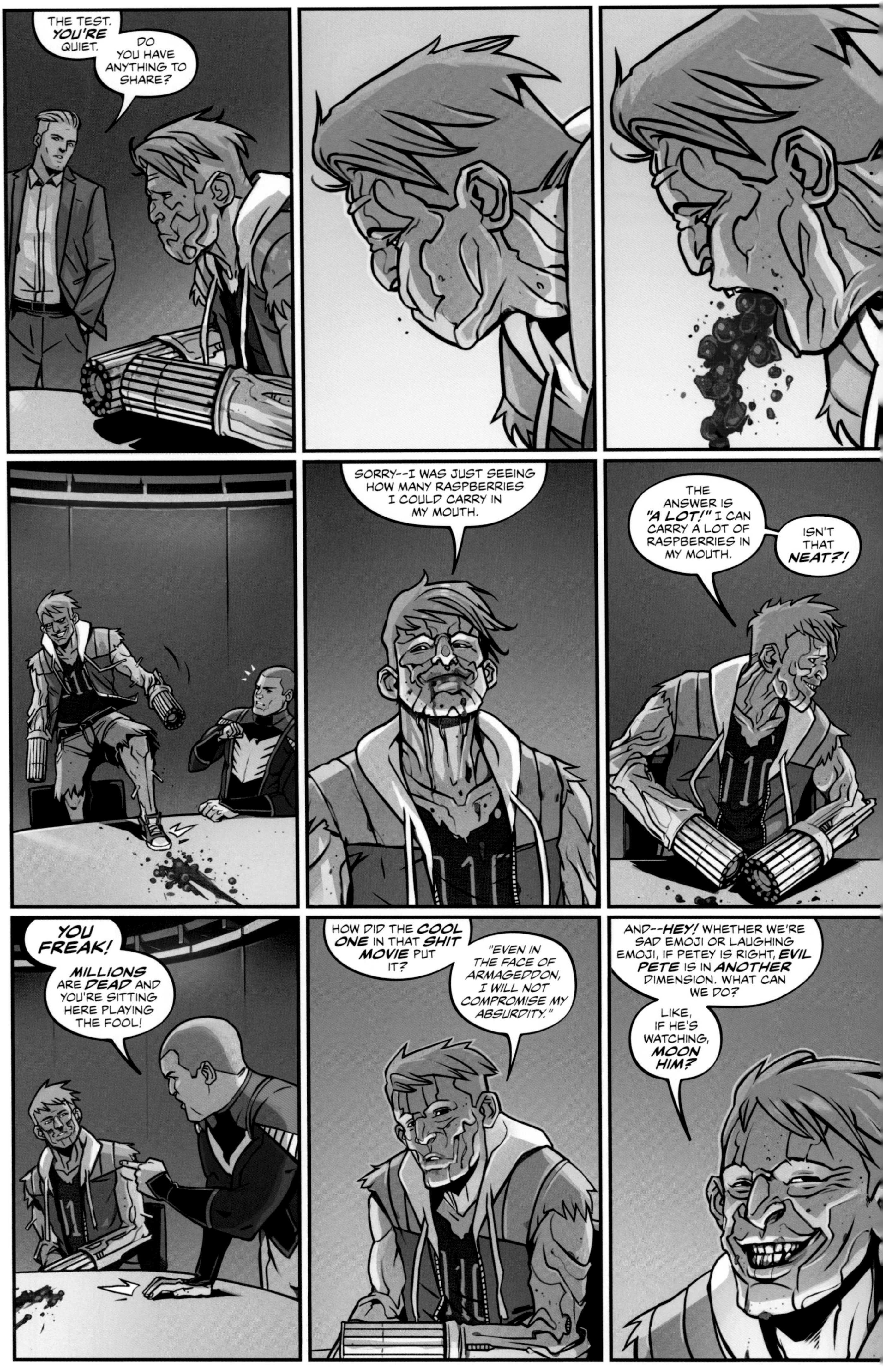
THE TEST. YOU'RE QUIET.
DO YOU HAVE ANYTHING TO SHARE?
SORRY--I WAS JUST SEEING HOW MANY RASPBERRIES I COULD CARRY IN MY MOUTH.
THE ANSWER IS "A LOT!" I CAN CARRY A LOT OF RASPBERRIES IN MY MOUTH.
ISN'T THAT NEAT?!
YOU FREAK!
MILLIONS ARE DEAD AND YOU'RE SITTING HERE PLAYING THE FOOL!
HOW DID THE COOL ONE IN THAT SHIT MOVIE PUT IT?
"EVEN IN THE FACE OF ARMAGEDDON, I WILL NOT COMPROMISE MY ABSURDITY."
AND--HEY! WHETHER WE'RE SAD EMOJI OR LAUGHING EMOJI, IF PETEY IS RIGHT, EVIL PETE IS IN ANOTHER DIMENSION. WHAT CAN WE DO?
LIKE, IF HE'S WATCHING, MOON HIM?

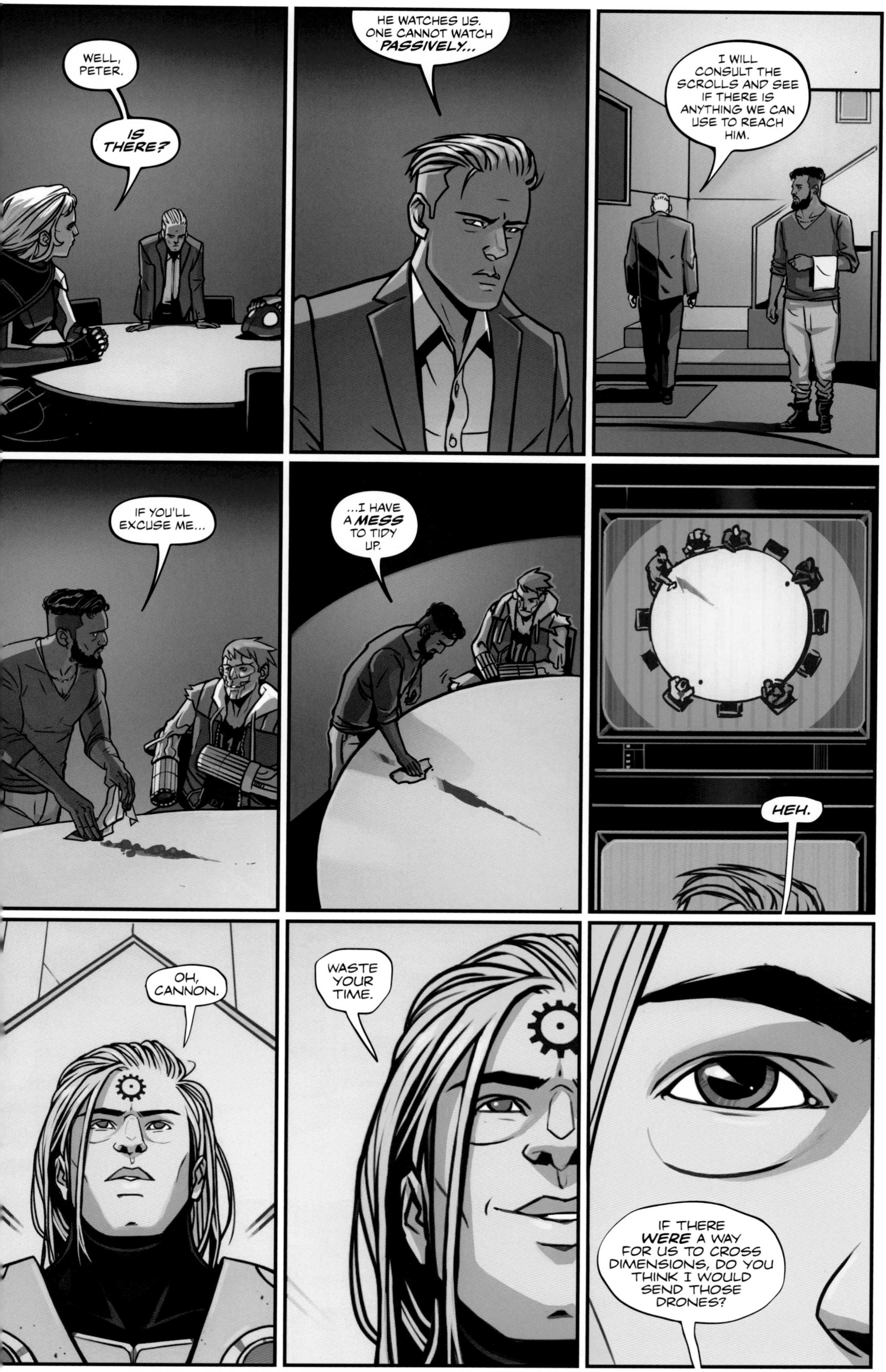
WELL, PETER.
IS THERE?
HE WATCHES US. ONE CANNOT WATCH PASSIVELY...
I WILL CONSULT THE SCROLLS AND SEE IF THERE IS ANYTHING WE CAN USE TO REACH HIM.
IF YOU'LL EXCUSE ME...
...I HAVE A MESS TO TIDY UP.
HEH.
OH, CANNON.
WASTE YOUR TIME.
IF THERE WERE A WAY FOR US TO CROSS DIMENSIONS, DO YOU THINK I WOULD SEND THOSE DRONES?

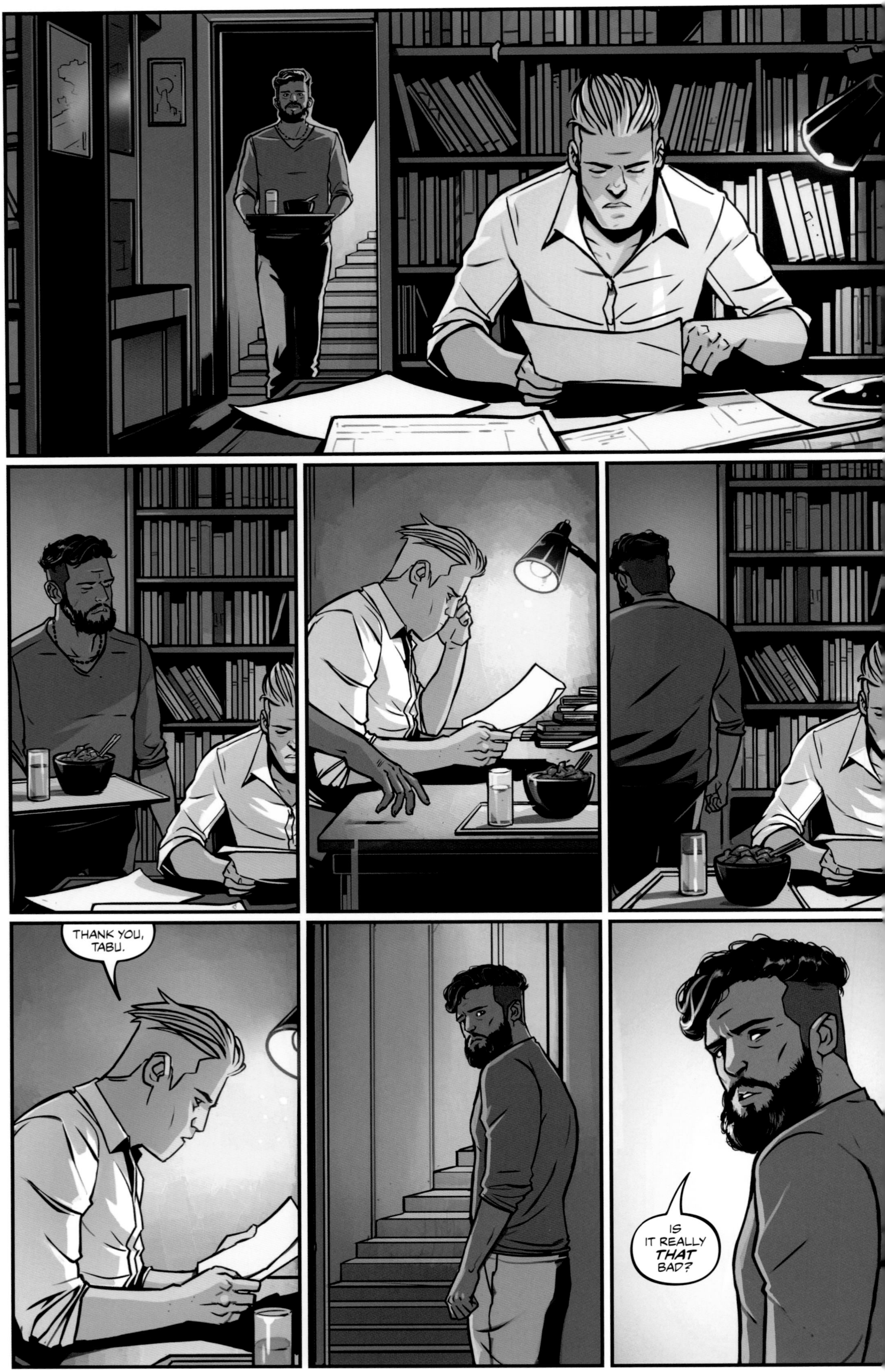
THANK YOU, TABU.
IS IT REALLY *THAT* BAD?

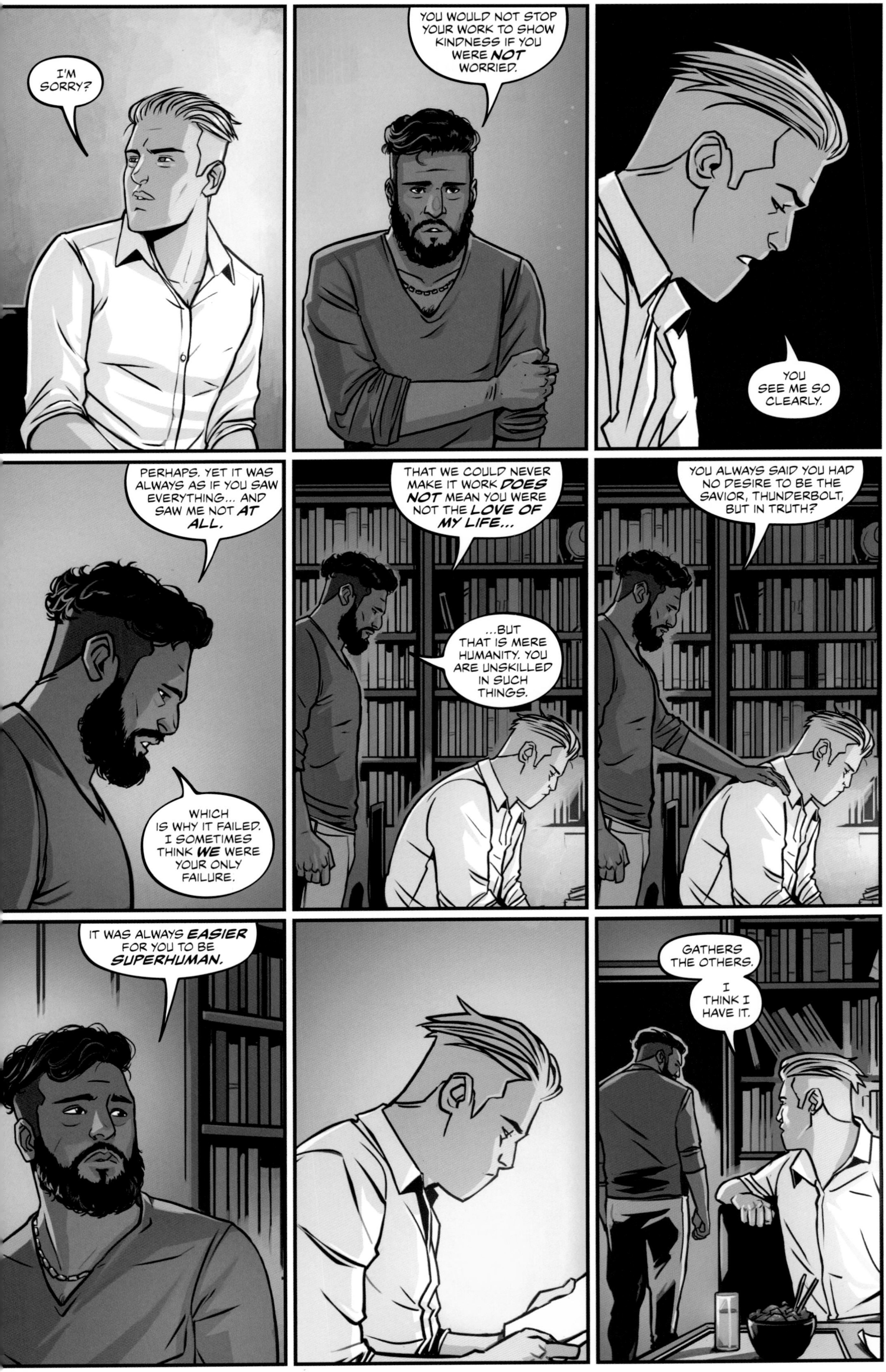

I'M SORRY?
YOU WOULD NOT STOP YOUR WORK TO SHOW KINDNESS IF YOU WERE NOT WORRIED.
YOU SEE ME SO CLEARLY.
PERHAPS. YET IT WAS ALWAYS AS IF YOU SAW EVERYTHING... AND SAW ME NOT AT ALL.
WHICH IS WHY IT FAILED. I SOMETIMES THINK WE WERE YOUR ONLY FAILURE.
THAT WE COULD NEVER MAKE IT WORK DOES NOT MEAN YOU WERE NOT THE LOVE OF MY LIFE...
...BUT THAT IS MERE HUMANITY. YOU ARE UNSKILLED IN SUCH THINGS.
YOU ALWAYS SAID YOU HAD NO DESIRE TO BE THE SAVIOR, THUNDERBOLT, BUT IN TRUTH?
IT WAS ALWAYS EASIER FOR YOU TO BE SUPERHUMAN.
GATHERS THE OTHERS.
I THINK I HAVE IT.

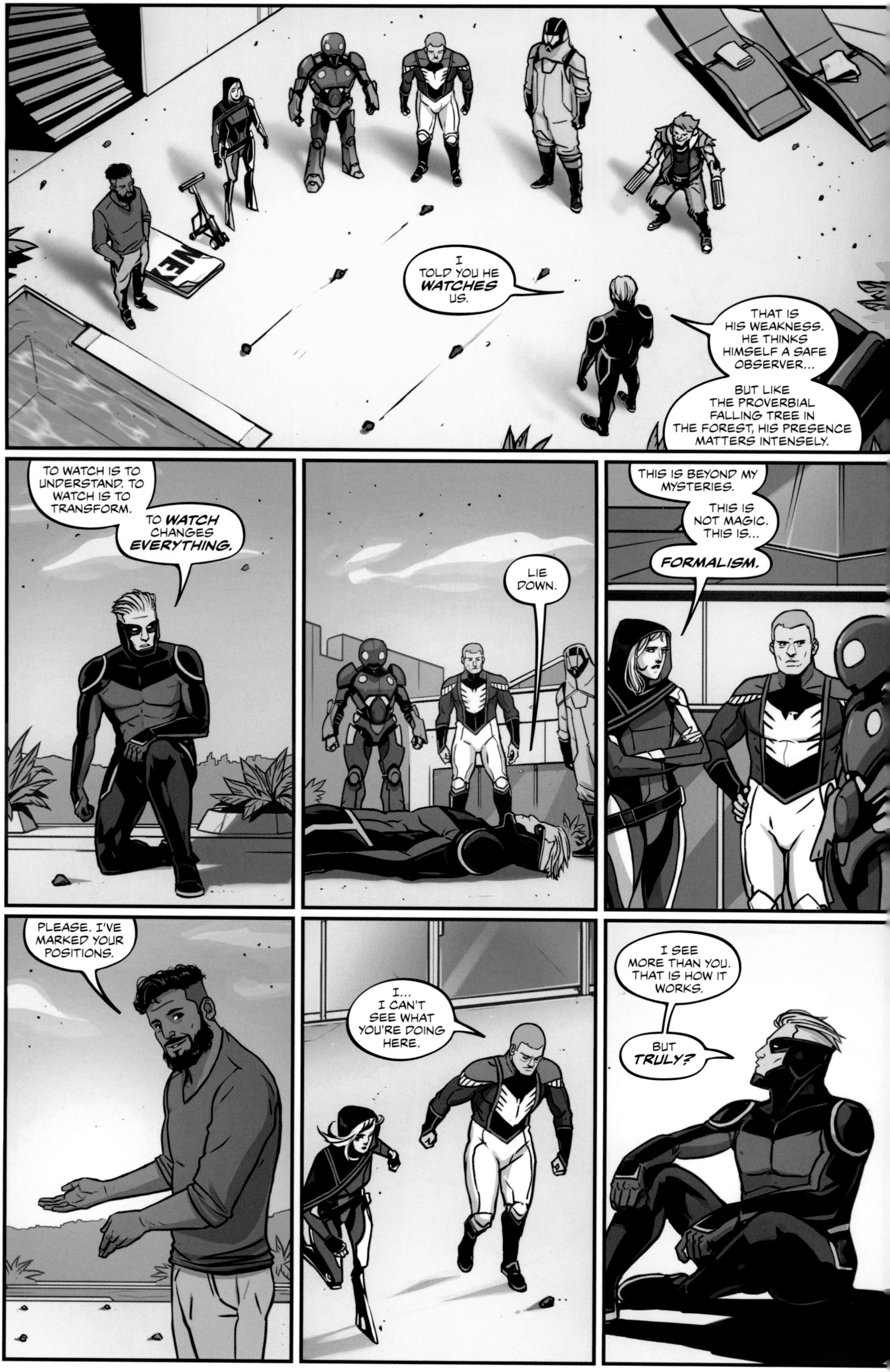
I TOLD YOU HE WATCHES US.
THAT IS HIS WEAKNESS. HE THINKS HIMSELF A SAFE OBSERVER...
BUT LIKE THE PROVERBIAL FALLING TREE IN THE FOREST, HIS PRESENCE MATTERS INTENSELY.
TO WATCH IS TO UNDERSTAND. TO WATCH IS TO TRANSFORM.
TO WATCH CHANGES EVERYTHING.
LIE DOWN.
THIS IS BEYOND MY MYSTERIES.
THIS IS NOT MAGIC. THIS IS...
FORMALISM.
PLEASE. I'VE MARKED YOUR POSITIONS.
I... I CAN'T SEE WHAT YOU'RE DOING HERE.
I SEE MORE THAN YOU. THAT IS HOW IT WORKS.
BUT TRULY?

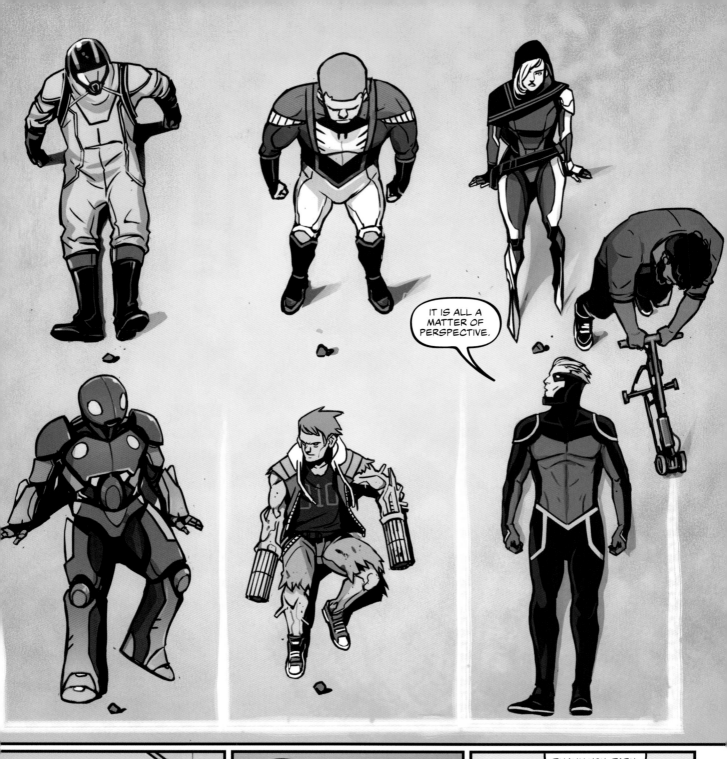

IT IS ALL A MATTER OF PERSPECTIVE.

HMMM.

DONE.

THANK YOU, TABU. NOW...

STEP BACK.

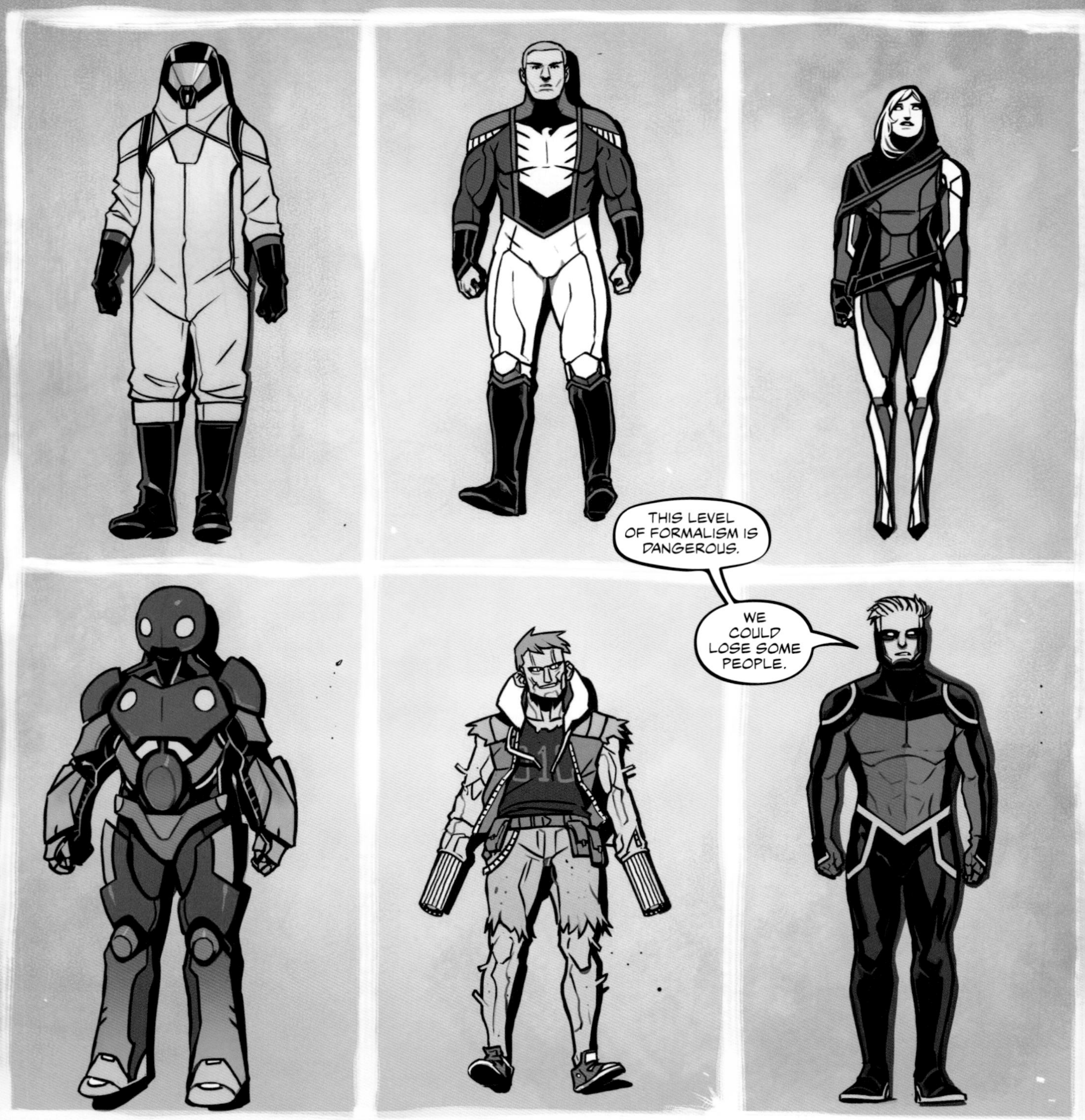
THIS LEVEL OF FORMALISM IS DANGEROUS.
WE COULD LOSE SOME PEOPLE.

NEXT: THE CROSSOVER

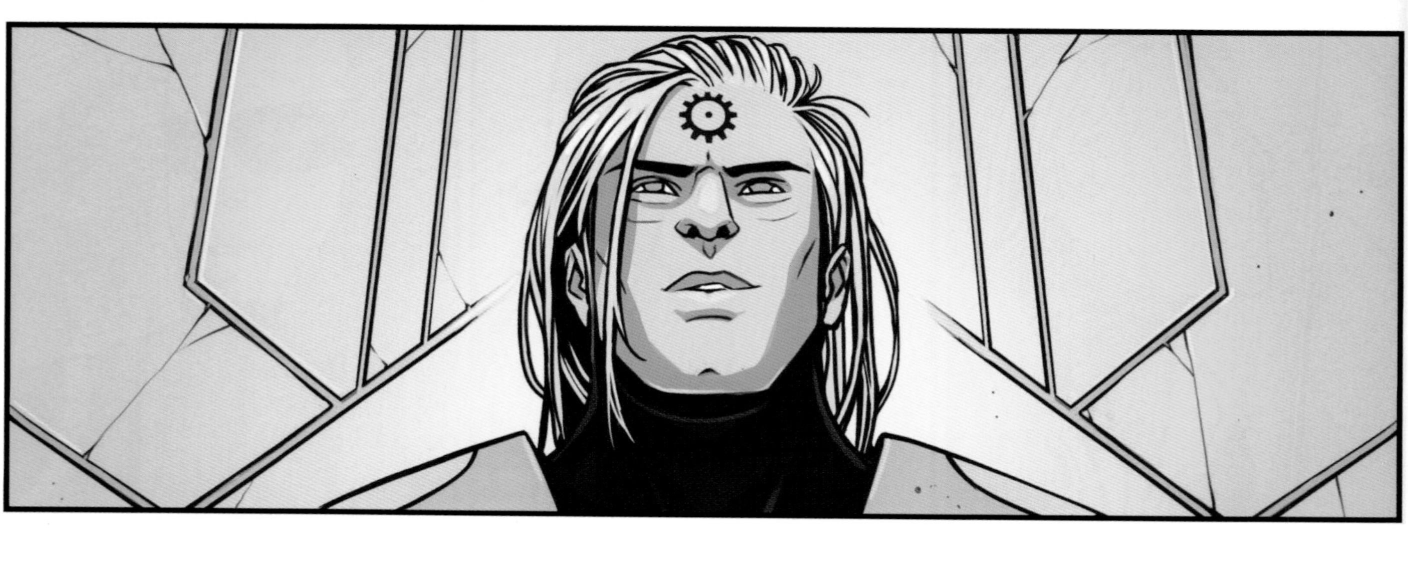

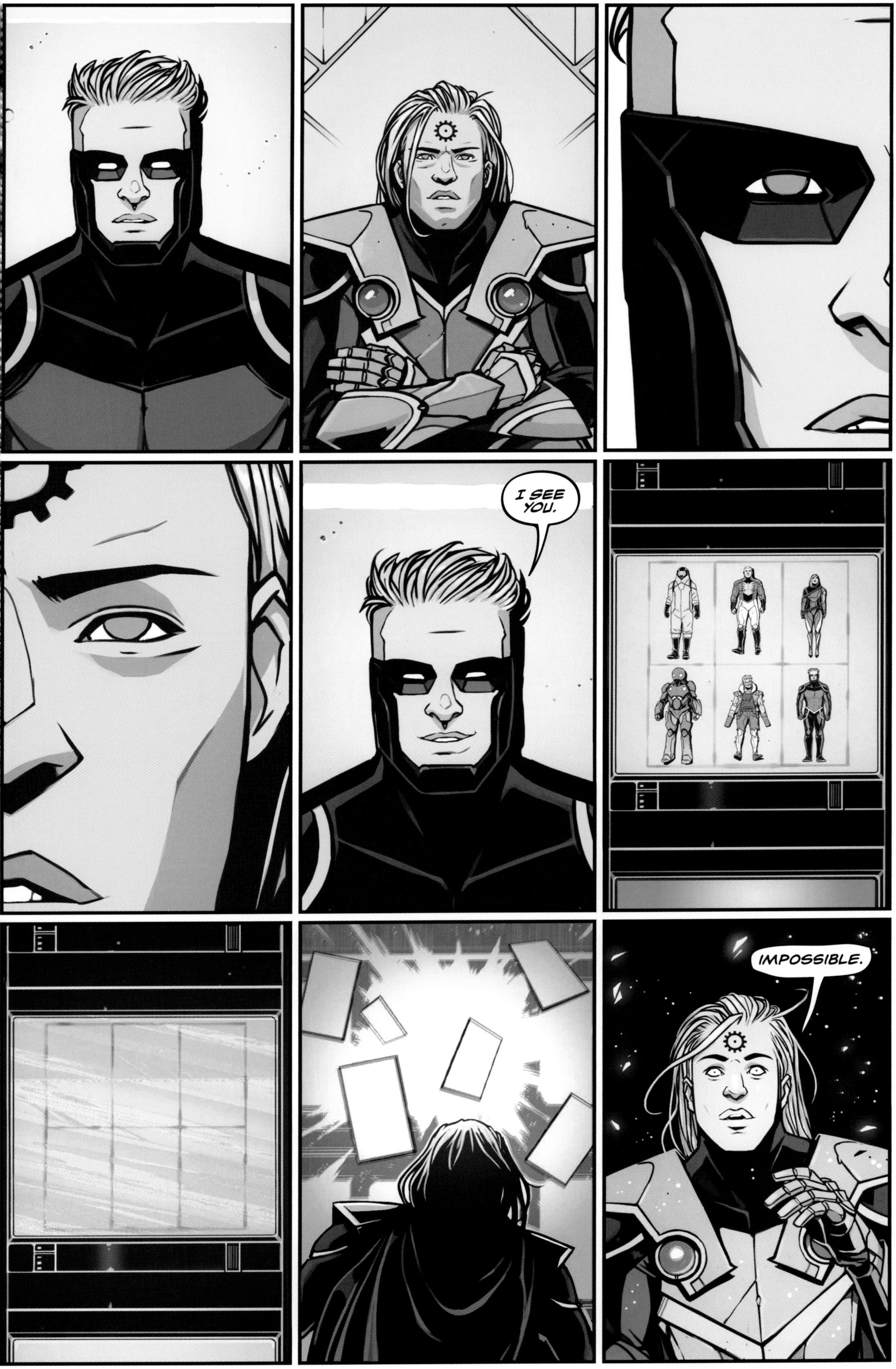
I SEE YOU.
IMPOSSIBLE.

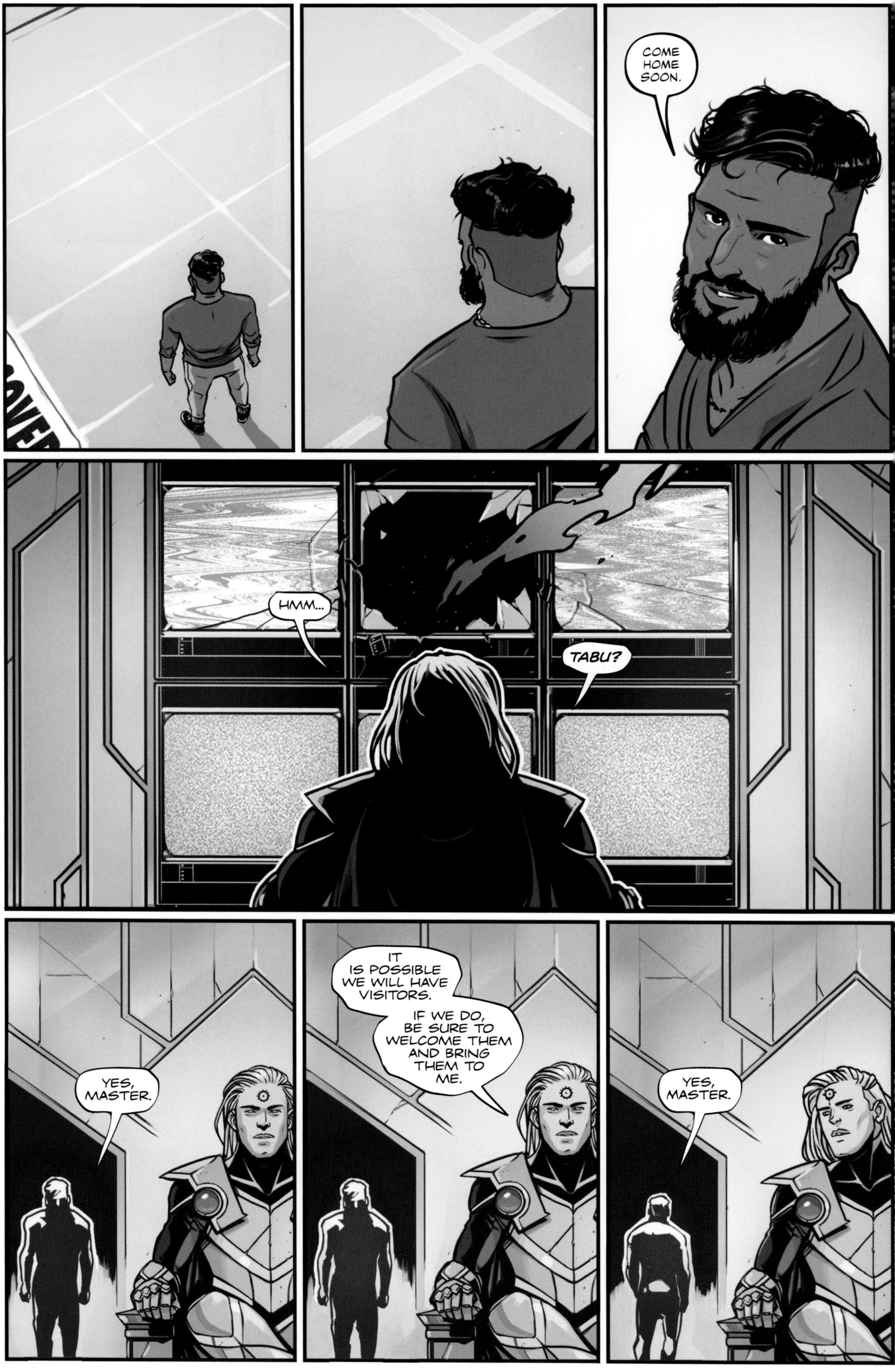
COME HOME SOON.
HMM...
TABU?
YES, MASTER.
IT IS POSSIBLE WE WILL HAVE VISITORS.
IF WE DO, BE SURE TO WELCOME THEM AND BRING THEM TO ME.
YES, MASTER.

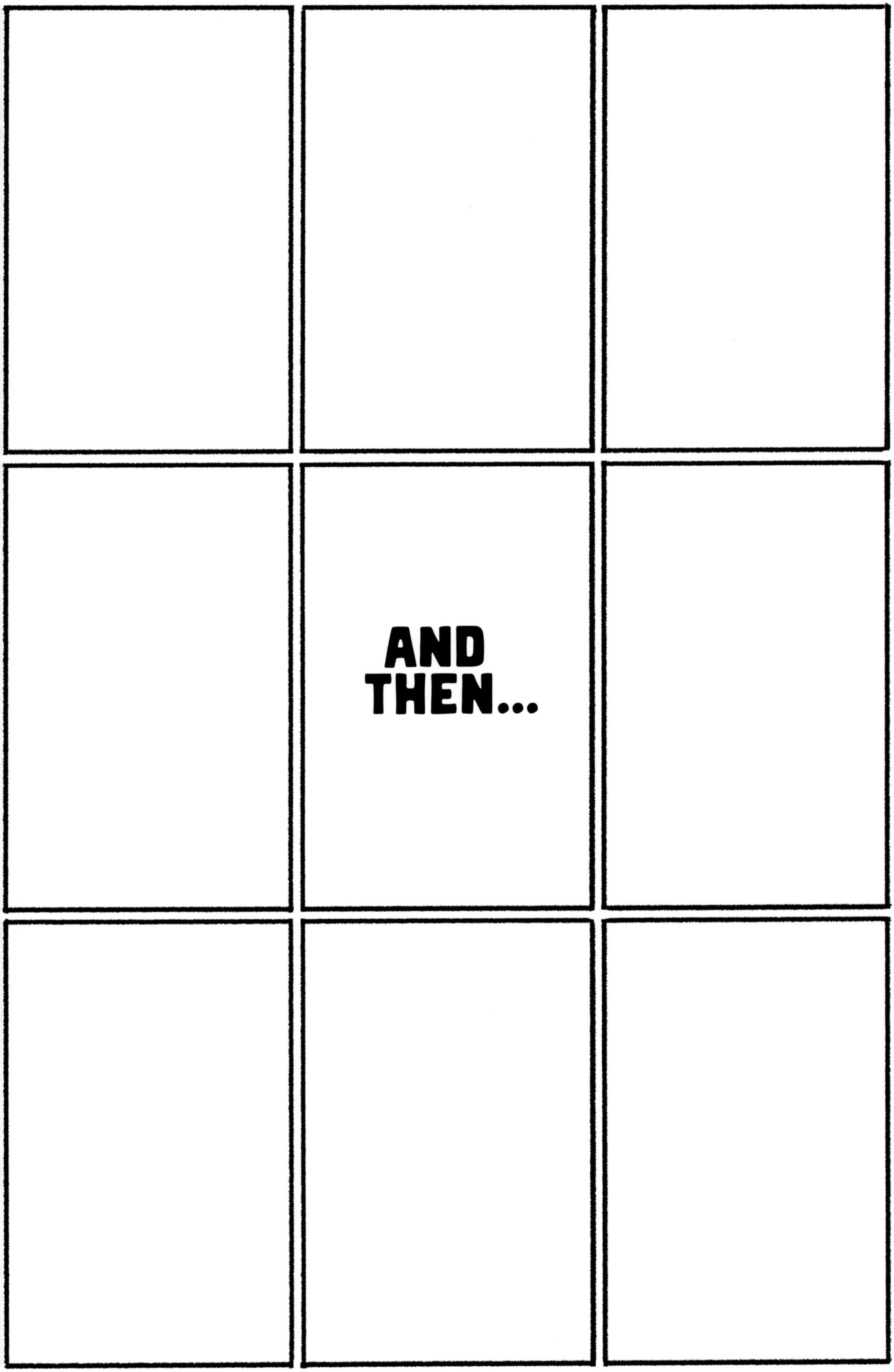
AND THEN...

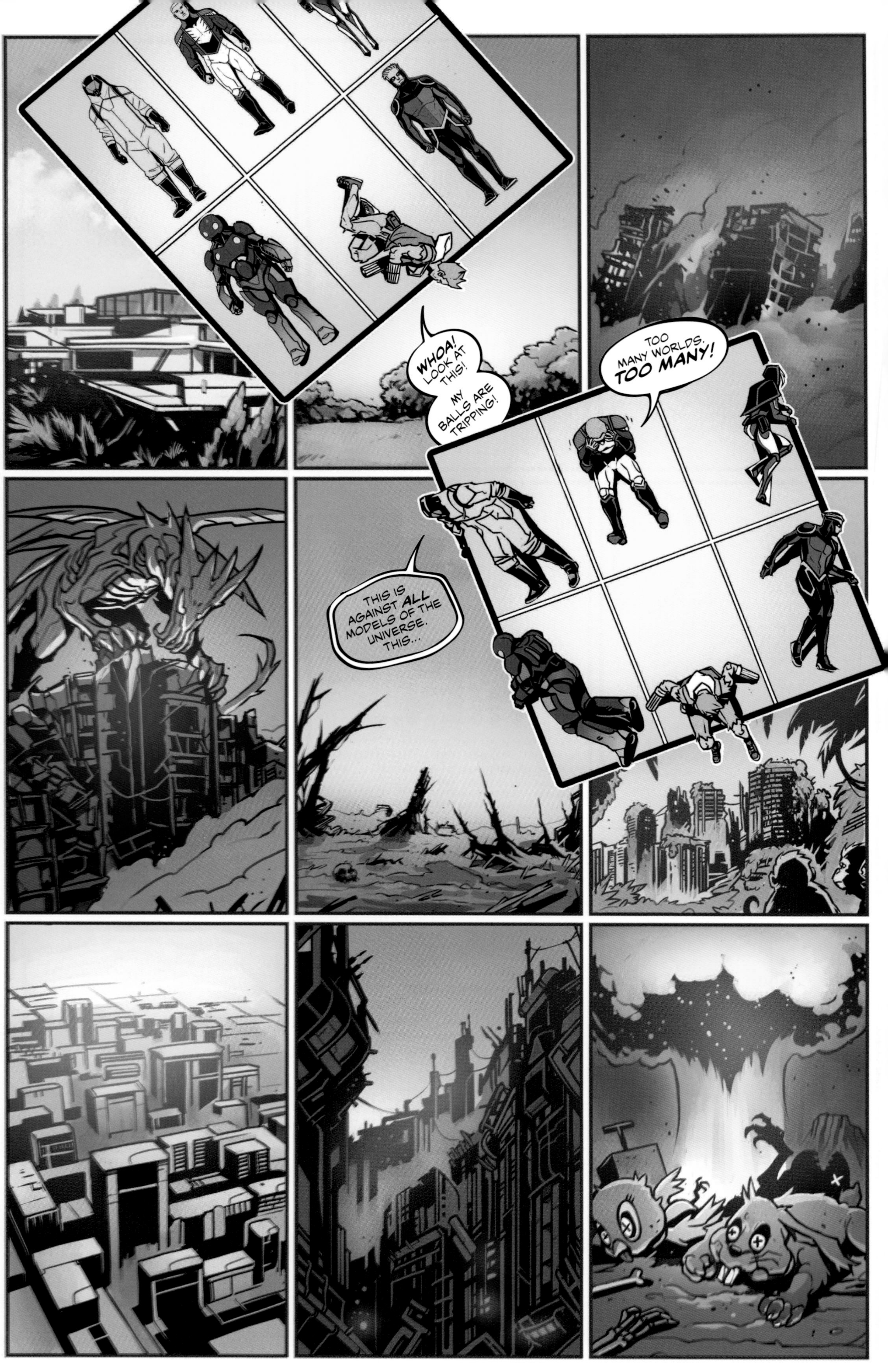
WHOA! LOOK AT THIS!
MY BALLS ARE TRIPPING!
TOO MANY WORLDS. TOO MANY!
THIS IS AGAINST ALL MODELS OF THE UNIVERSE. THIS...

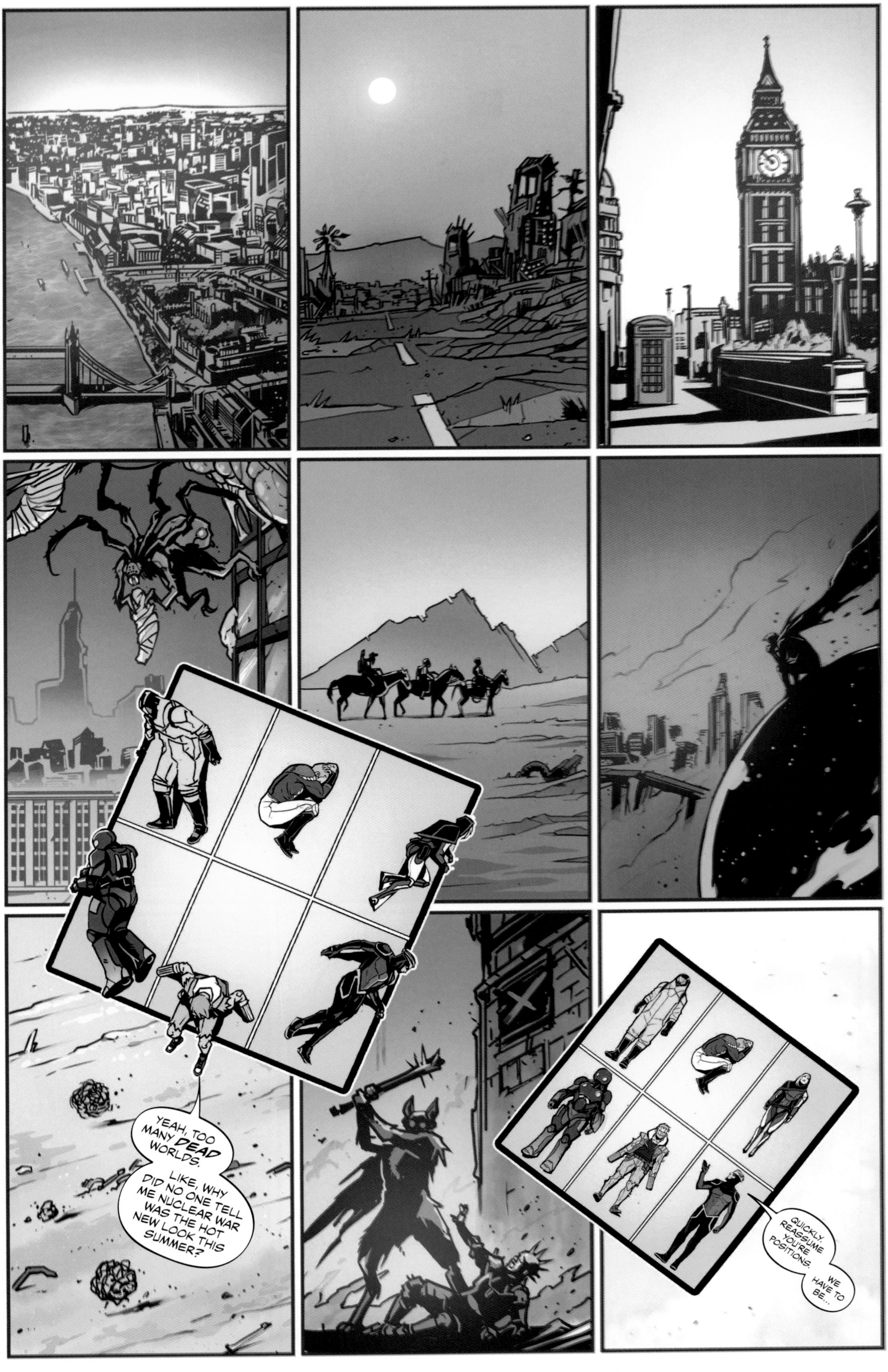

YEAH, TOO MANY DEAD WORLDS.
LIKE, WHY DID NO ONE TELL ME NUCLEAR WAR WAS THE HOT NEW LOOK THIS SUMMER?
QUICKLY. REASSUME YOU'RE POSITIONS.
WE HAVE TO BE...

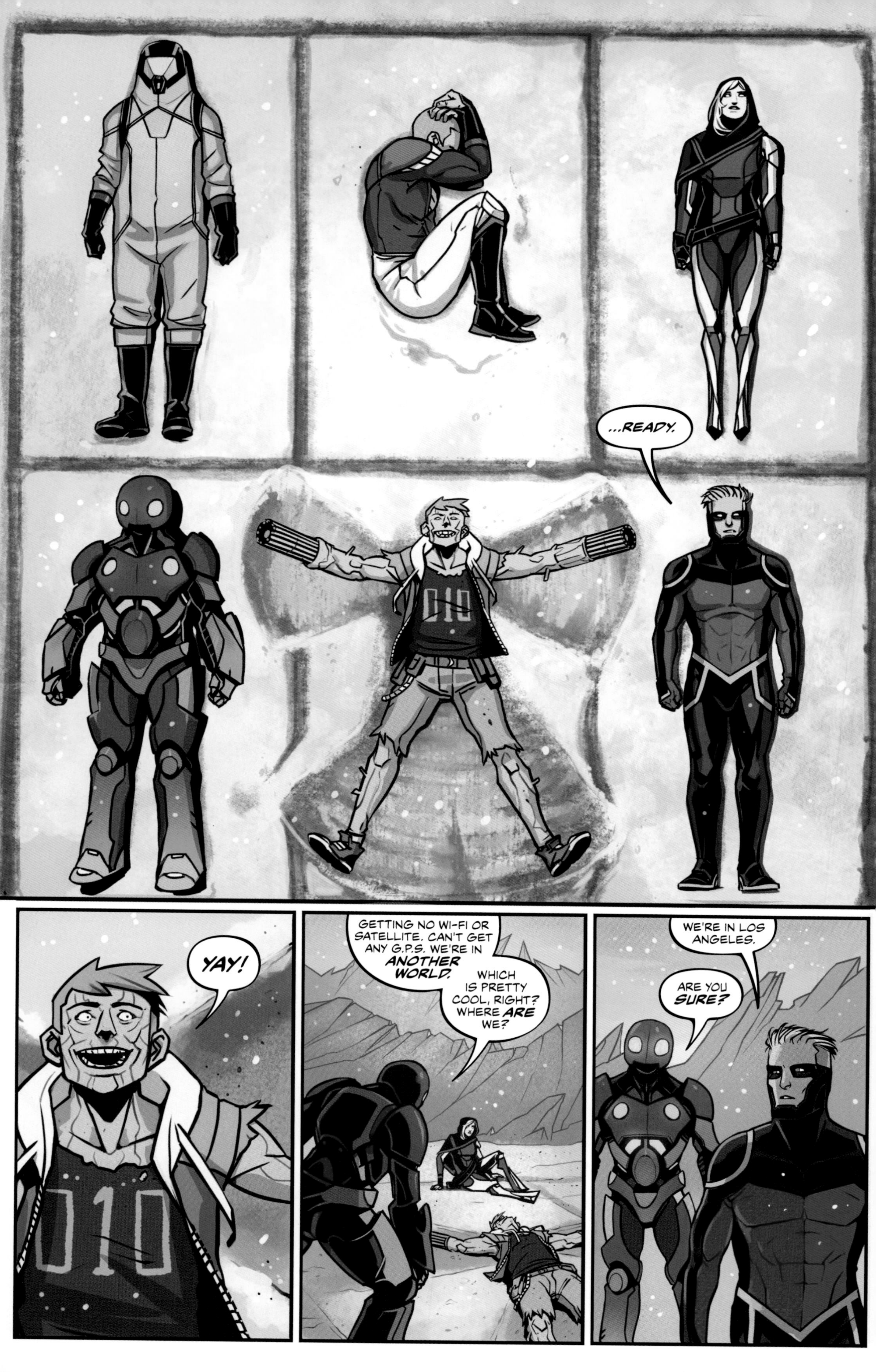
...READY.
YAY!
GETTING NO WI-FI OR SATELLITE. CAN'T GET ANY G.P.S. WE'RE IN ANOTHER WORLD.
WHICH IS PRETTY COOL, RIGHT? WHERE ARE WE?
WE'RE IN LOS ANGELES.
ARE YOU SURE?

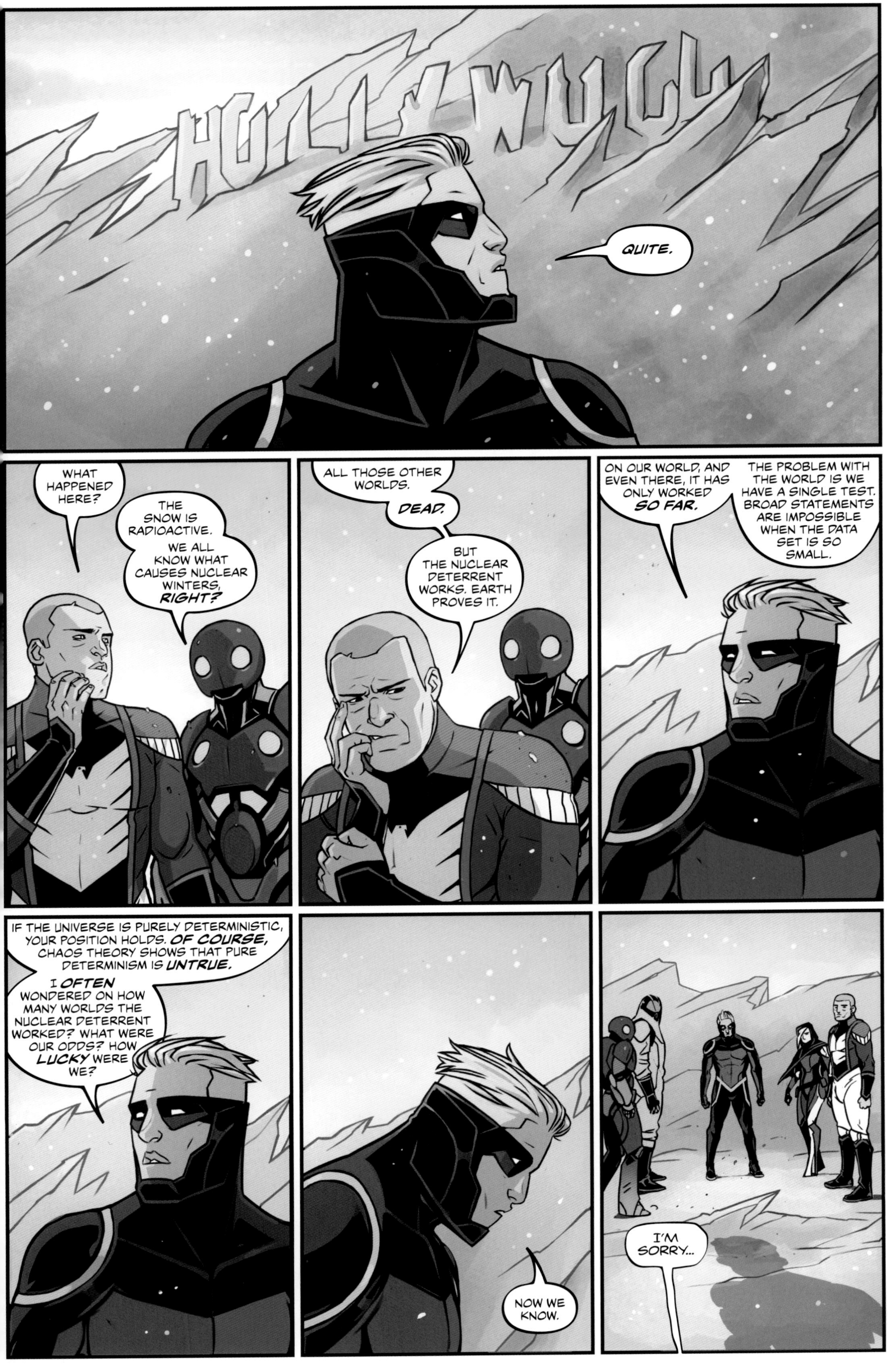
QUITE.
WHAT HAPPENED HERE?
THE SNOW IS RADIOACTIVE.
WE ALL KNOW WHAT CAUSES NUCLEAR WINTERS, RIGHT?
ALL THOSE OTHER WORLDS.
DEAD.
BUT THE NUCLEAR DETERRENT WORKS. EARTH PROVES IT.
ON OUR WORLD, AND EVEN THERE, IT HAS ONLY WORKED SO FAR.
THE PROBLEM WITH THE WORLD IS WE HAVE A SINGLE TEST. BROAD STATEMENTS ARE IMPOSSIBLE WHEN THE DATA SET IS SO SMALL.
IF THE UNIVERSE IS PURELY DETERMINISTIC, YOUR POSITION HOLDS. OF COURSE, CHAOS THEORY SHOWS THAT PURE DETERMINISM IS UNTRUE.
I OFTEN WONDERED ON HOW MANY WORLDS THE NUCLEAR DETERRENT WORKED? WHAT WERE OUR ODDS? HOW LUCKY WERE WE?
NOW WE KNOW.
I'M SORRY...

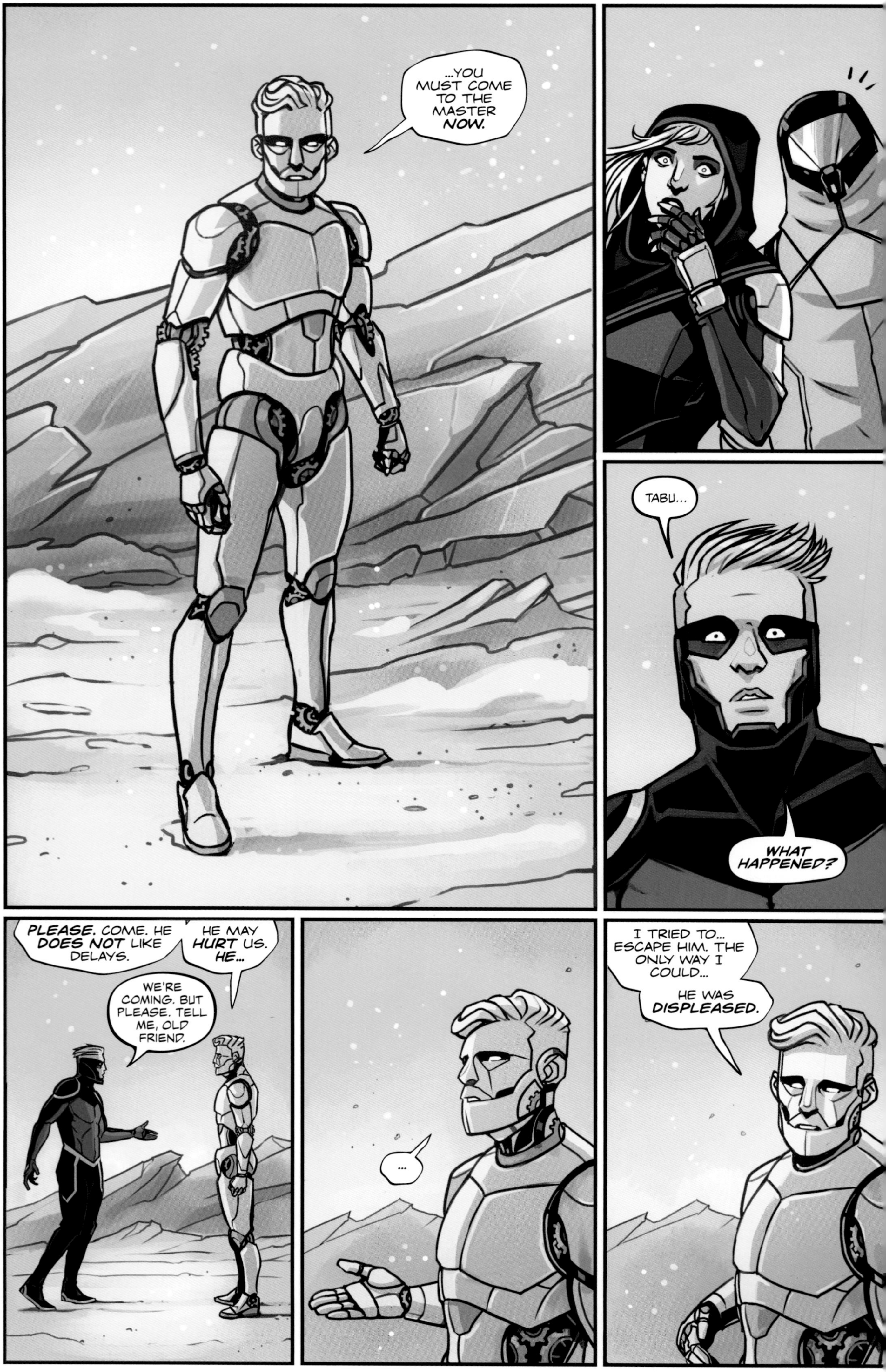
...YOU MUST COME TO THE MASTER NOW.
TABU...
WHAT HAPPENED?
PLEASE. COME. HE DOES NOT LIKE DELAYS.
HE MAY HURT US. HE...
WE'RE COMING. BUT PLEASE. TELL ME, OLD FRIEND.
...
I TRIED TO... ESCAPE HIM. THE ONLY WAY I COULD...
HE WAS DISPLEASED.

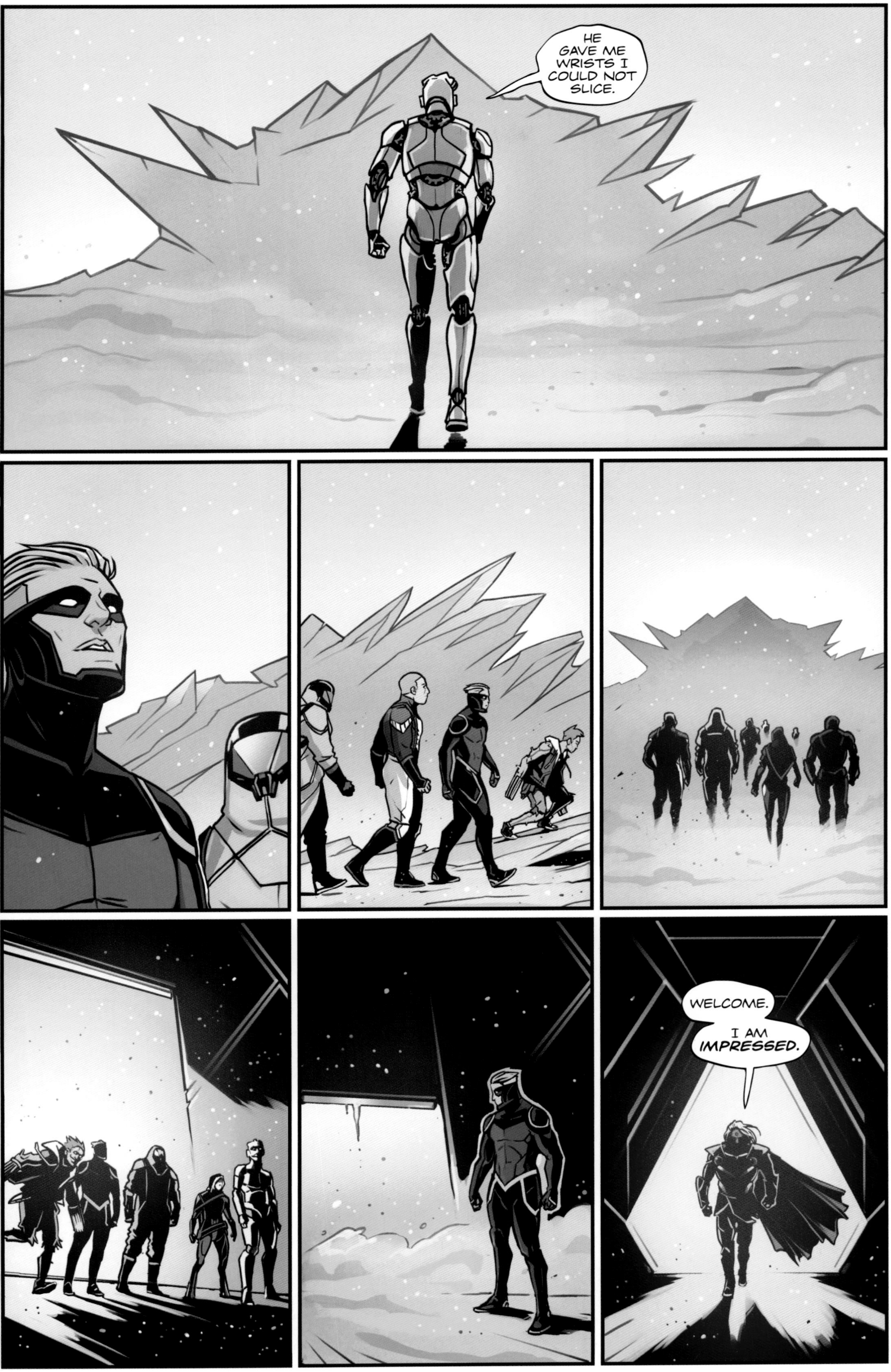
HE GAVE ME WRISTS I COULD NOT SLICE.
WELCOME.
I AM *IMPRESSED.*

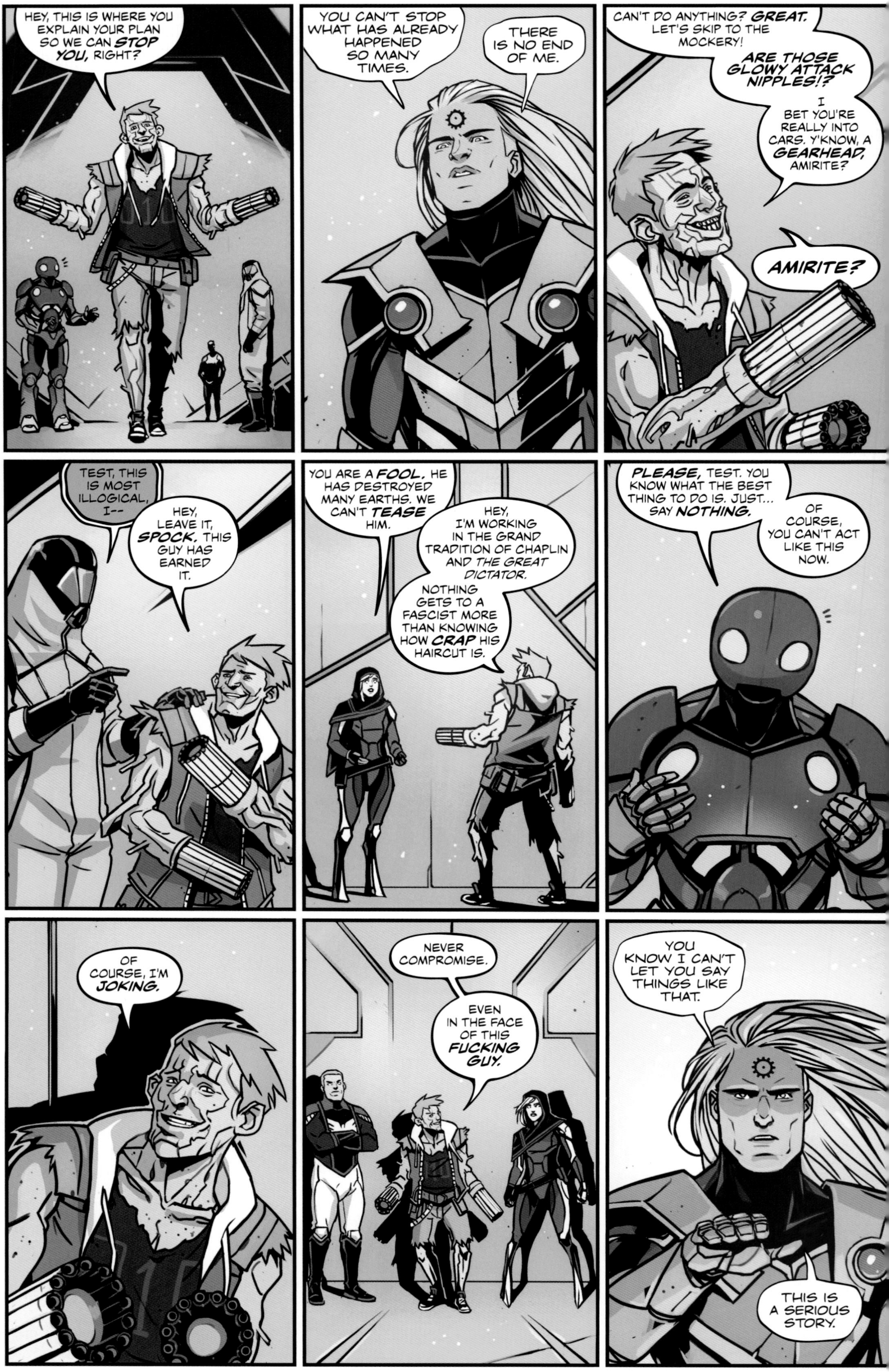
HEY, THIS IS WHERE YOU EXPLAIN YOUR PLAN SO WE CAN STOP YOU, RIGHT?
YOU CAN'T STOP WHAT HAS ALREADY HAPPENED SO MANY TIMES.
THERE IS NO END OF ME.
CAN'T DO ANYTHING? GREAT. LET'S SKIP TO THE MOCKERY!
ARE THOSE GLOWY ATTACK NIPPLES!?
I BET YOU'RE REALLY INTO CARS. Y'KNOW, A GEARHEAD, AMIRITE?
AMIRITE?
TEST, THIS IS MOST ILLOGICAL, I--
HEY, LEAVE IT, SPOCK. THIS GUY HAS EARNED IT.
YOU ARE A FOOL. HE HAS DESTROYED MANY EARTHS. WE CAN'T TEASE HIM.
HEY, I'M WORKING IN THE GRAND TRADITION OF CHAPLIN AND THE GREAT DICTATOR.
NOTHING GETS TO A FASCIST MORE THAN KNOWING HOW CRAP HIS HAIRCUT IS.
PLEASE, TEST. YOU KNOW WHAT THE BEST THING TO DO IS. JUST... SAY NOTHING.
OF COURSE, YOU CAN'T ACT LIKE THIS NOW.
OF COURSE, I'M JOKING.
NEVER COMPROMISE.
EVEN IN THE FACE OF THIS FUCKING GUY.
YOU KNOW I CAN'T LET YOU SAY THINGS LIKE THAT.
THIS IS A SERIOUS STORY.

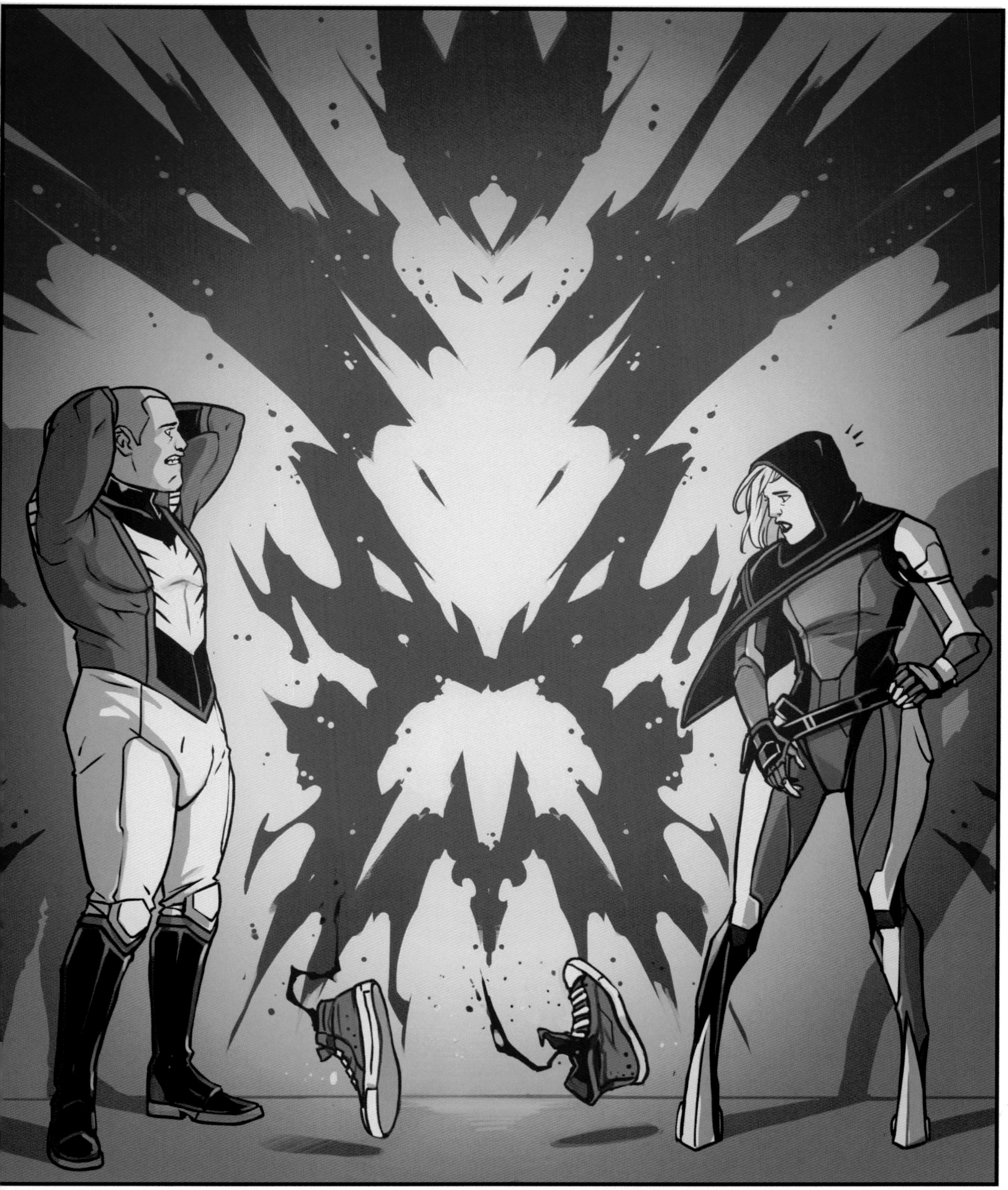

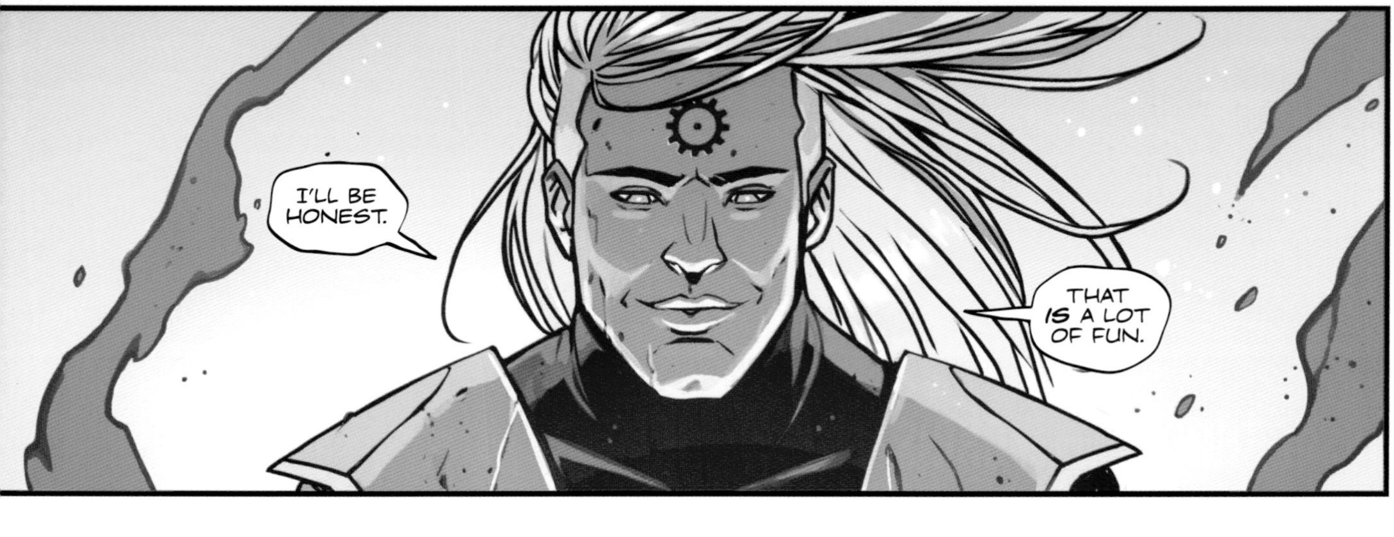
I'LL BE HONEST.
THAT IS A LOT OF FUN.

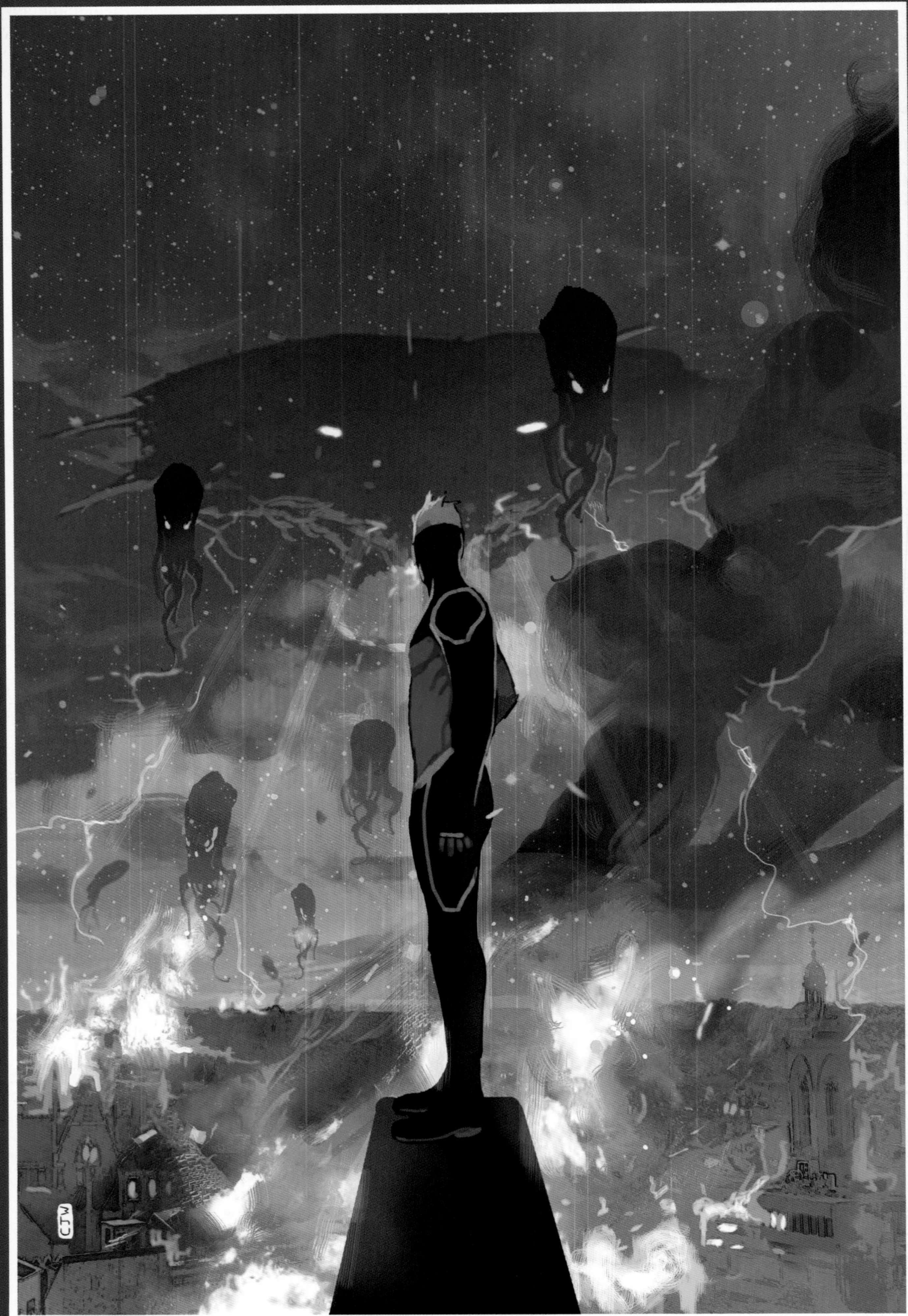
CJW

ISSUE THREE COVER BY CHRISTIAN WARD

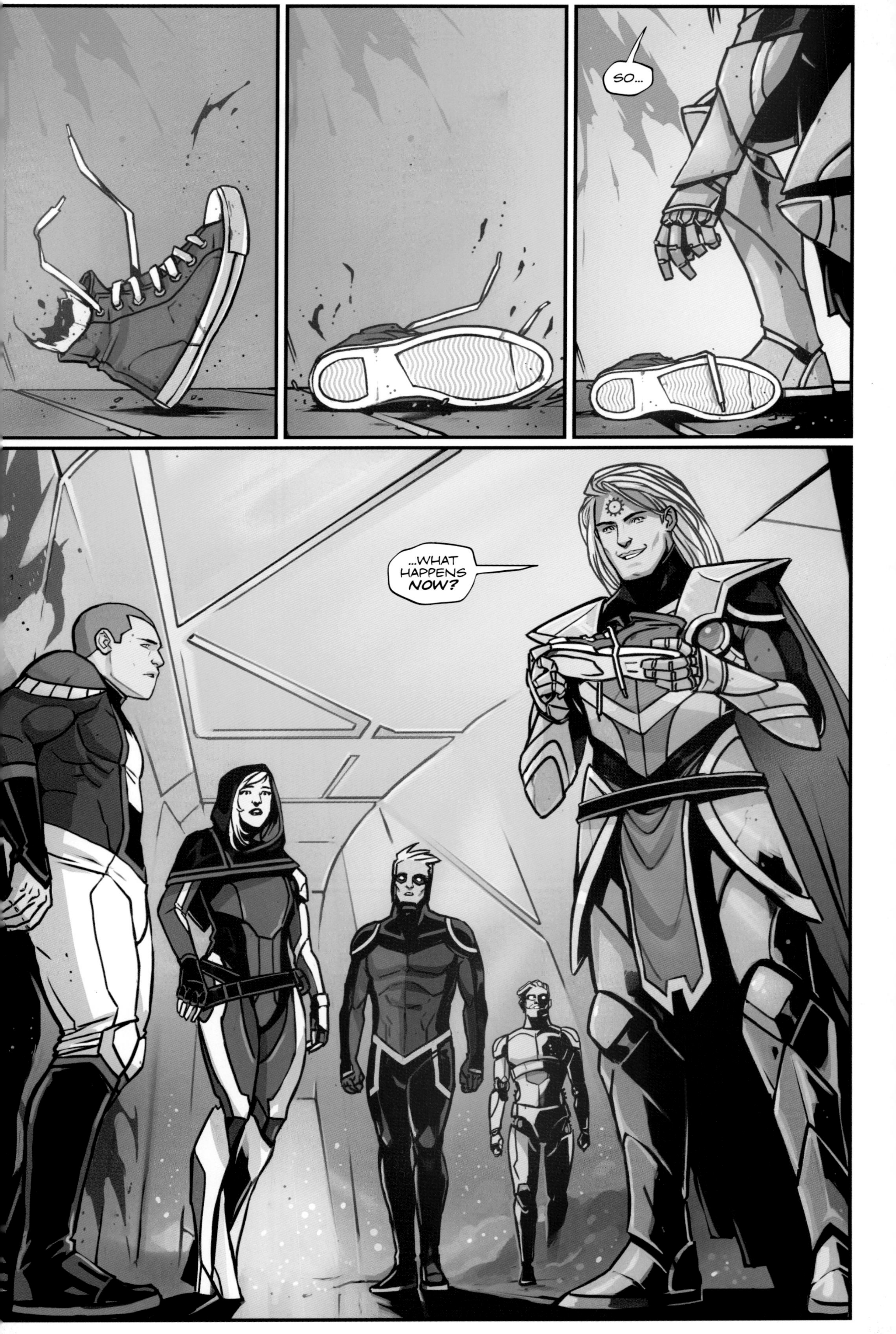
SO...
...WHAT HAPPENS NOW?

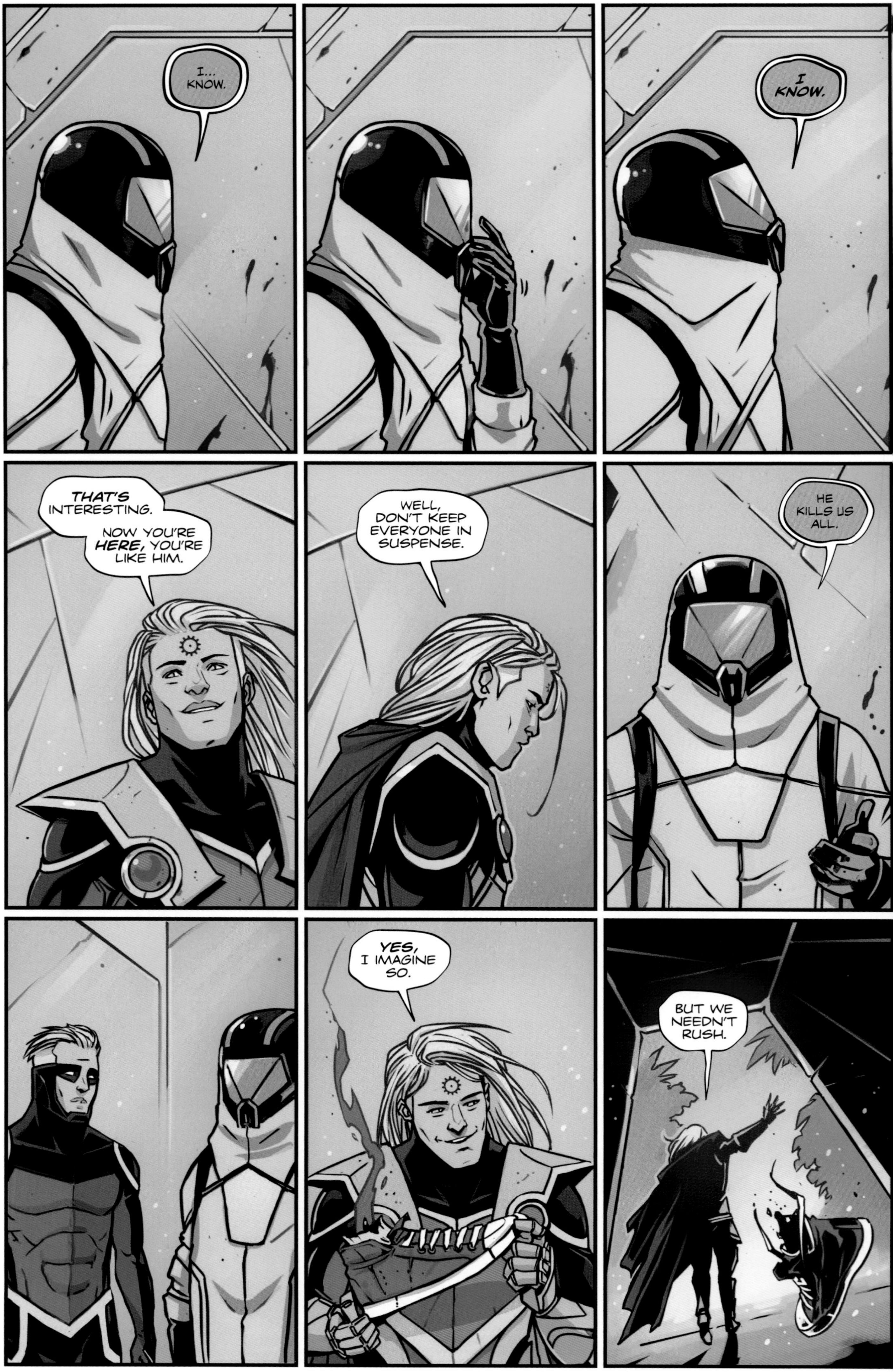
I... KNOW.
I KNOW.
THAT'S INTERESTING.
NOW YOU'RE HERE, YOU'RE LIKE HIM.
WELL, DON'T KEEP EVERYONE IN SUSPENSE.
HE KILLS US ALL.
YES, I IMAGINE SO.
BUT WE NEEDN'T RUSH.

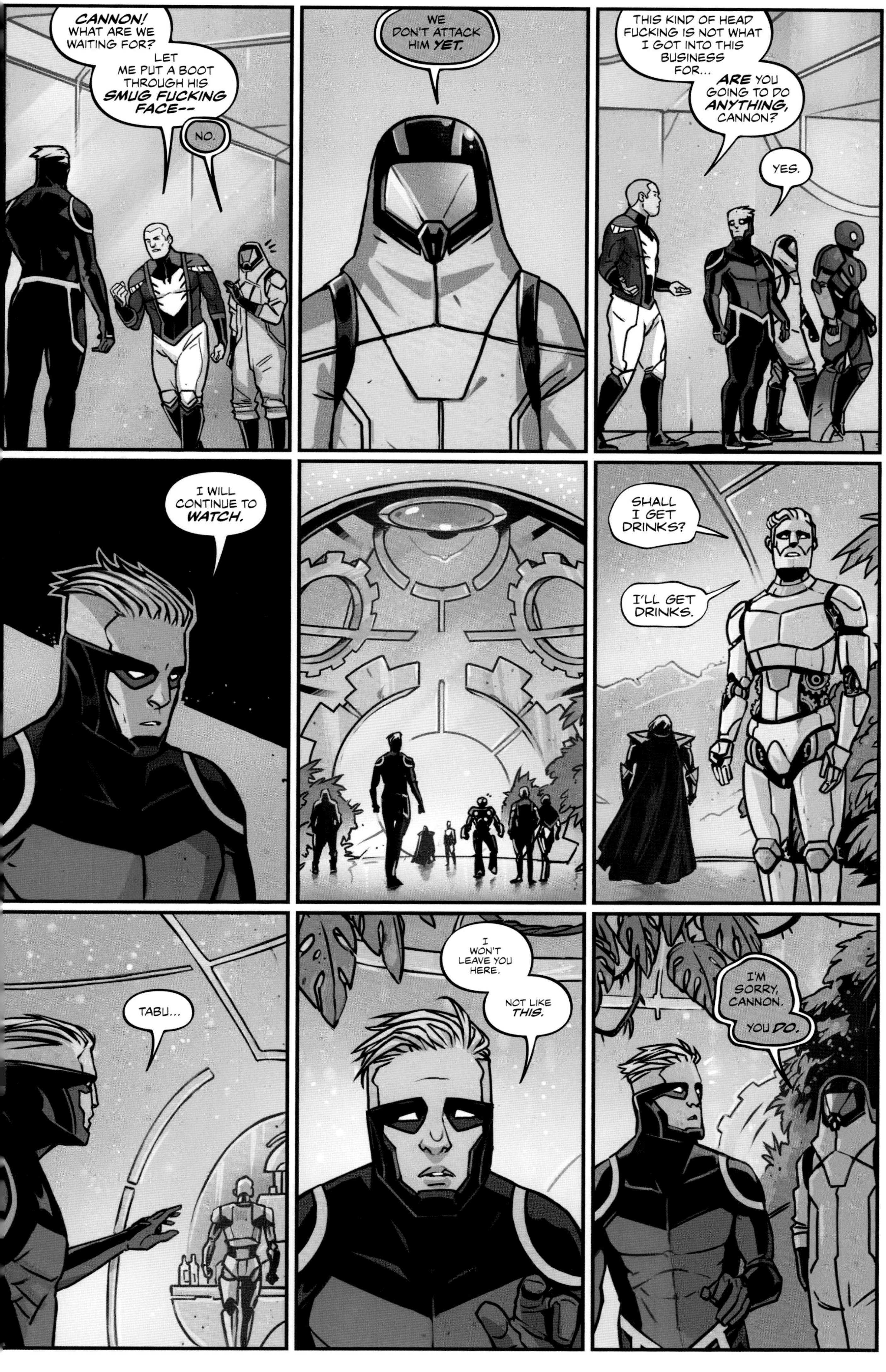
CANNON! WHAT ARE WE WAITING FOR?
LET ME PUT A BOOT THROUGH HIS SMUG FUCKING FACE--
NO.
WE DON'T ATTACK HIM YET.
THIS KIND OF HEAD FUCKING IS NOT WHAT I GOT INTO THIS BUSINESS FOR...
ARE YOU GOING TO DO ANYTHING, CANNON?
YES.
I WILL CONTINUE TO WATCH.
SHALL I GET DRINKS?
I'LL GET DRINKS.
TABU...
I WON'T LEAVE YOU HERE.
NOT LIKE THIS.
I'M SORRY, CANNON.
YOU DO.

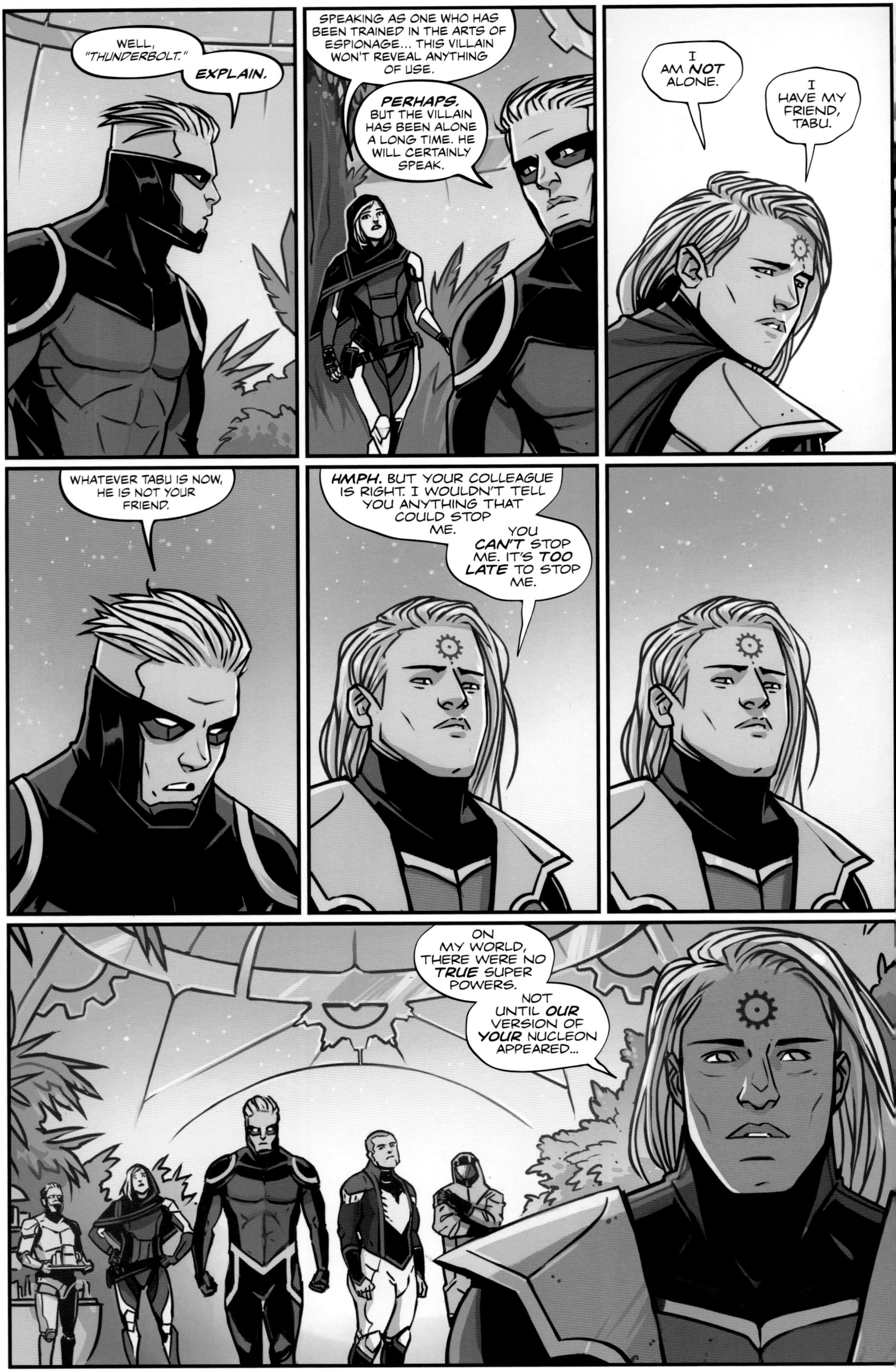
WELL, "THUNDERBOLT." EXPLAIN.
SPEAKING AS ONE WHO HAS BEEN TRAINED IN THE ARTS OF ESPIONAGE... THIS VILLAIN WON'T REVEAL ANYTHING OF USE.
PERHAPS. BUT THE VILLAIN HAS BEEN ALONE A LONG TIME. HE WILL CERTAINLY SPEAK.
I AM NOT ALONE.
I HAVE MY FRIEND, TABU.
WHATEVER TABU IS NOW, HE IS NOT YOUR FRIEND.
HMPH. BUT YOUR COLLEAGUE IS RIGHT. I WOULDN'T TELL YOU ANYTHING THAT COULD STOP ME.
YOU CAN'T STOP ME. IT'S TOO LATE TO STOP ME.
ON MY WORLD, THERE WERE NO TRUE SUPER POWERS.
NOT UNTIL OUR VERSION OF YOUR NUCLEON APPEARED...

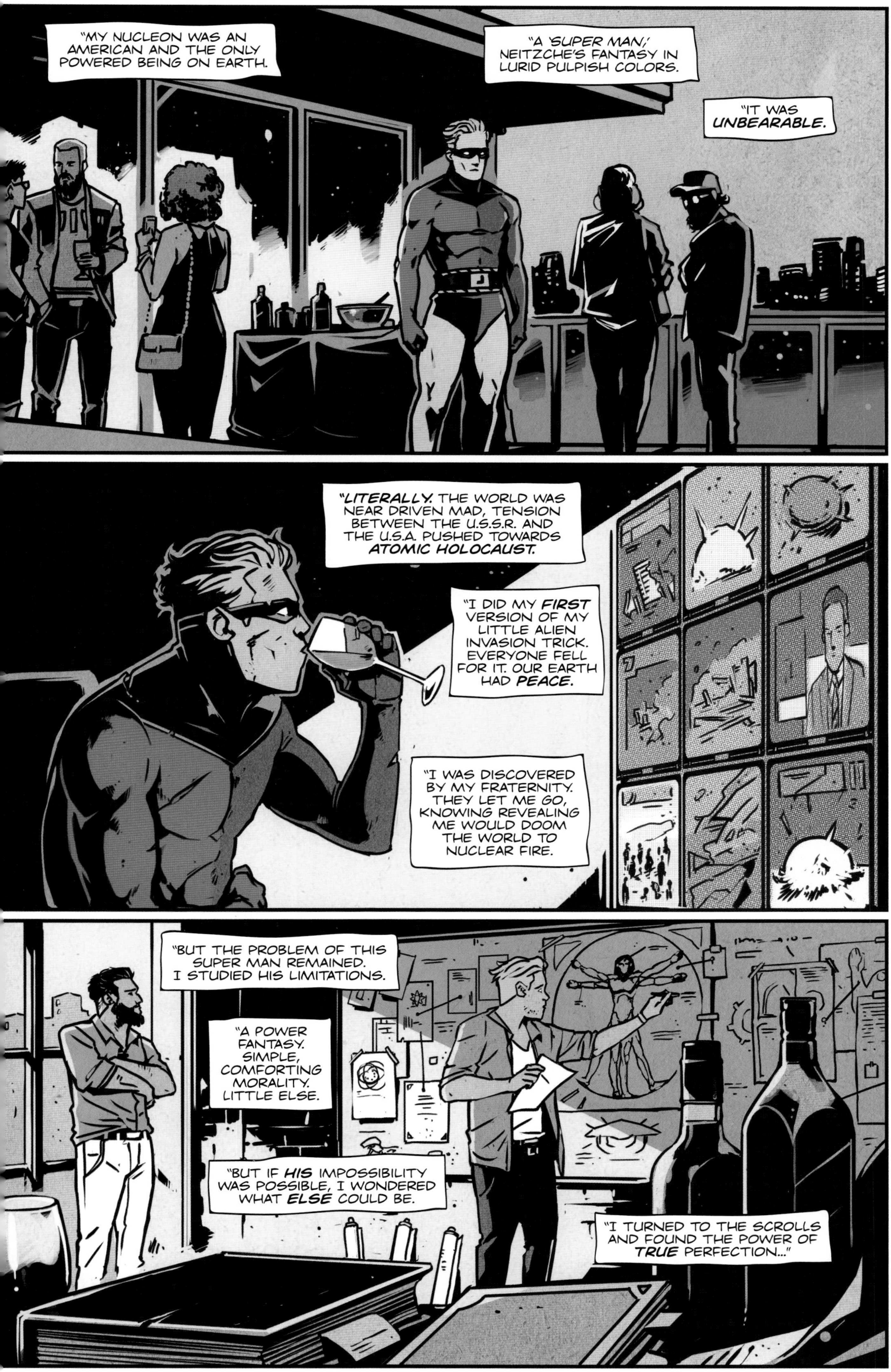
"MY NUCLEON WAS AN AMERICAN AND THE ONLY POWERED BEING ON EARTH.
"A 'SUPER MAN,' NEITZCHE'S FANTASY IN LURID PULPISH COLORS.
"IT WAS UNBEARABLE.
"LITERALLY. THE WORLD WAS NEAR DRIVEN MAD, TENSION BETWEEN THE U.S.S.R. AND THE U.S.A. PUSHED TOWARDS ATOMIC HOLOCAUST.
"I DID MY FIRST VERSION OF MY LITTLE ALIEN INVASION TRICK. EVERYONE FELL FOR IT. OUR EARTH HAD PEACE.
"I WAS DISCOVERED BY MY FRATERNITY. THEY LET ME GO, KNOWING REVEALING ME WOULD DOOM THE WORLD TO NUCLEAR FIRE.
"BUT THE PROBLEM OF THIS SUPER MAN REMAINED. I STUDIED HIS LIMITATIONS.
"A POWER FANTASY. SIMPLE, COMFORTING MORALITY. LITTLE ELSE.
"BUT IF HIS IMPOSSIBILITY WAS POSSIBLE, I WONDERED WHAT ELSE COULD BE.
"I TURNED TO THE SCROLLS AND FOUND THE POWER OF TRUE PERFECTION..."

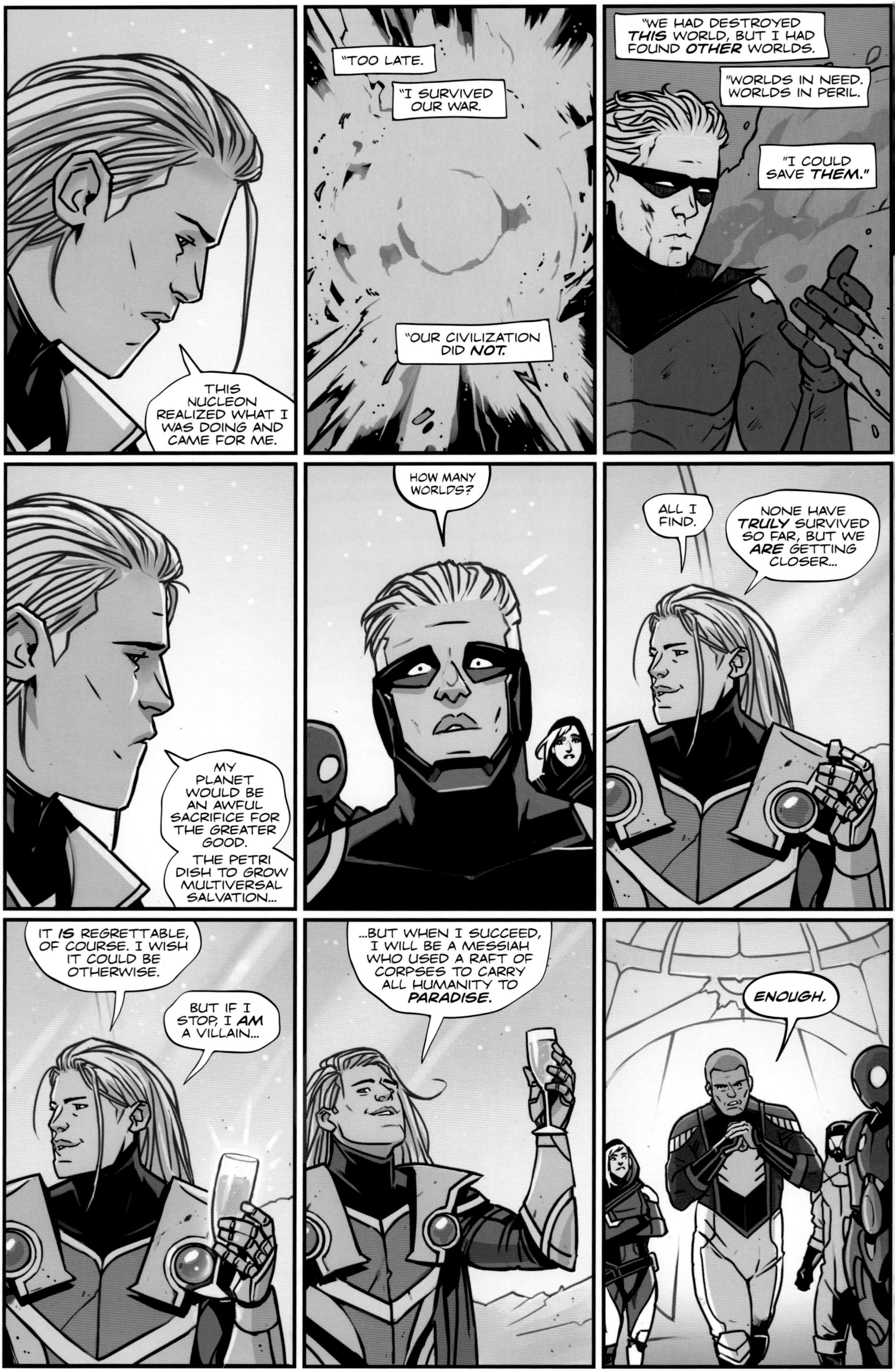
THIS NUCLEON REALIZED WHAT I WAS DOING AND CAME FOR ME.
"TOO LATE.
"I SURVIVED OUR WAR.
"OUR CIVILIZATION DID NOT.
"WE HAD DESTROYED THIS WORLD, BUT I HAD FOUND OTHER WORLDS.
"WORLDS IN NEED. WORLDS IN PERIL.
"I COULD SAVE THEM."
MY PLANET WOULD BE AN AWFUL SACRIFICE FOR THE GREATER GOOD.
THE PETRI DISH TO GROW MULTIVERSAL SALVATION...
HOW MANY WORLDS?
ALL I FIND.
NONE HAVE TRULY SURVIVED SO FAR, BUT WE ARE GETTING CLOSER...
IT IS REGRETTABLE, OF COURSE. I WISH IT COULD BE OTHERWISE.
BUT IF I STOP, I AM A VILLAIN...
...BUT WHEN I SUCCEED, I WILL BE A MESSIAH WHO USED A RAFT OF CORPSES TO CARRY ALL HUMANITY TO PARADISE.
ENOUGH.

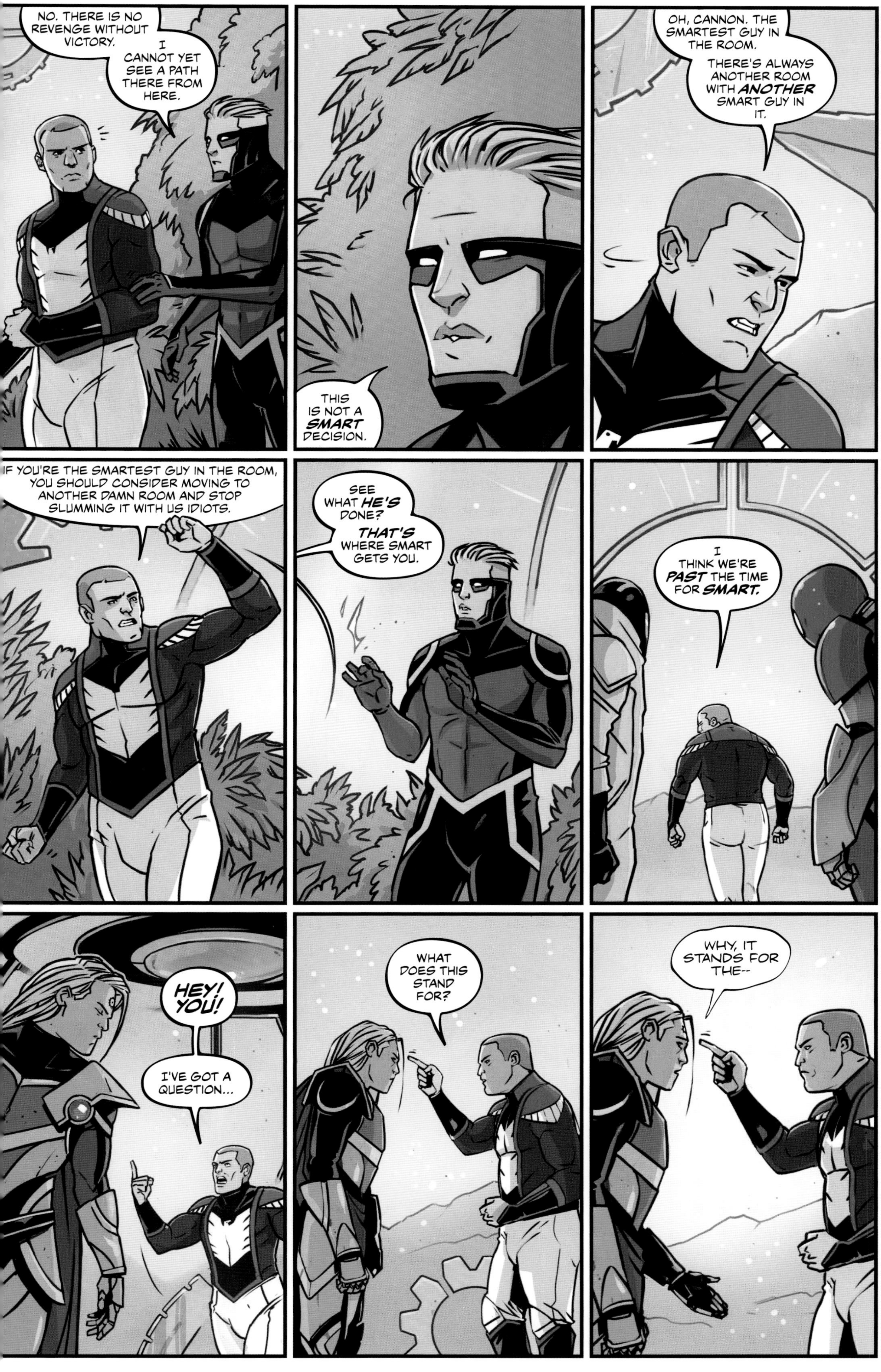
NO. THERE IS NO REVENGE WITHOUT VICTORY.
I CANNOT YET SEE A PATH THERE FROM HERE.
THIS IS NOT A SMART DECISION.
OH, CANNON. THE SMARTEST GUY IN THE ROOM.
THERE'S ALWAYS ANOTHER ROOM WITH ANOTHER SMART GUY IN IT.
IF YOU'RE THE SMARTEST GUY IN THE ROOM, YOU SHOULD CONSIDER MOVING TO ANOTHER DAMN ROOM AND STOP SLUMMING IT WITH US IDIOTS.
SEE WHAT HE'S DONE?
THAT'S WHERE SMART GETS YOU.
I THINK WE'RE PAST THE TIME FOR SMART.
HEY! YOU!
I'VE GOT A QUESTION...
WHAT DOES THIS STAND FOR?
WHY, IT STANDS FOR THE--

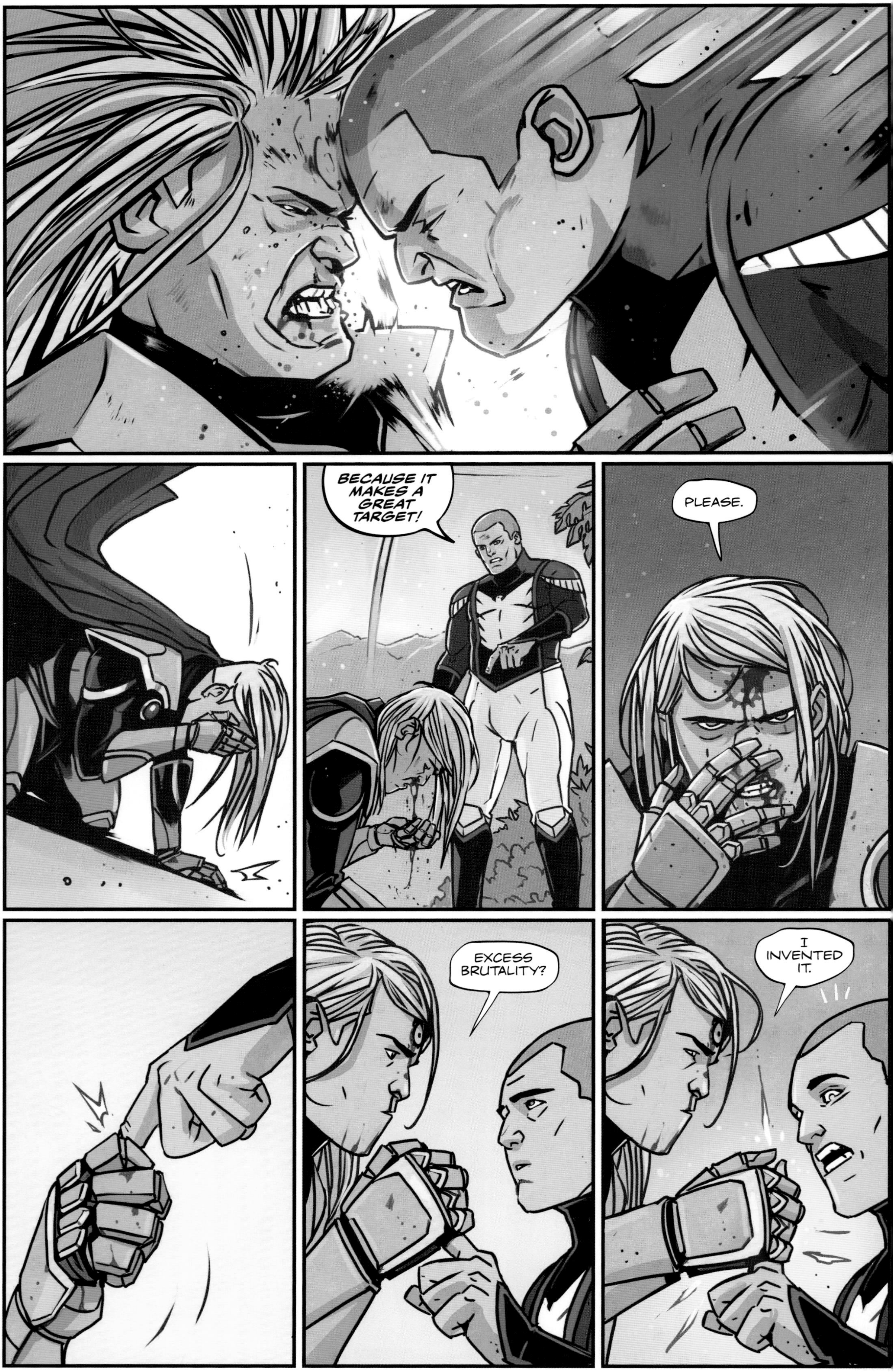
BECAUSE IT MAKES A GREAT TARGET!
PLEASE.
EXCESS BRUTALITY?
I INVENTED IT.

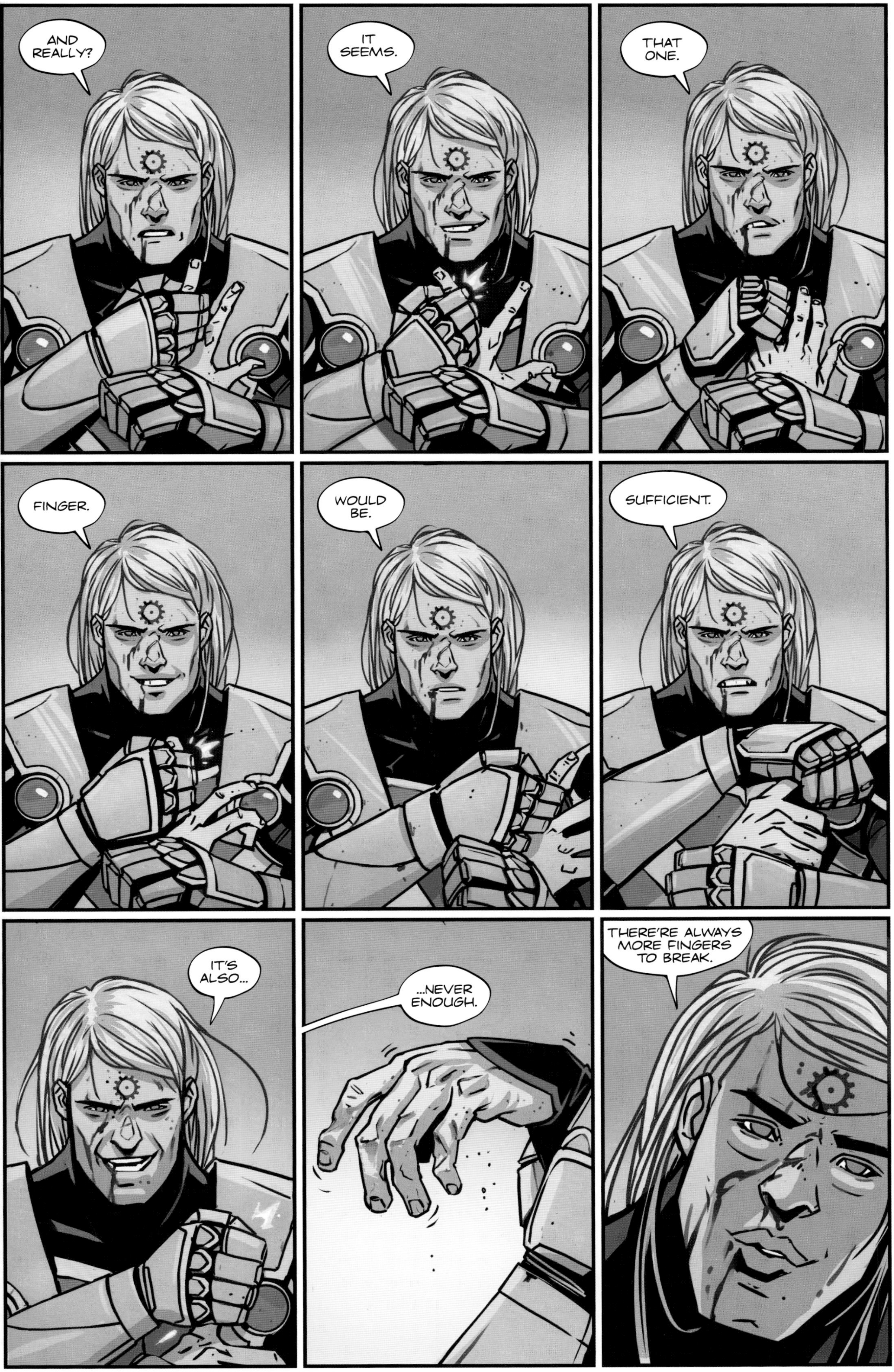
AND REALLY?
IT SEEMS.
THAT ONE.
FINGER.
WOULD BE.
SUFFICIENT.
IT'S ALSO...
...NEVER ENOUGH.
THERE'RE ALWAYS MORE FINGERS TO BREAK.

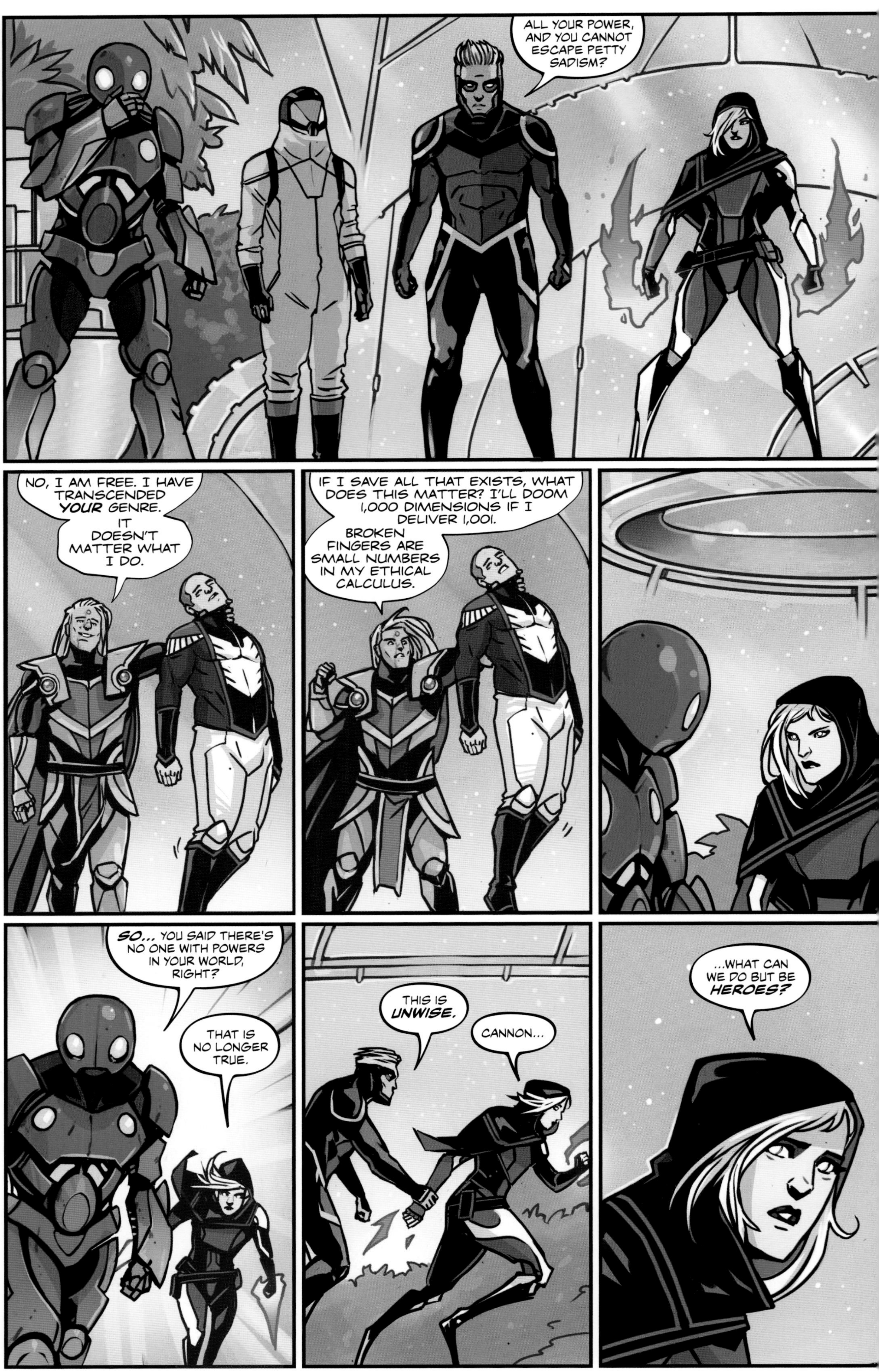
ALL YOUR POWER, AND YOU CANNOT ESCAPE PETTY SADISM?
NO, I AM FREE. I HAVE TRANSCENDED YOUR GENRE.
IT DOESN'T MATTER WHAT I DO.
IF I SAVE ALL THAT EXISTS, WHAT DOES THIS MATTER? I'LL DOOM 1,000 DIMENSIONS IF I DELIVER 1,001.
BROKEN FINGERS ARE SMALL NUMBERS IN MY ETHICAL CALCULUS.
SO... YOU SAID THERE'S NO ONE WITH POWERS IN YOUR WORLD, RIGHT?
THAT IS NO LONGER TRUE.
THIS IS UNWISE.
CANNON...
...WHAT CAN WE DO BUT BE HEROES?

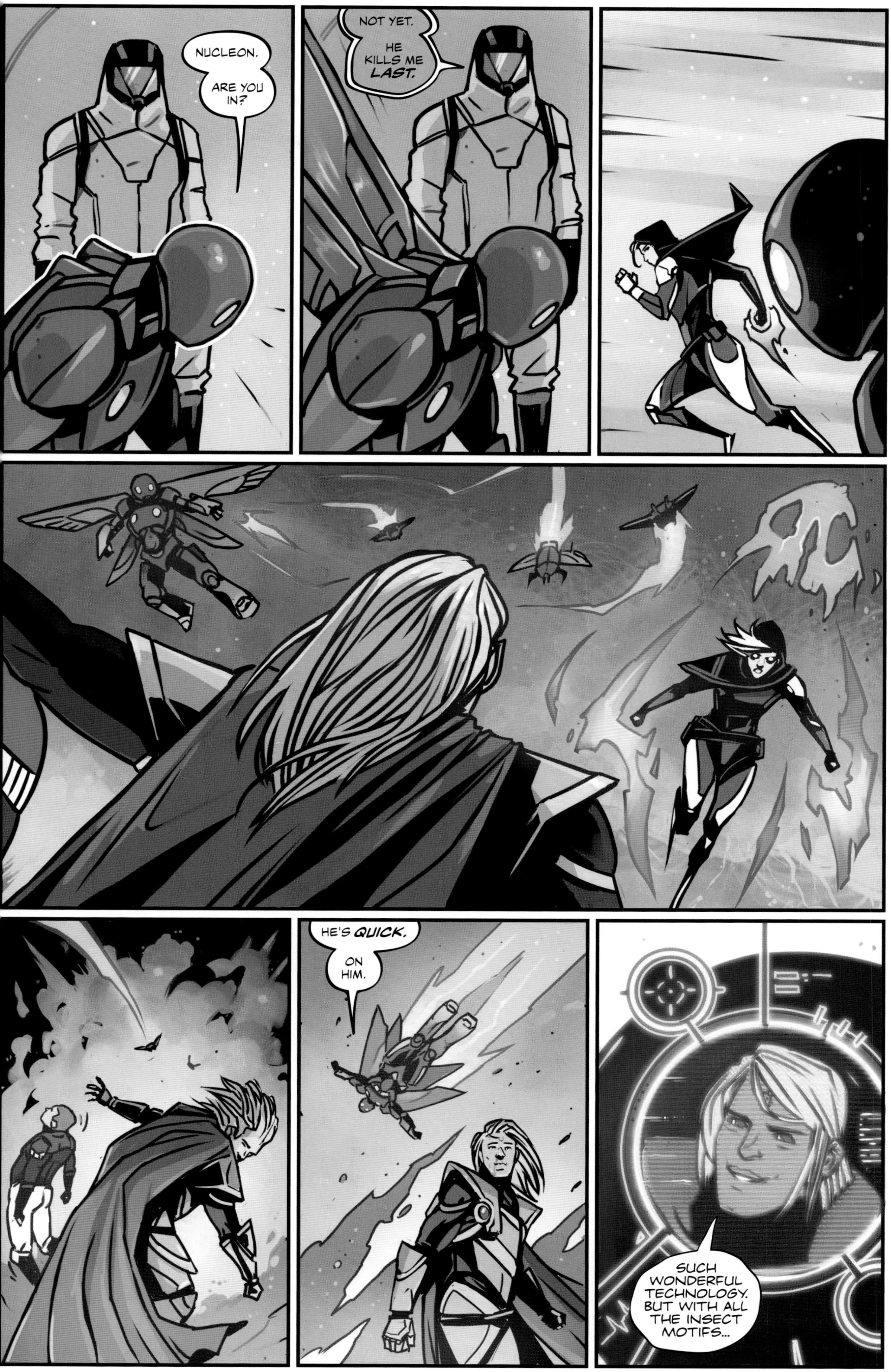
NUCLEON.
ARE YOU IN?
NOT YET.
HE KILLS ME ***LAST.***
HE'S ***QUICK.***
ON HIM.
SUCH WONDERFUL TECHNOLOGY. BUT WITH ALL THE INSECT MOTIFS...

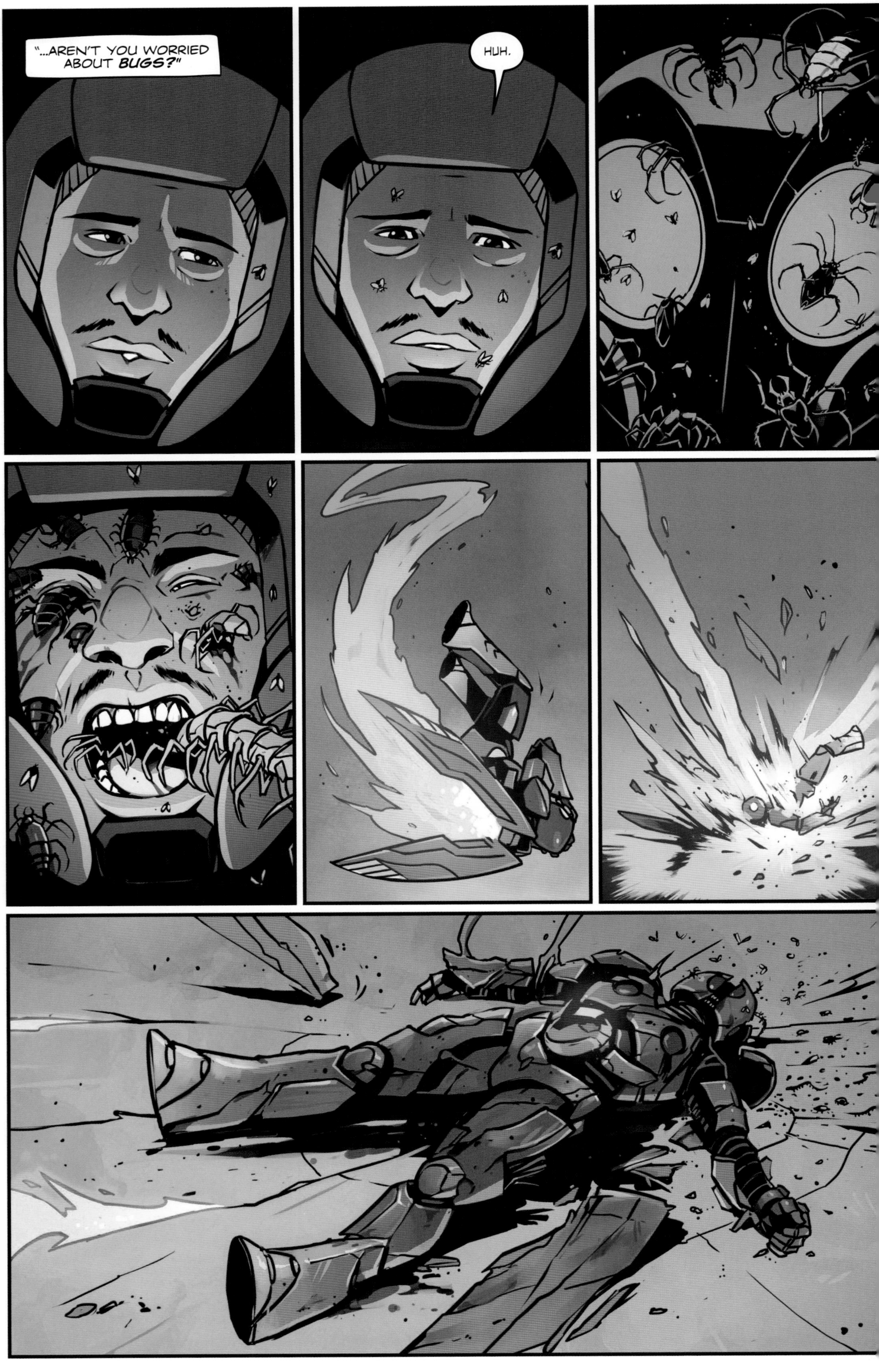
"...AREN'T YOU WORRIED ABOUT BUGS?"
HUH.

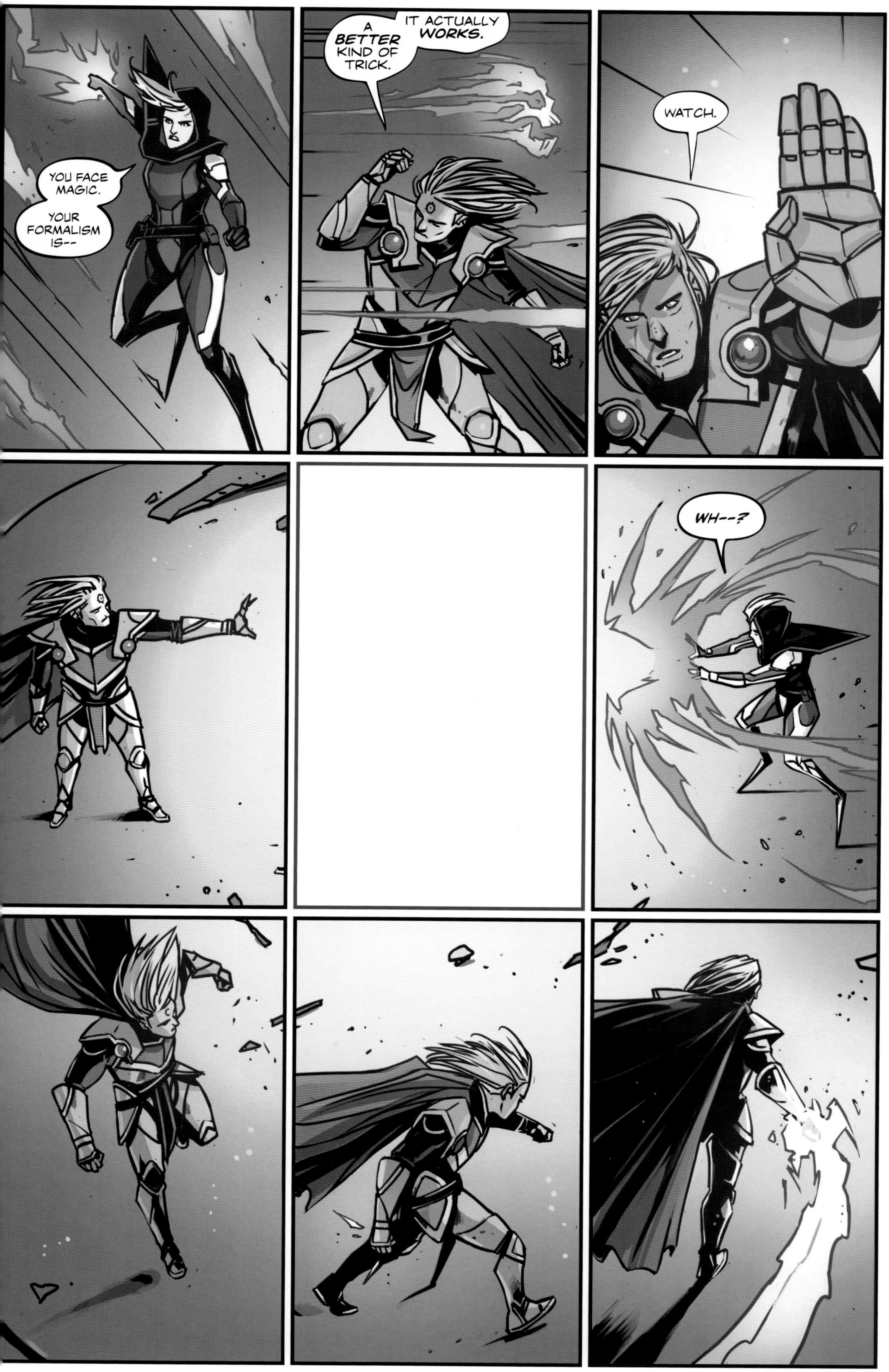
YOU FACE MAGIC.
YOUR FORMALISM IS--
A BETTER KIND OF TRICK.
IT ACTUALLY WORKS.
WATCH.
WH--?

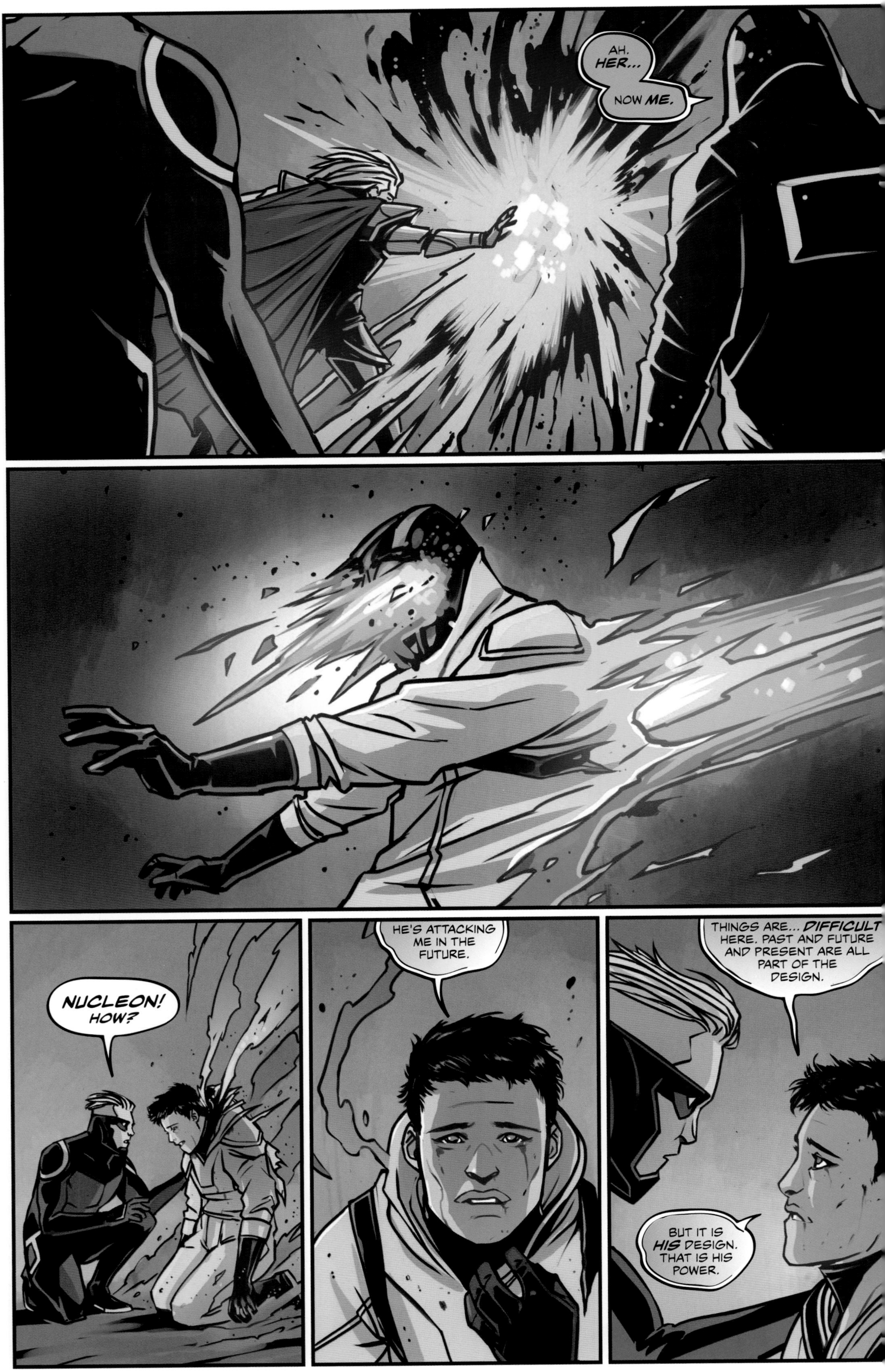
AH. HER...
NOW ME.
NUCLEON! HOW?
HE'S ATTACKING ME IN THE FUTURE.
THINGS ARE... DIFFICULT HERE. PAST AND FUTURE AND PRESENT ARE ALL PART OF THE DESIGN.
BUT IT IS HIS DESIGN. THAT IS HIS POWER.

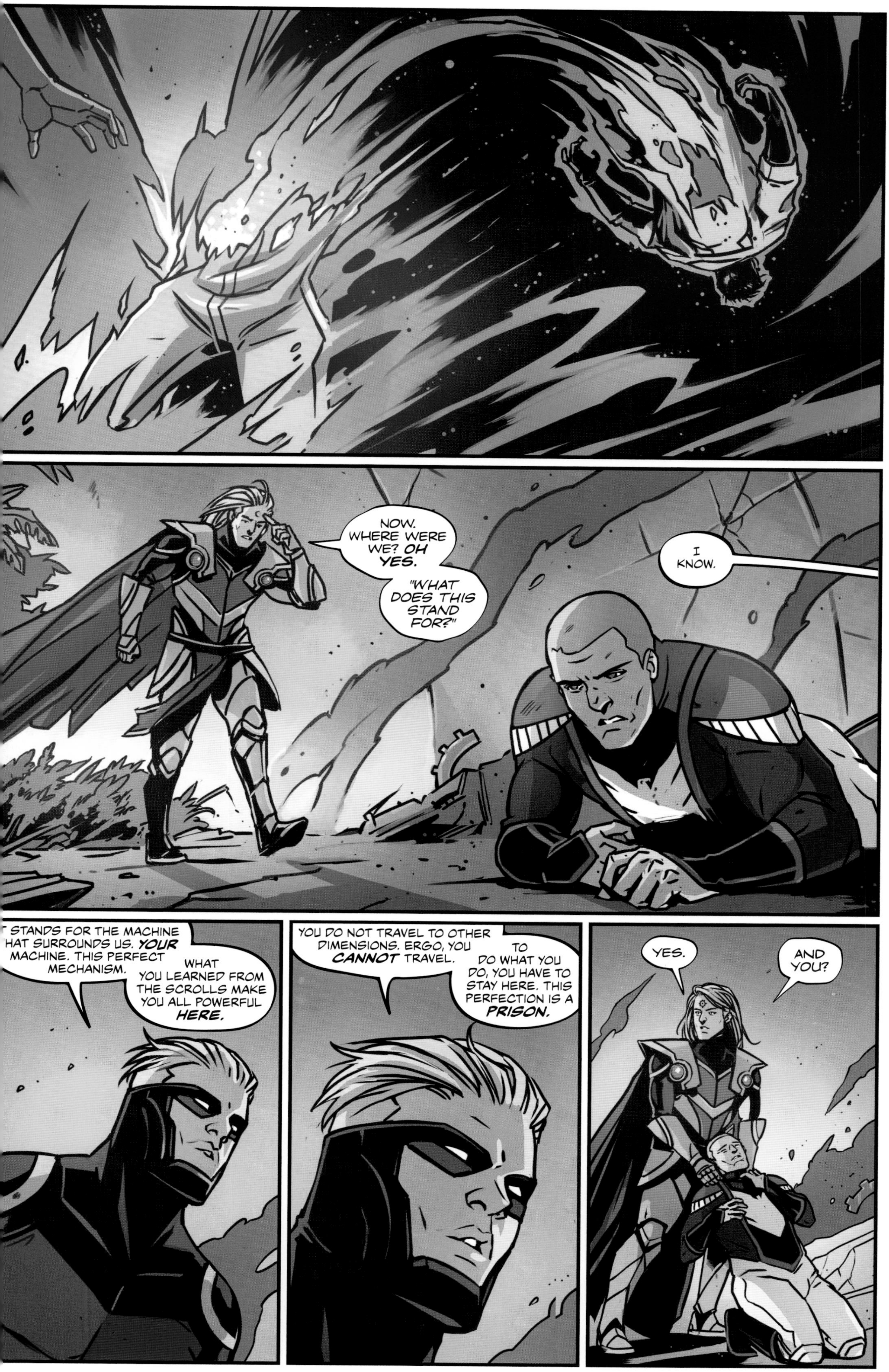

NOW. WHERE WERE WE? OH YES.
"WHAT DOES THIS STAND FOR?"
I KNOW.
T STANDS FOR THE MACHINE HAT SURROUNDS US. YOUR MACHINE. THIS PERFECT MECHANISM.
WHAT YOU LEARNED FROM THE SCROLLS MAKE YOU ALL POWERFUL HERE.
YOU DO NOT TRAVEL TO OTHER DIMENSIONS. ERGO, YOU CANNOT TRAVEL.
TO DO WHAT YOU DO, YOU HAVE TO STAY HERE. THIS PERFECTION IS A PRISON.
YES.
AND YOU?

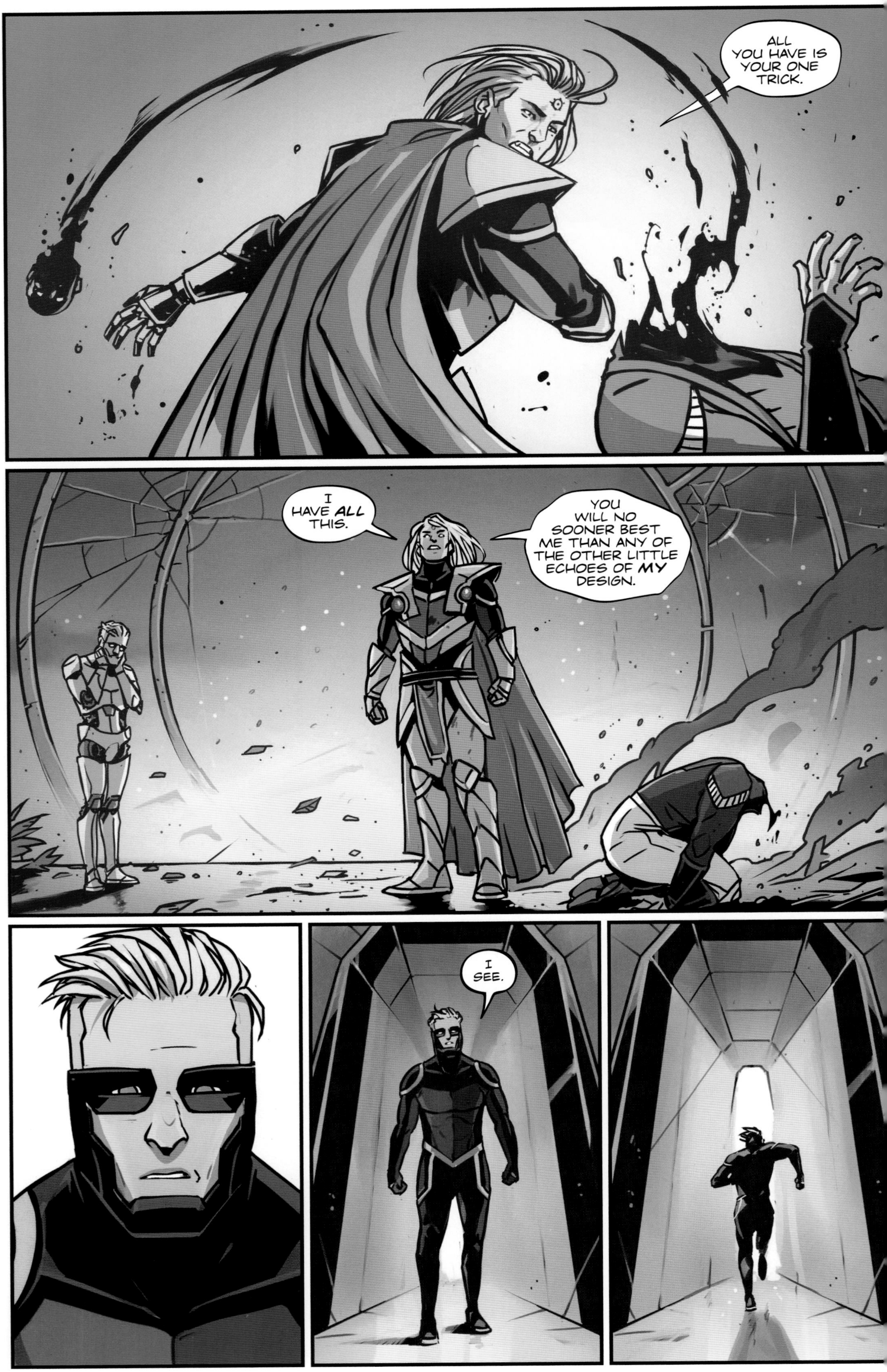
ALL YOU HAVE IS YOUR ONE TRICK.
I HAVE ALL THIS.
YOU WILL NO SOONER BEST ME THAN ANY OF THE OTHER LITTLE ECHOES OF MY DESIGN.
I SEE.

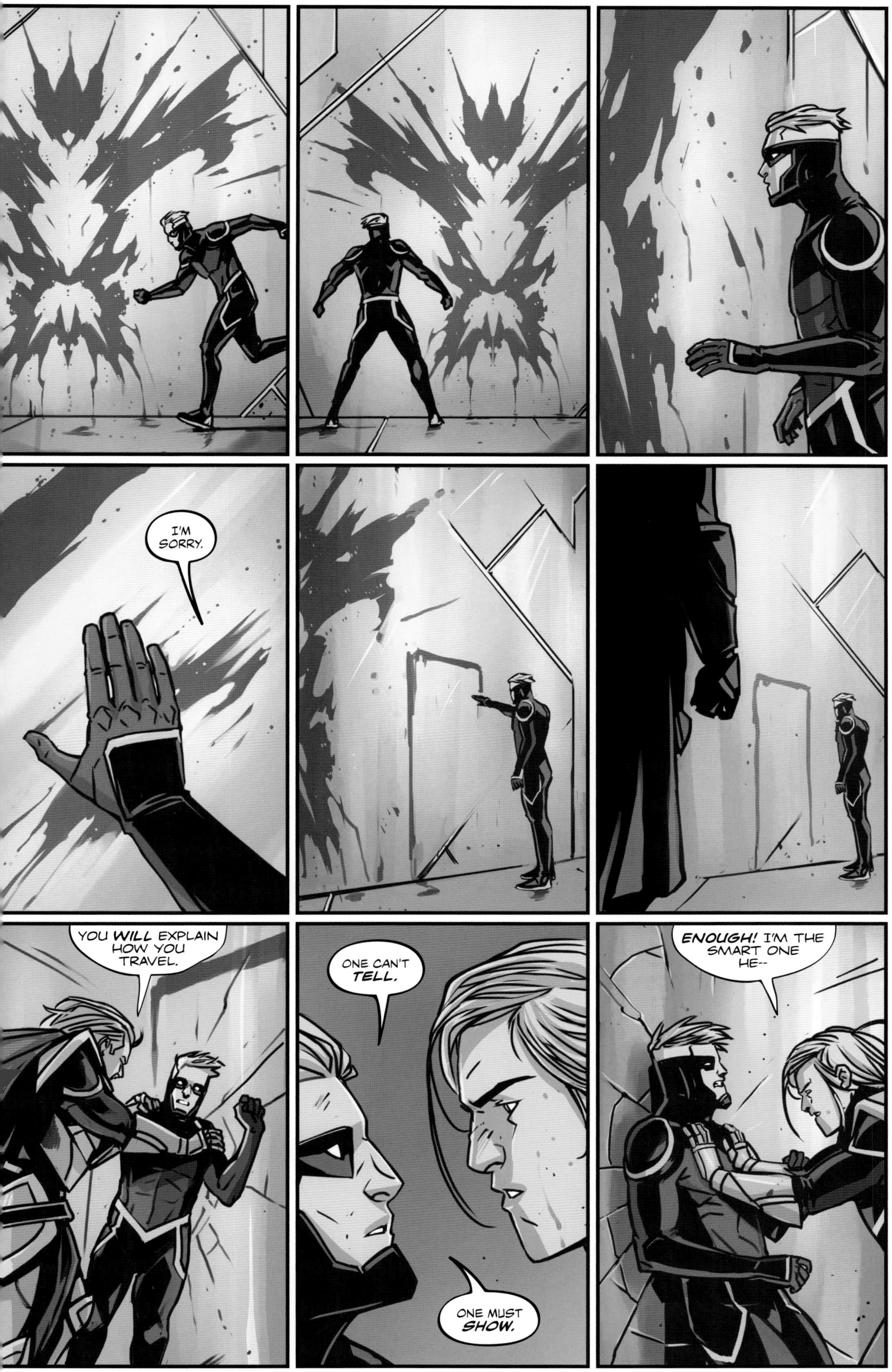
I'M SORRY.
YOU WILL EXPLAIN HOW YOU TRAVEL.
ONE CAN'T TELL.
ONE MUST SHOW.
ENOUGH! I'M THE SMART ONE HE--

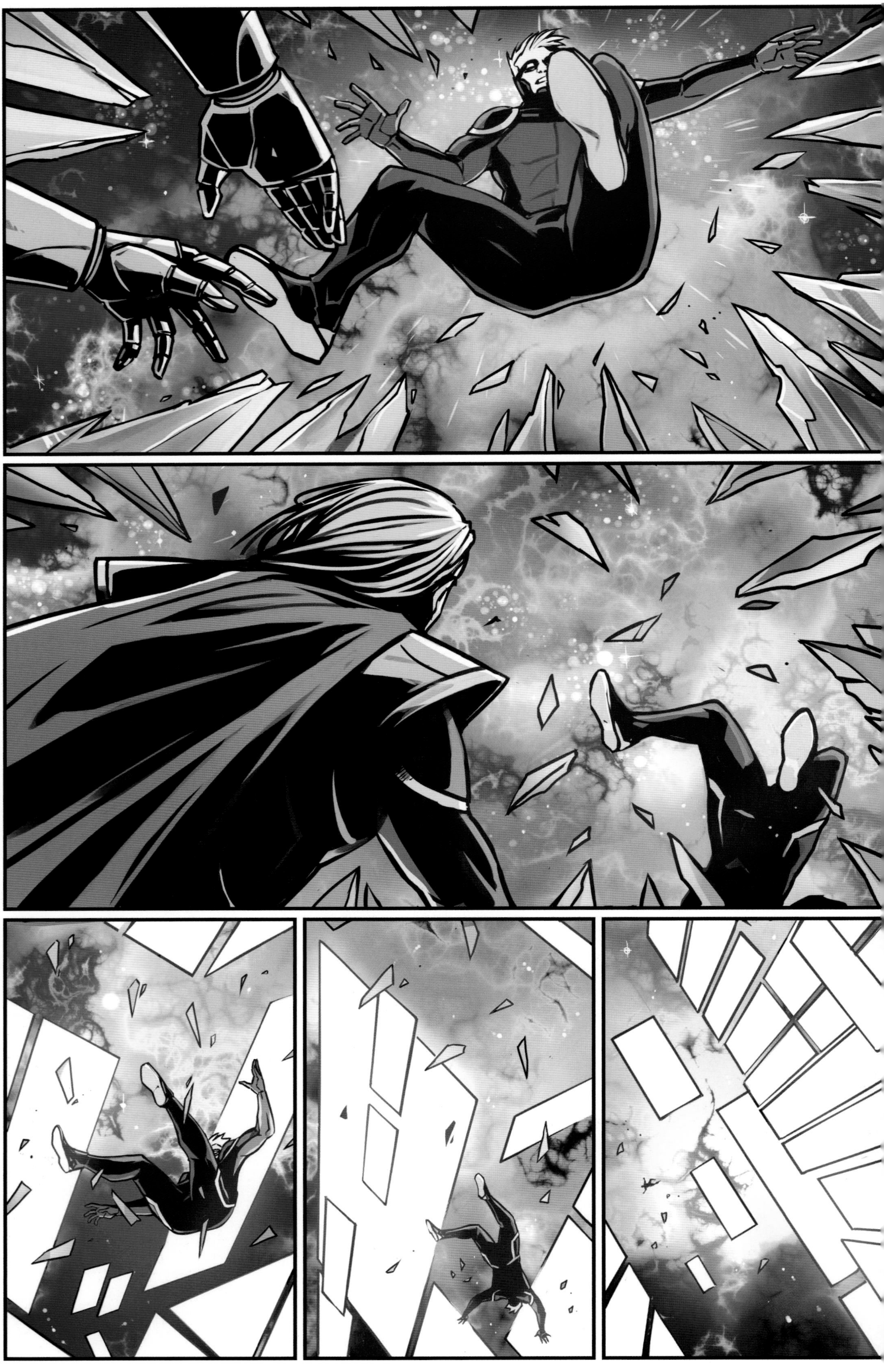

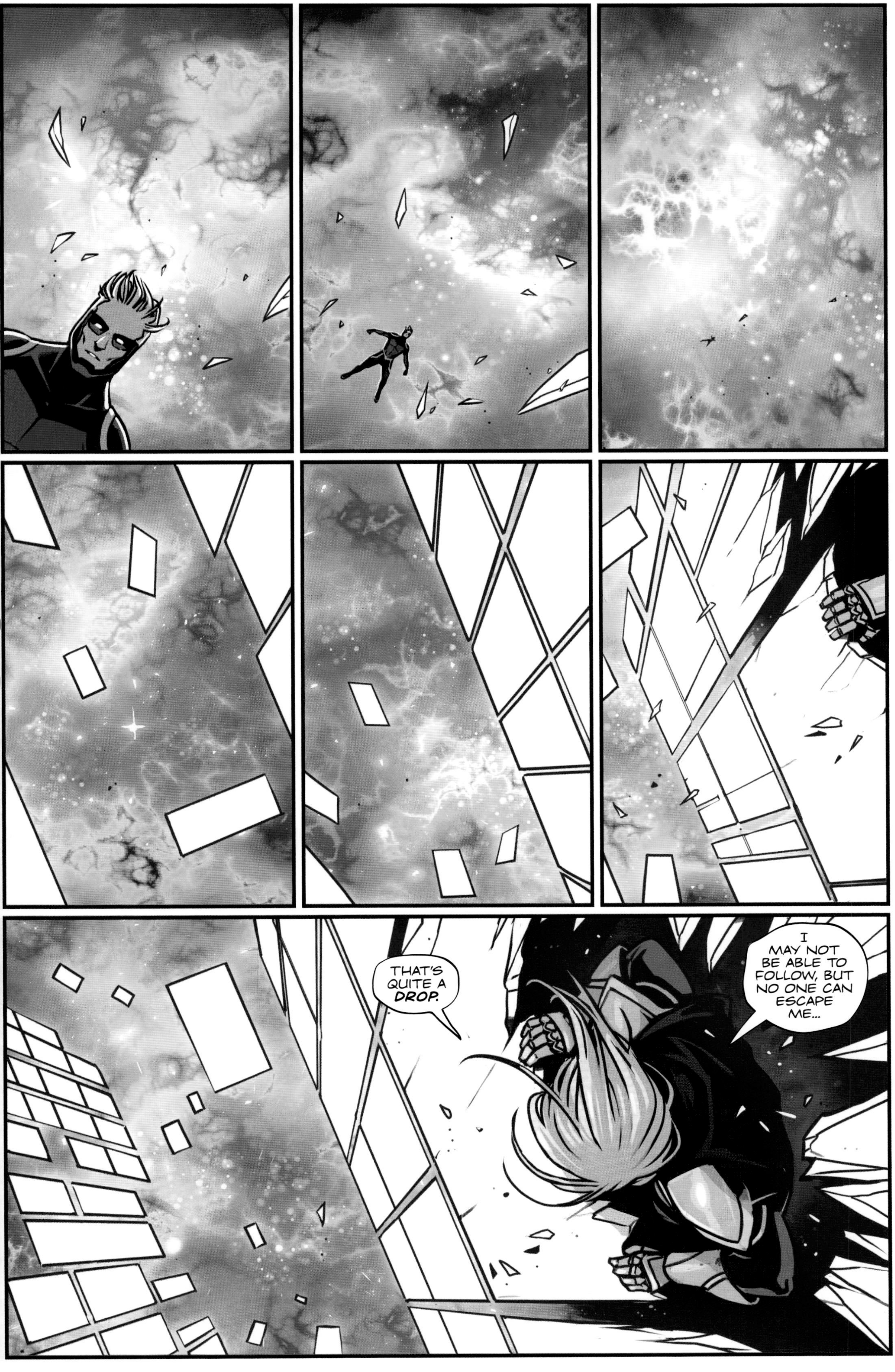
THAT'S QUITE A DROP.
I MAY NOT BE ABLE TO FOLLOW, BUT NO ONE CAN ESCAPE ME...

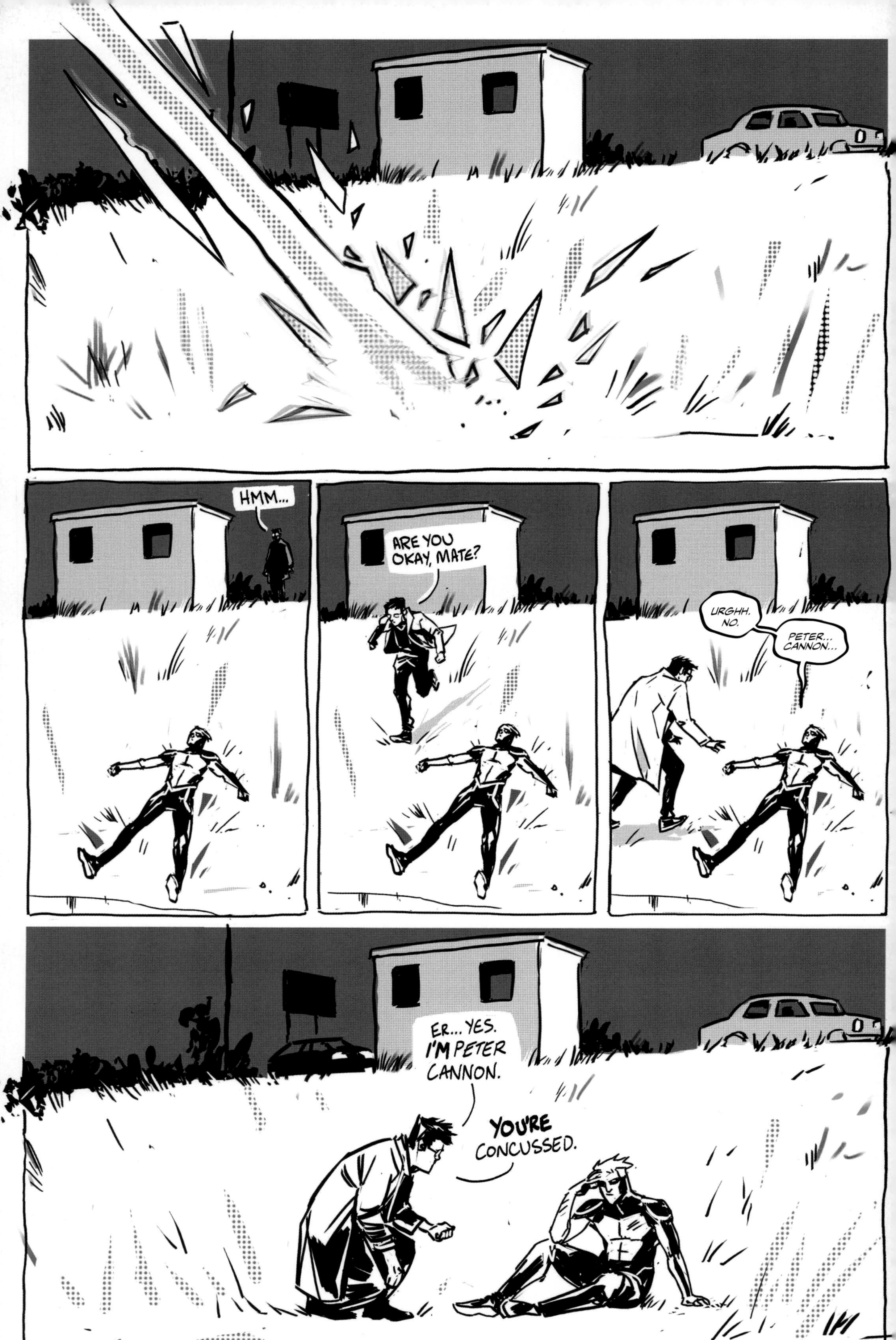
HMM...
ARE YOU OKAY, MATE?
URGHH. NO.
PETER... CANNON...
ER... YES. I'M PETER CANNON.
YOU'RE CONCUSSED.

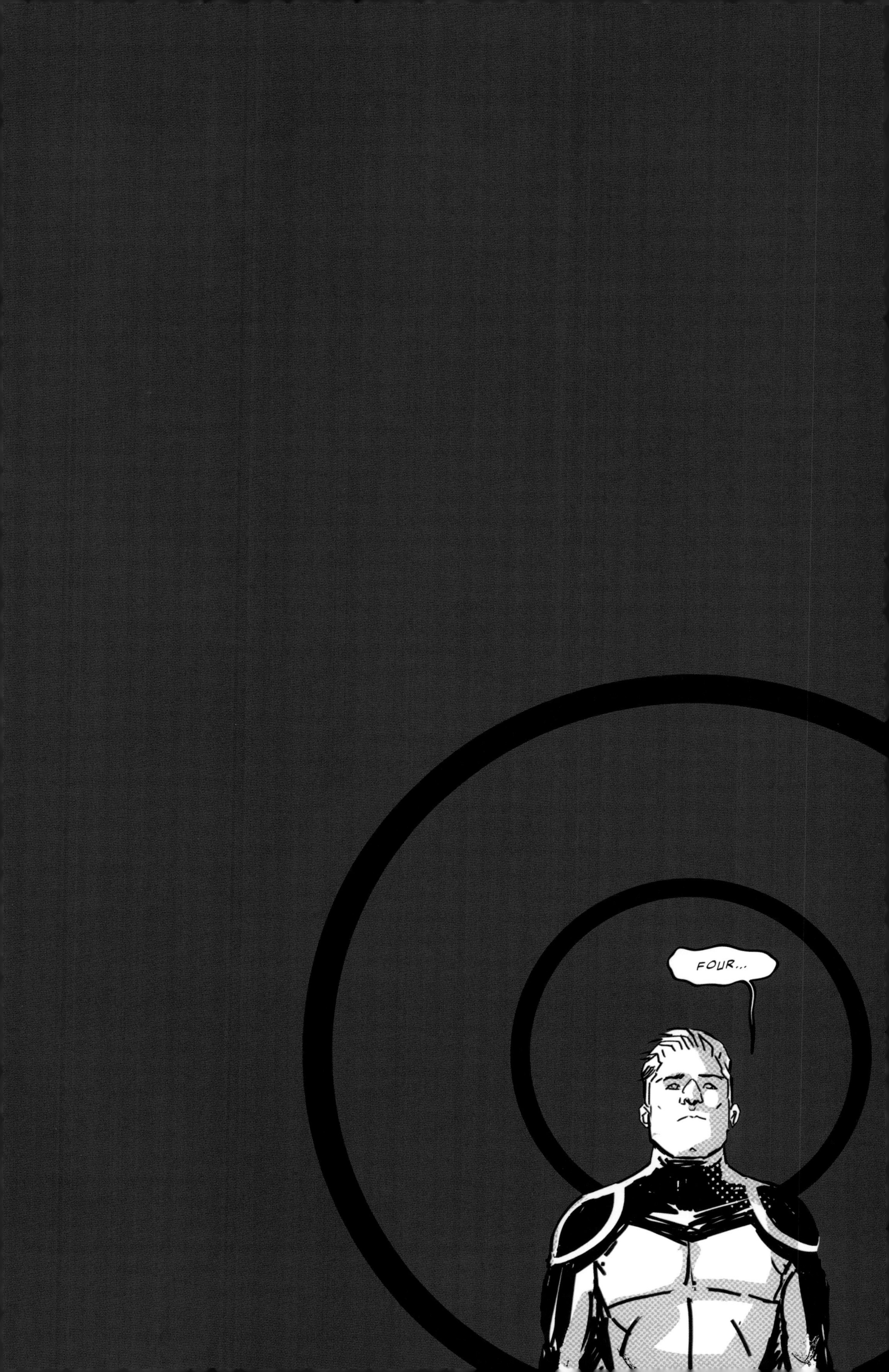
FOUR...

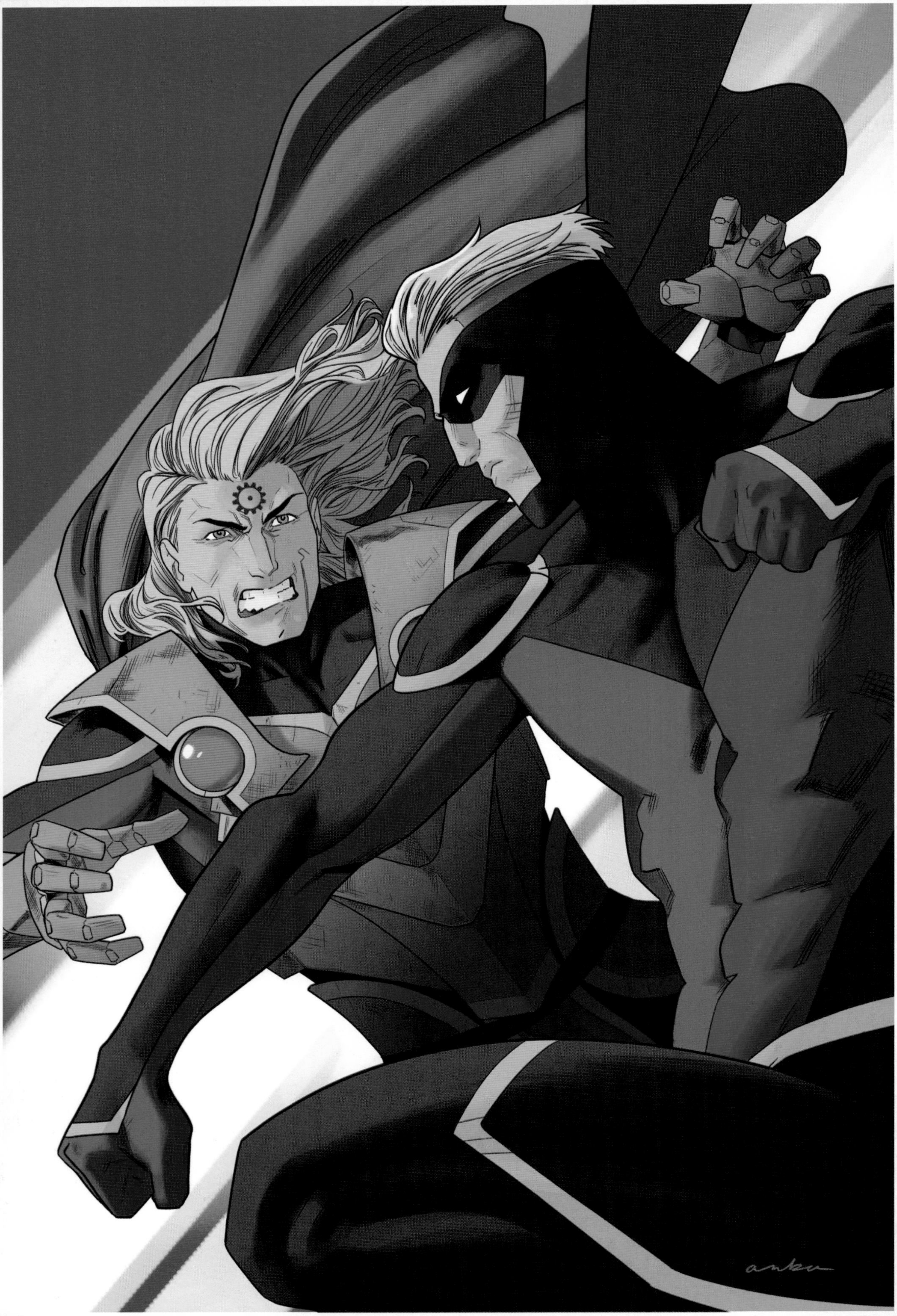
anka

ISSUE FOUR COVER BY KRIS ANKA

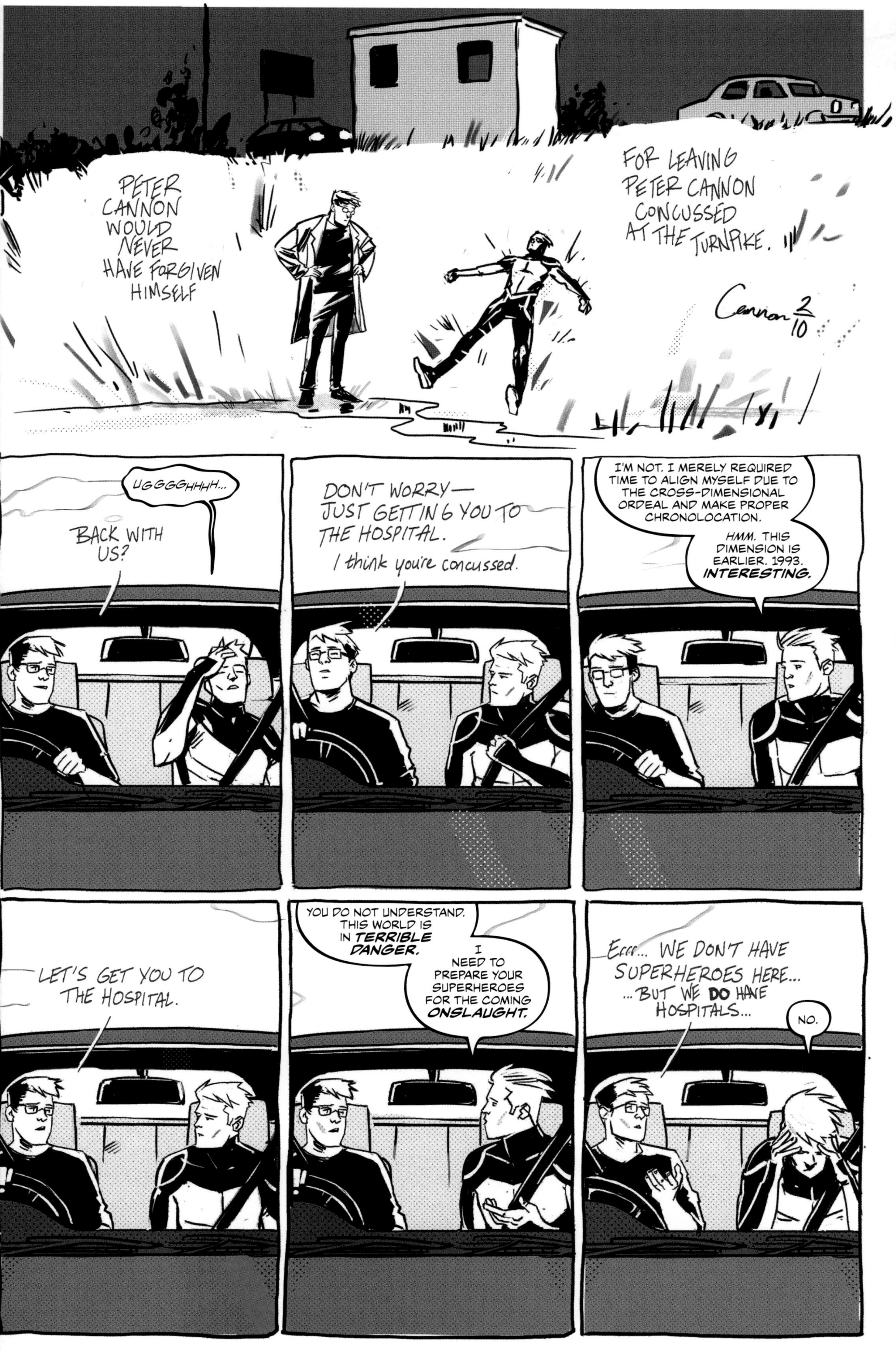

PETER CANNON WOULD NEVER HAVE FORGIVEN HIMSELF
FOR LEAVING PETER CANNON CONCUSSED AT THE TURNPIKE.
Cannon 2/10
UGGGGHHHH...
BACK WITH US?
DON'T WORRY— JUST GETTING YOU TO THE HOSPITAL.
I think you're concussed.
I'M NOT. I MERELY REQUIRED TIME TO ALIGN MYSELF DUE TO THE CROSS-DIMENSIONAL ORDEAL AND MAKE PROPER CHRONOLOCATION.
HMM. THIS DIMENSION IS EARLIER. 1993. INTERESTING.
LET'S GET YOU TO THE HOSPITAL.
YOU DO NOT UNDERSTAND. THIS WORLD IS IN TERRIBLE DANGER.
I NEED TO PREPARE YOUR SUPERHEROES FOR THE COMING ONSLAUGHT.
Errr... WE DON'T HAVE SUPERHEROES HERE... ...BUT WE DO HAVE HOSPITALS...
NO.

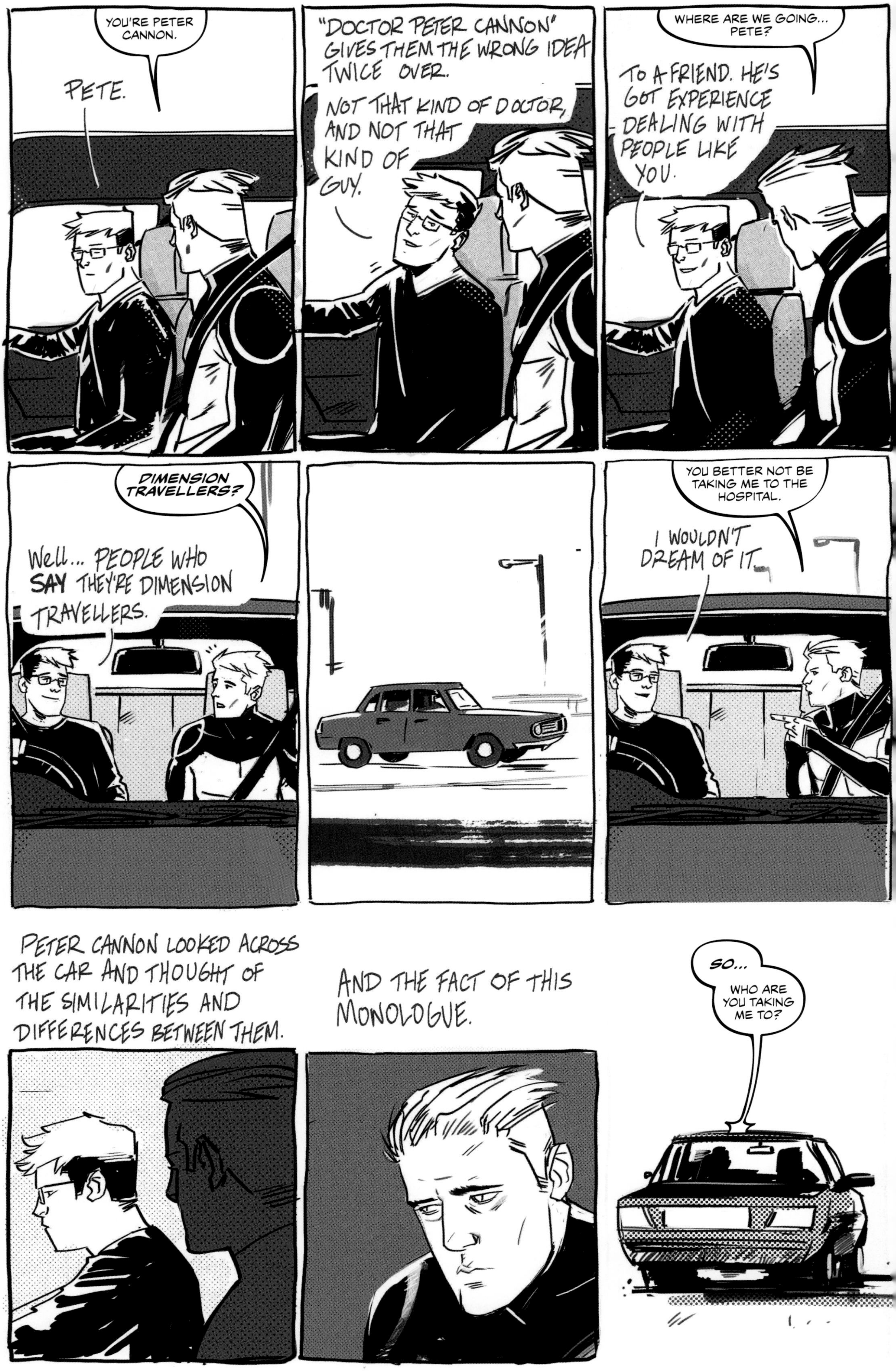
YOU'RE PETER CANNON.
PETE.
"DOCTOR PETER CANNON" GIVES THEM THE WRONG IDEA TWICE OVER.
NOT THAT KIND OF DOCTOR, AND NOT THAT KIND OF GUY.
WHERE ARE WE GOING... PETE?
TO A FRIEND. HE'S GOT EXPERIENCE DEALING WITH PEOPLE LIKE YOU.
DIMENSION TRAVELLERS?
WELL... PEOPLE WHO SAY THEY'RE DIMENSION TRAVELLERS.
YOU BETTER NOT BE TAKING ME TO THE HOSPITAL.
I WOULDN'T DREAM OF IT.
PETER CANNON LOOKED ACROSS THE CAR AND THOUGHT OF THE SIMILARITIES AND DIFFERENCES BETWEEN THEM.
AND THE FACT OF THIS MONOLOGUE.
SO...
WHO ARE YOU TAKING ME TO?

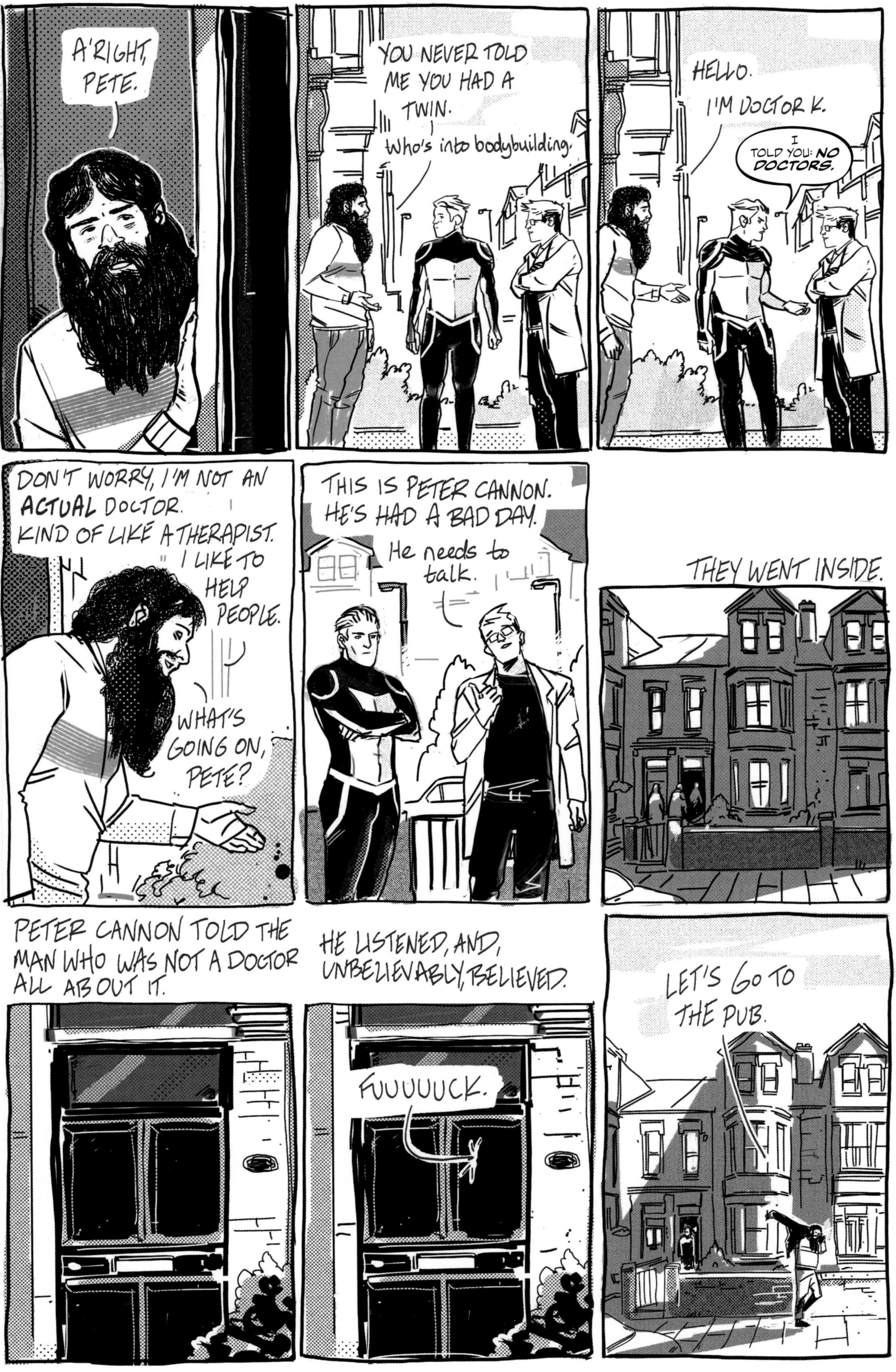
A'RIGHT, PETE.
YOU NEVER TOLD ME YOU HAD A TWIN.
Who's into bodybuilding.
HELLO.
I'M DOCTOR K.
I TOLD YOU: NO DOCTORS.
DON'T WORRY, I'M NOT AN ACTUAL DOCTOR. KIND OF LIKE A THERAPIST.
I LIKE TO HELP PEOPLE.
WHAT'S GOING ON, PETE?
THIS IS PETER CANNON. HE'S HAD A BAD DAY.
He needs to talk.
THEY WENT INSIDE.
PETER CANNON TOLD THE MAN WHO WAS NOT A DOCTOR ALL ABOUT IT.
HE LISTENED, AND, UNBELIEVABLY, BELIEVED.
FUUUUUCK.
LET'S GO TO THE PUB.

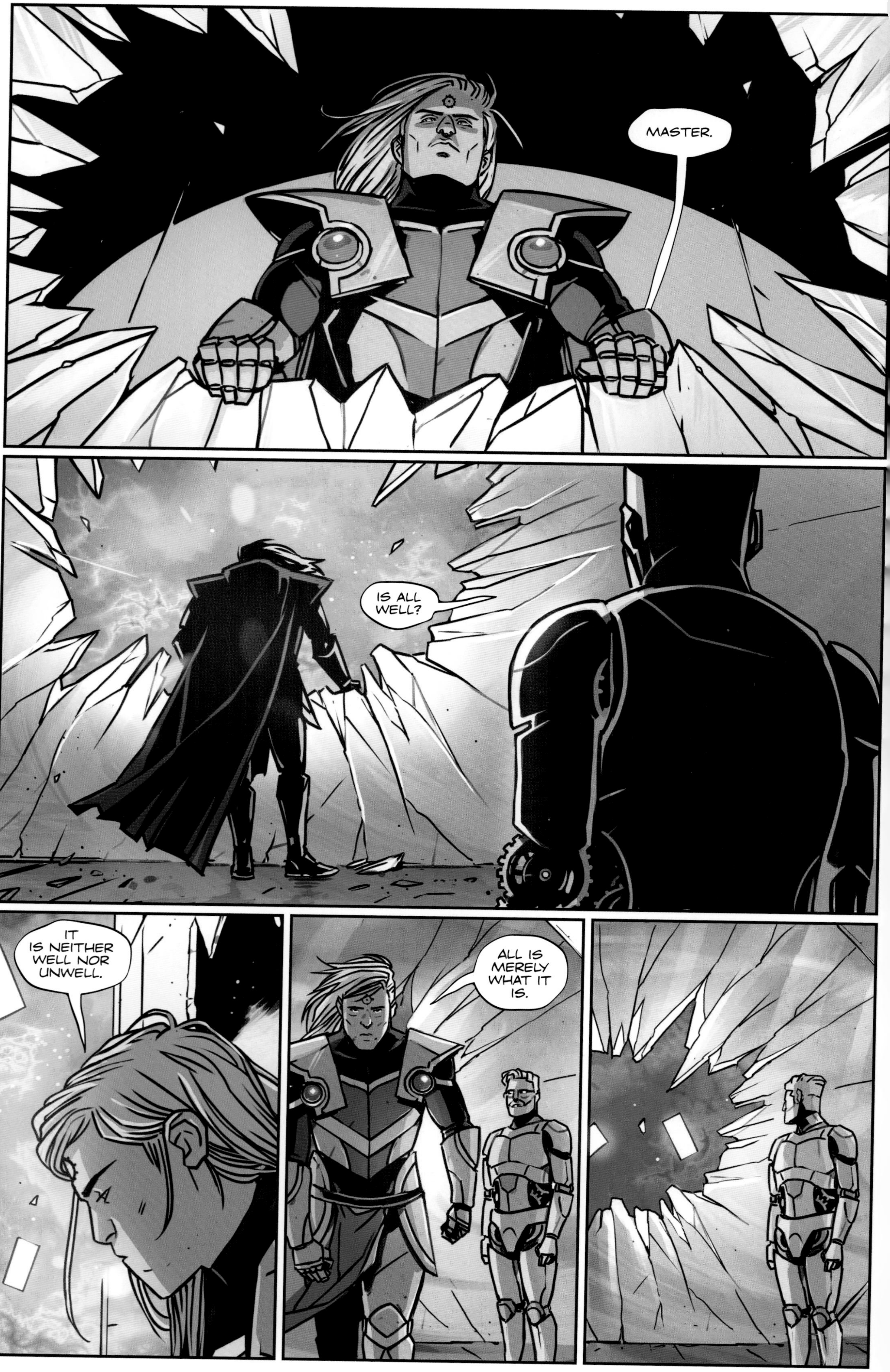
MASTER.
IS ALL WELL?
IT IS NEITHER WELL NOR UNWELL.
ALL IS MERELY WHAT IT IS.

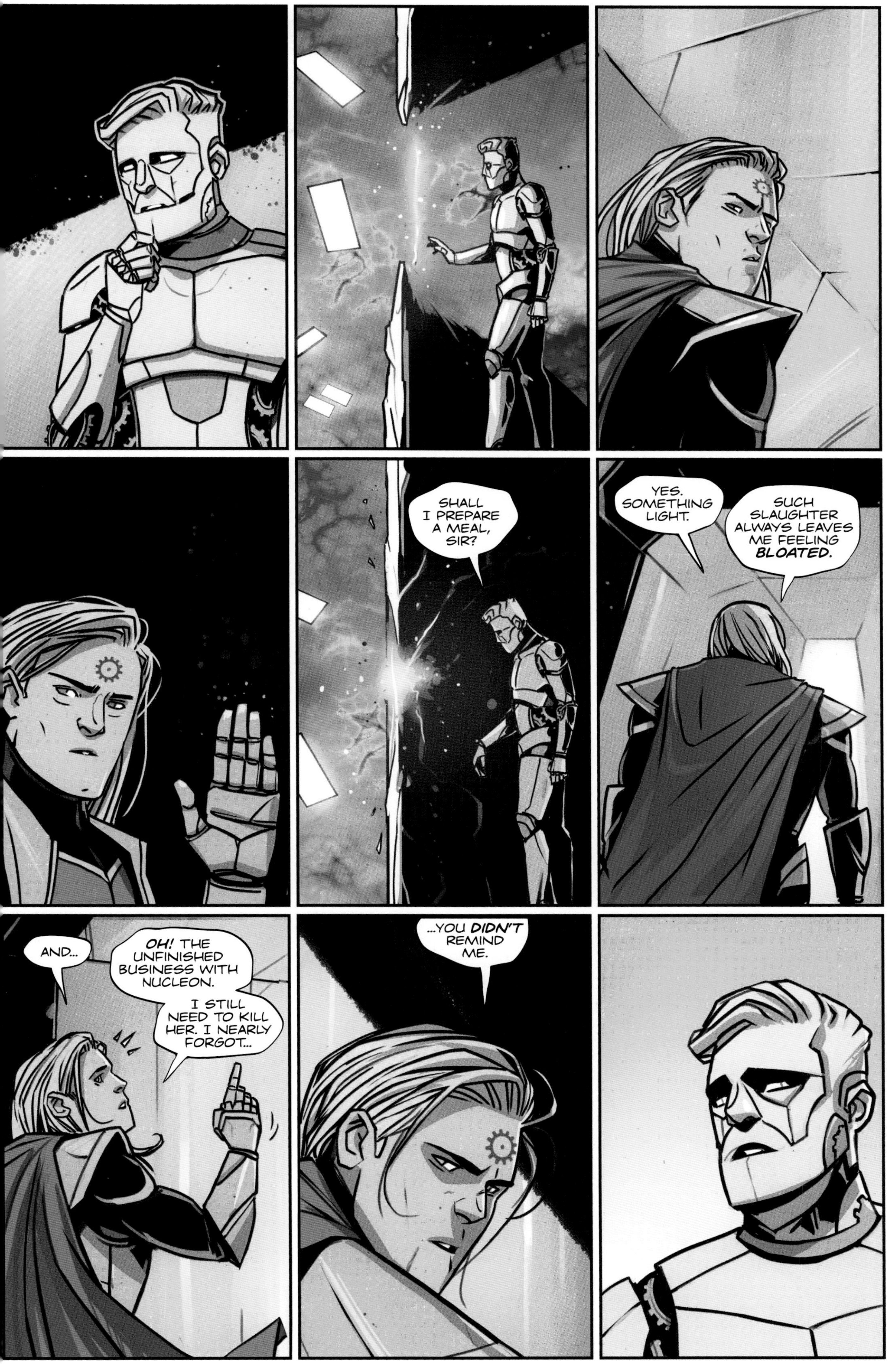
SHALL I PREPARE A MEAL, SIR?
YES. SOMETHING LIGHT.
SUCH SLAUGHTER ALWAYS LEAVES ME FEELING *BLOATED.*
AND...
OH! THE UNFINISHED BUSINESS WITH NUCLEON.
I STILL NEED TO KILL HER. I NEARLY FORGOT...
...YOU *DIDN'T* REMIND ME.

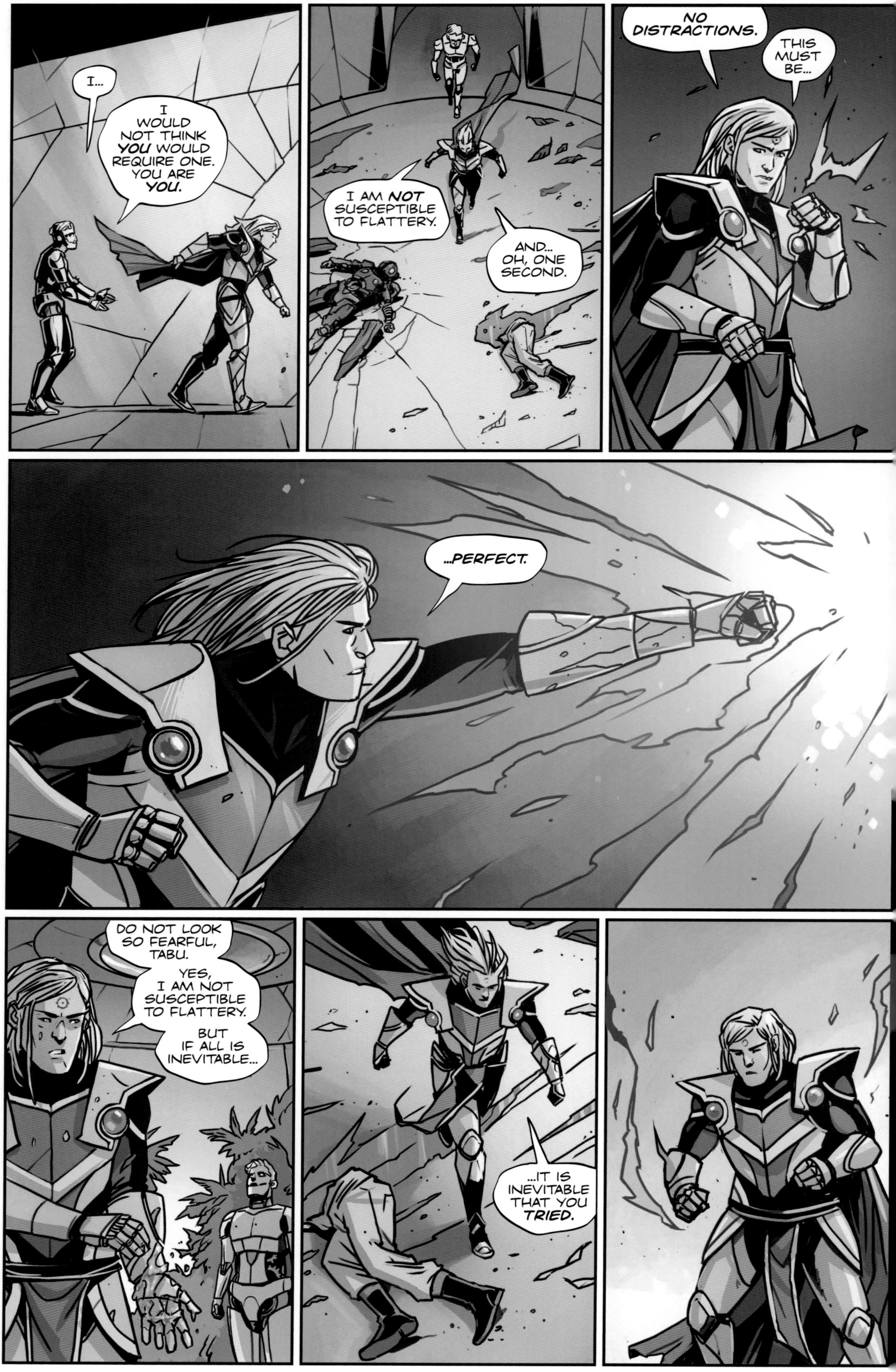
I...
I WOULD NOT THINK YOU WOULD REQUIRE ONE. YOU ARE YOU.
I AM NOT SUSCEPTIBLE TO FLATTERY.
AND... OH, ONE SECOND.
NO DISTRACTIONS.
THIS MUST BE...
...PERFECT.
DO NOT LOOK SO FEARFUL, TABU.
YES, I AM NOT SUSCEPTIBLE TO FLATTERY.
BUT IF ALL IS INEVITABLE...
...IT IS INEVITABLE THAT YOU TRIED.

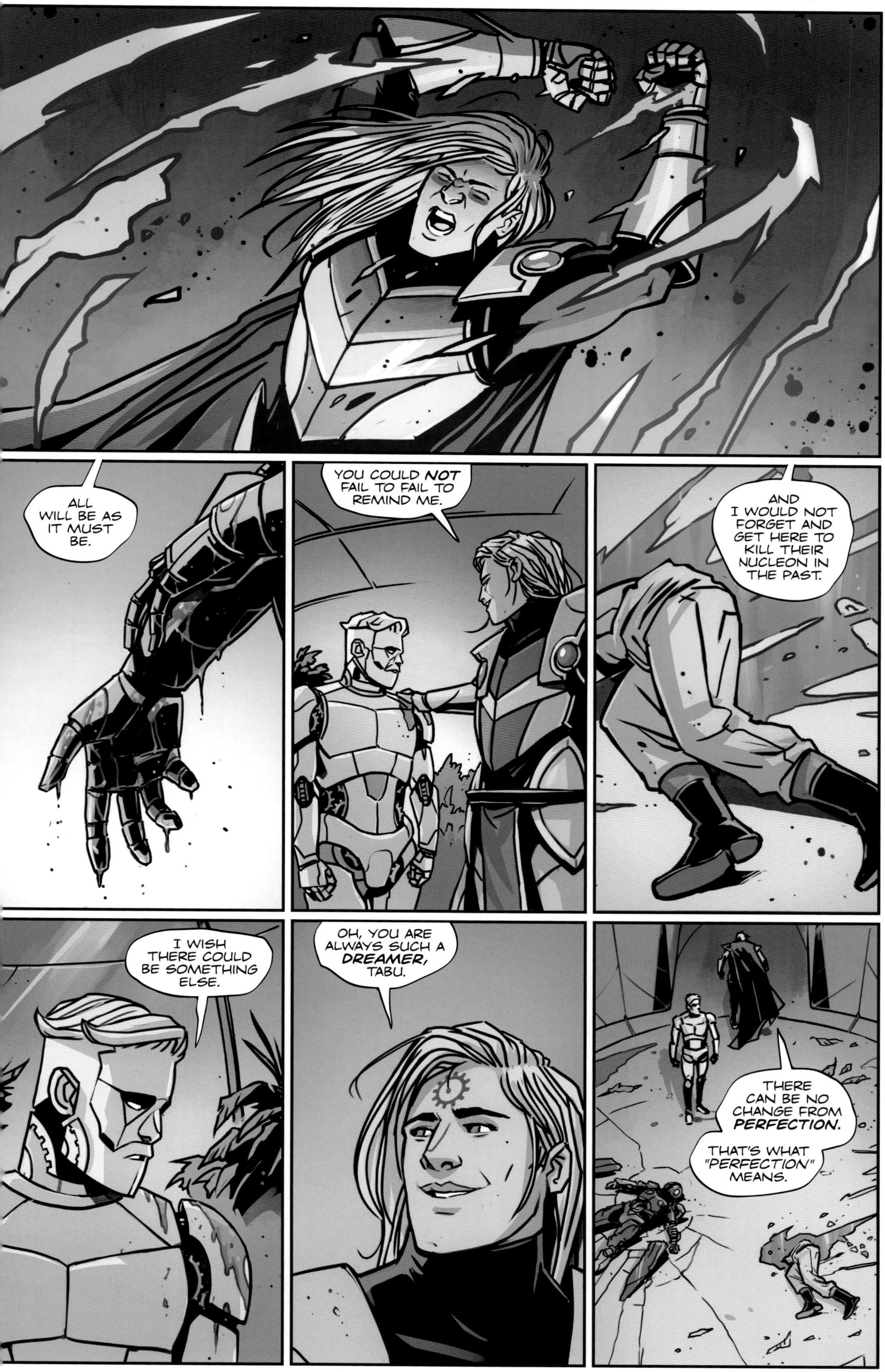
ALL WILL BE AS IT MUST BE.
YOU COULD NOT FAIL TO FAIL TO REMIND ME.
AND I WOULD NOT FORGET AND GET HERE TO KILL THEIR NUCLEON IN THE PAST.
I WISH THERE COULD BE SOMETHING ELSE.
OH, YOU ARE ALWAYS SUCH A DREAMER, TABU.
THERE CAN BE NO CHANGE FROM PERFECTION.
THAT'S WHAT "PERFECTION" MEANS.

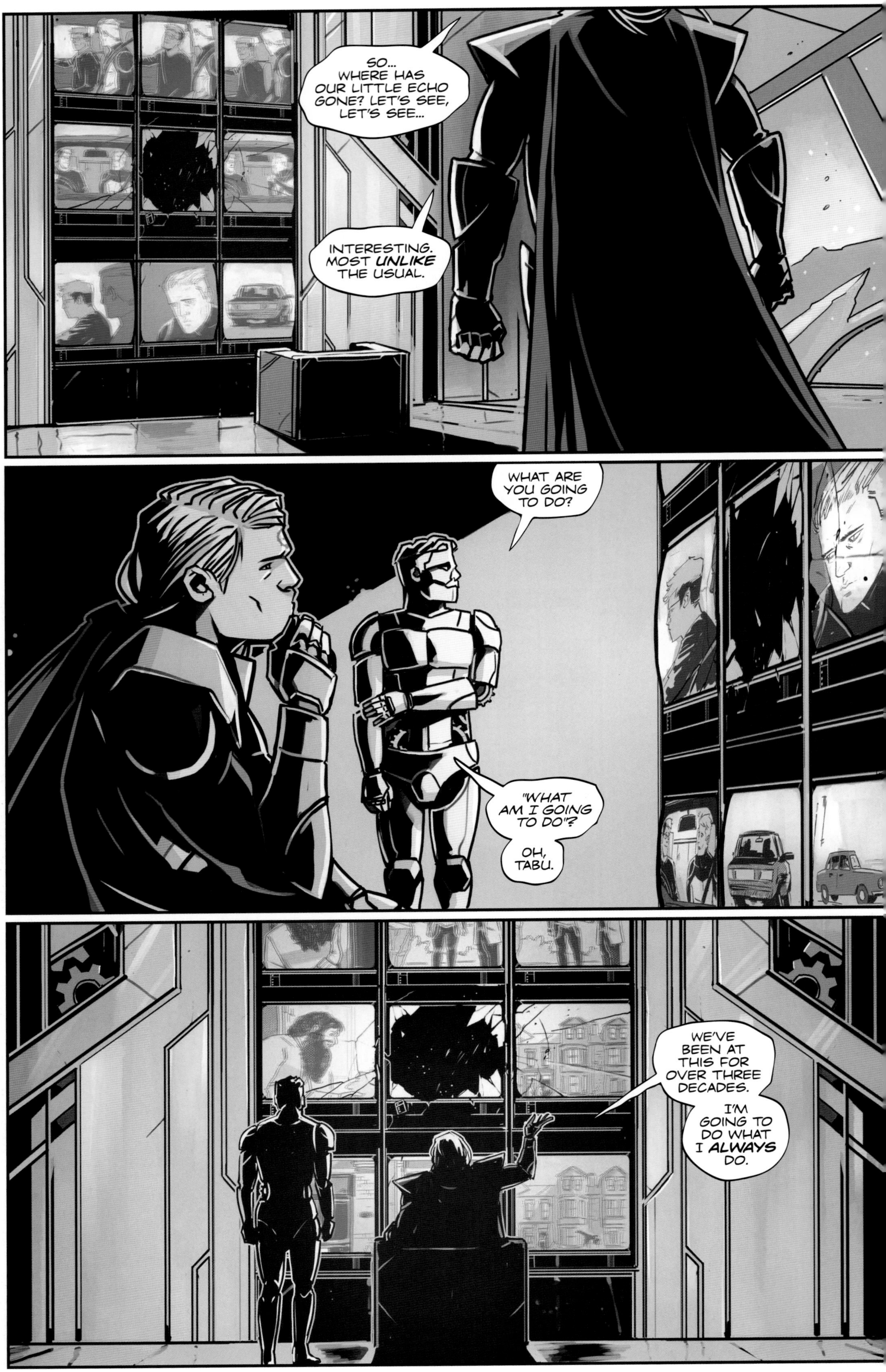
SO... WHERE HAS OUR LITTLE ECHO GONE? LET'S SEE, LET'S SEE...
INTERESTING. MOST UNLIKE THE USUAL.
WHAT ARE YOU GOING TO DO?
"WHAT AM I GOING TO DO"?
OH, TABU.
WE'VE BEEN AT THIS FOR OVER THREE DECADES.
I'M GOING TO DO WHAT I ALWAYS DO.

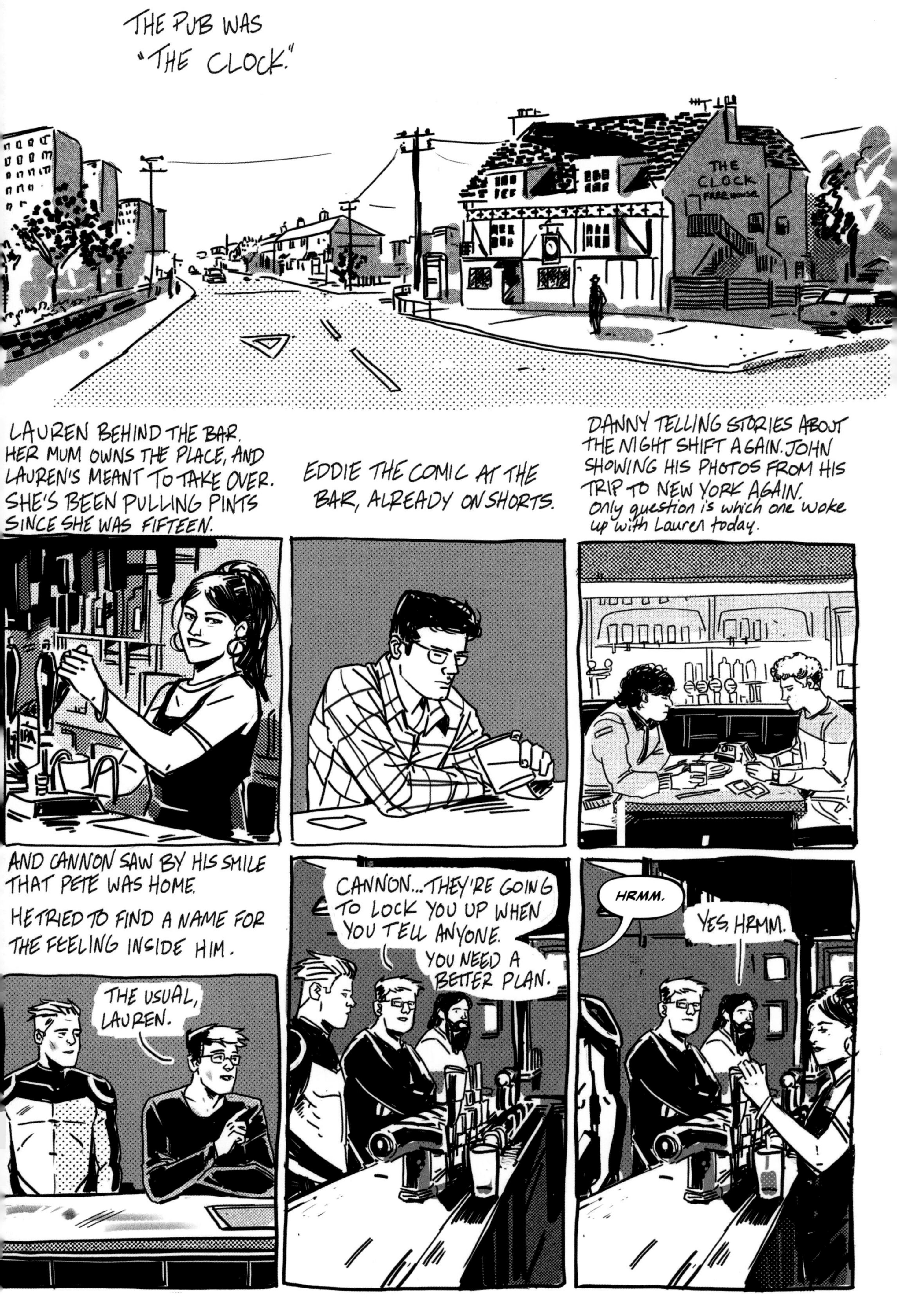
THE PUB WAS "THE CLOCK."
THE CLOCK FREE HOUSE
LAUREN BEHIND THE BAR. HER MUM OWNS THE PLACE, AND LAUREN'S MEANT TO TAKE OVER. SHE'S BEEN PULLING PINTS SINCE SHE WAS FIFTEEN.
EDDIE THE COMIC AT THE BAR, ALREADY ON SHORTS.
DANNY TELLING STORIES ABOUT THE NIGHT SHIFT AGAIN. JOHN SHOWING HIS PHOTOS FROM HIS TRIP TO NEW YORK AGAIN.
Only question is which one woke up with Lauren today.
AND CANNON SAW BY HIS SMILE THAT PETE WAS HOME.
HE TRIED TO FIND A NAME FOR THE FEELING INSIDE HIM.
THE USUAL, LAUREN.
CANNON... THEY'RE GOING TO LOCK YOU UP WHEN YOU TELL ANYONE.
YOU NEED A BETTER PLAN.
HRMM.
YES, HRMM.

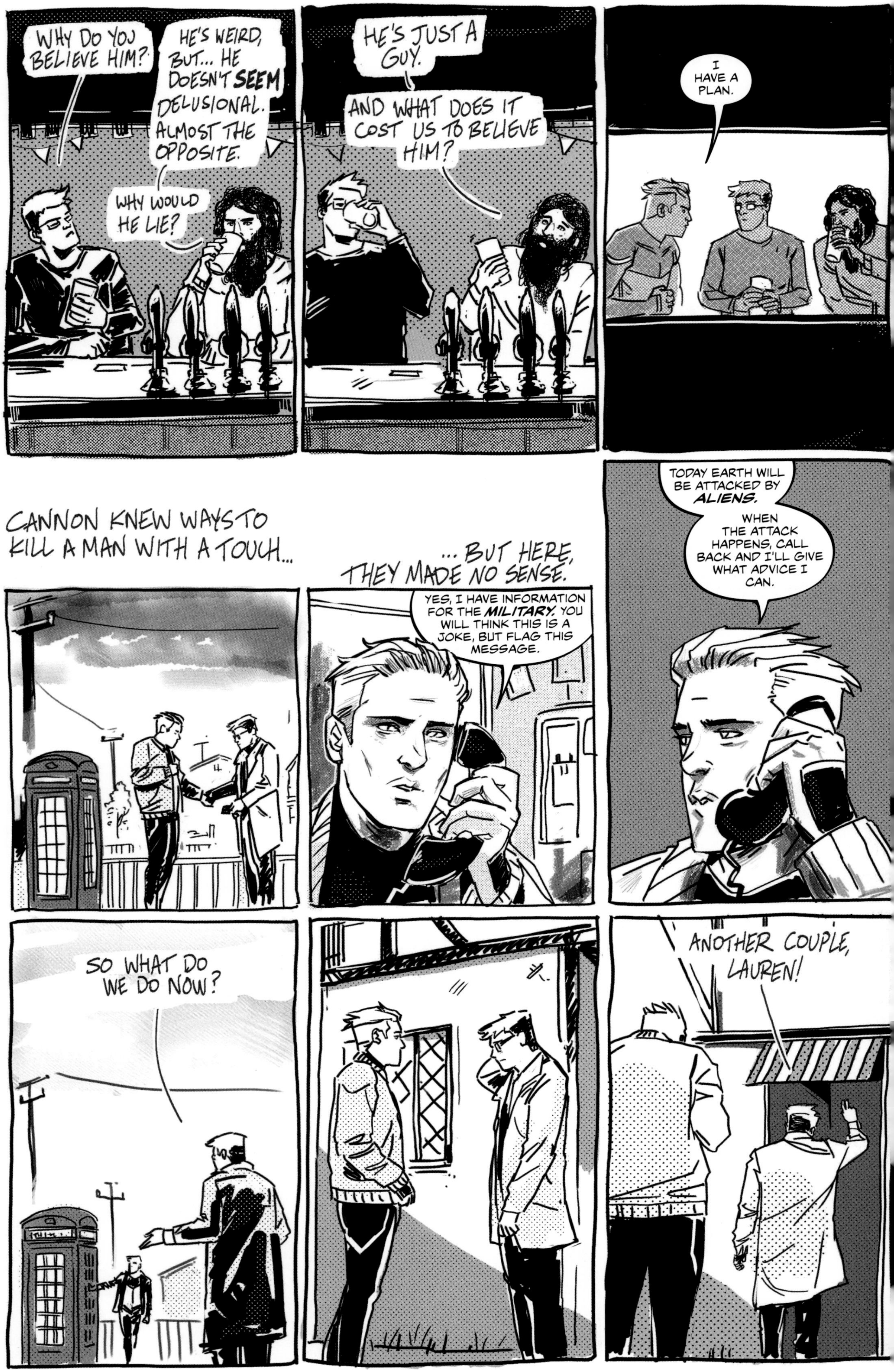
WHY DO YOU BELIEVE HIM?
HE'S WEIRD, BUT... HE DOESN'T SEEM DELUSIONAL. ALMOST THE OPPOSITE.
WHY WOULD HE LIE?
HE'S JUST A GUY.
AND WHAT DOES IT COST US TO BELIEVE HIM?
I HAVE A PLAN.
CANNON KNEW WAYS TO KILL A MAN WITH A TOUCH...
...BUT HERE, THEY MADE NO SENSE.
YES, I HAVE INFORMATION FOR THE MILITARY. YOU WILL THINK THIS IS A JOKE, BUT FLAG THIS MESSAGE.
TODAY EARTH WILL BE ATTACKED BY ALIENS.
WHEN THE ATTACK HAPPENS, CALL BACK AND I'LL GIVE WHAT ADVICE I CAN.
SO WHAT DO WE DO NOW?
ANOTHER COUPLE, LAUREN!

"WHY DO YOU WANT TO HELP PEOPLE?"

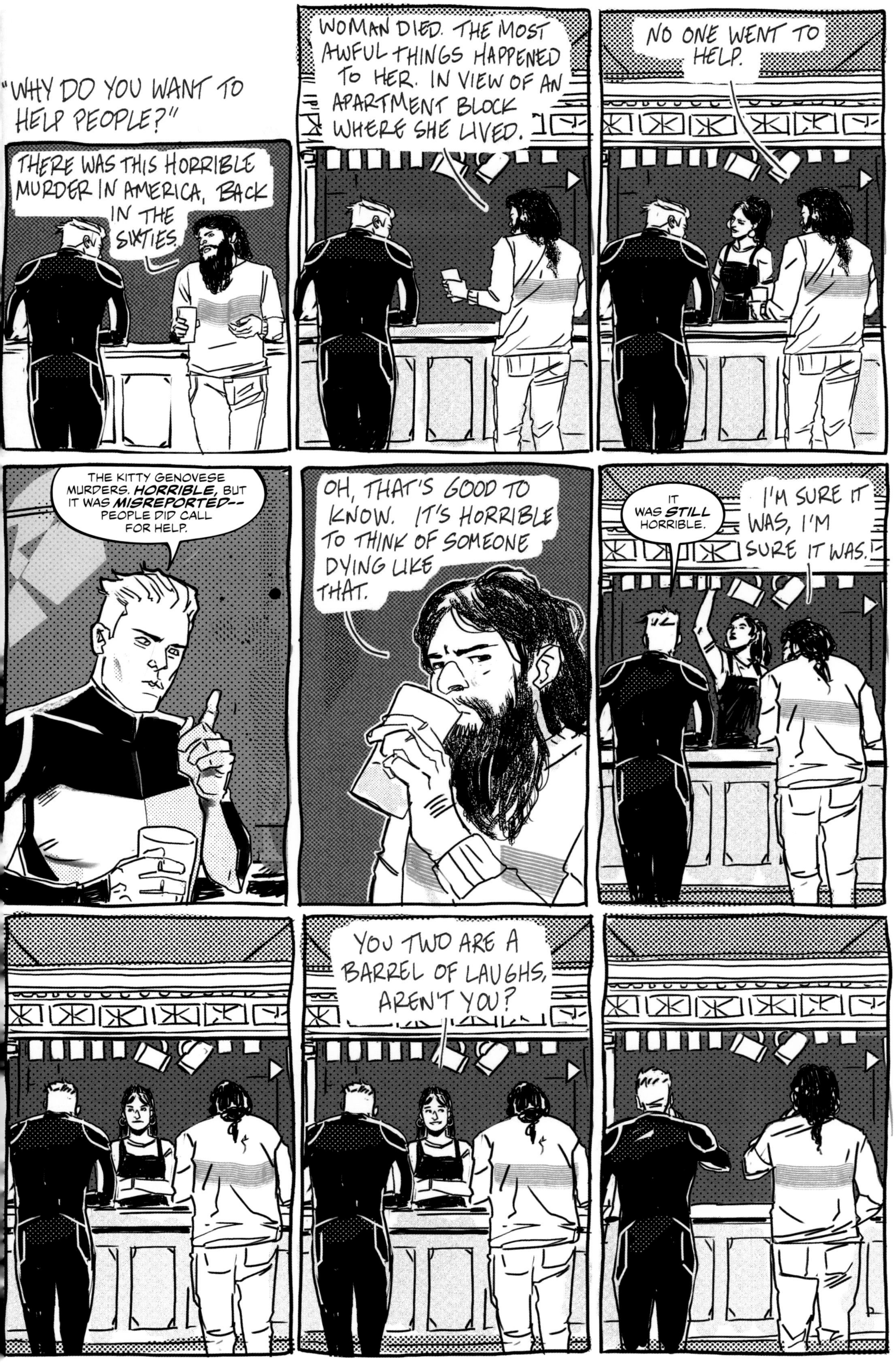
THERE WAS THIS HORRIBLE MURDER IN AMERICA, BACK IN THE SIXTIES.
WOMAN DIED. THE MOST AWFUL THINGS HAPPENED TO HER. IN VIEW OF AN APARTMENT BLOCK WHERE SHE LIVED.
NO ONE WENT TO HELP.
THE KITTY GENOVESE MURDERS. HORRIBLE, BUT IT WAS MISREPORTED-- PEOPLE DID CALL FOR HELP.
OH, THAT'S GOOD TO KNOW. IT'S HORRIBLE TO THINK OF SOMEONE DYING LIKE THAT.
IT WAS STILL HORRIBLE.
I'M SURE IT WAS, I'M SURE IT WAS.
YOU TWO ARE A BARREL OF LAUGHS, AREN'T YOU?

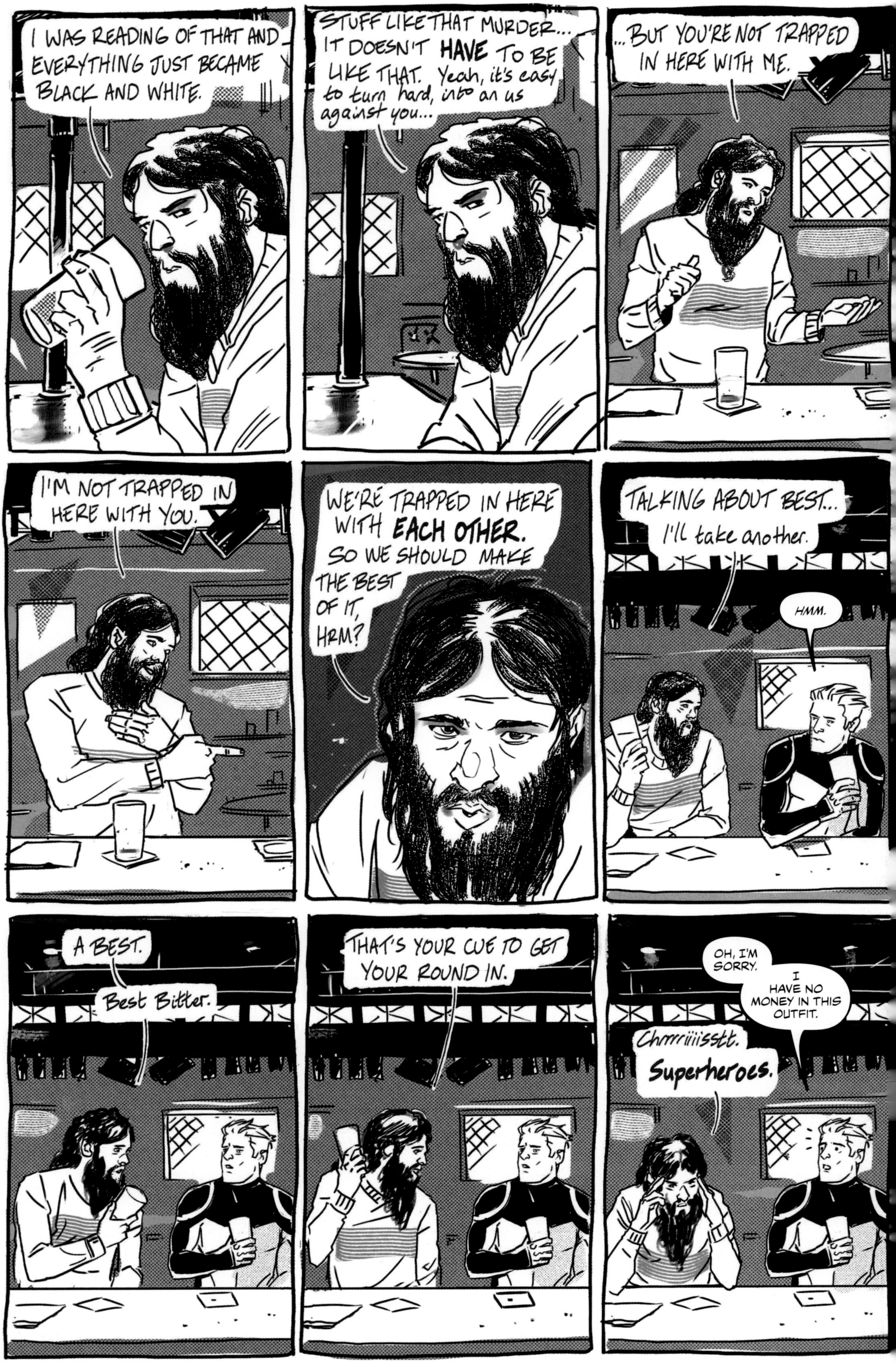
I WAS READING OF THAT AND EVERYTHING JUST BECAME BLACK AND WHITE.
STUFF LIKE THAT MURDER... IT DOESN'T **HAVE** TO BE LIKE THAT. Yeah, it's easy to turn hard, into an us against you...
...BUT YOU'RE NOT TRAPPED IN HERE WITH ME.
I'M NOT TRAPPED IN HERE WITH YOU.
WE'RE TRAPPED IN HERE WITH **EACH OTHER.** SO WE SHOULD MAKE THE BEST OF IT, HRM?
TALKING ABOUT BEST... I'll take another.
HMM.
A BEST.
Best Bitter.
THAT'S YOUR CUE TO GET YOUR ROUND IN.
OH, I'M SORRY.
I HAVE NO MONEY IN THIS OUTFIT.
Chrrriiiissttt.
Superheroes.

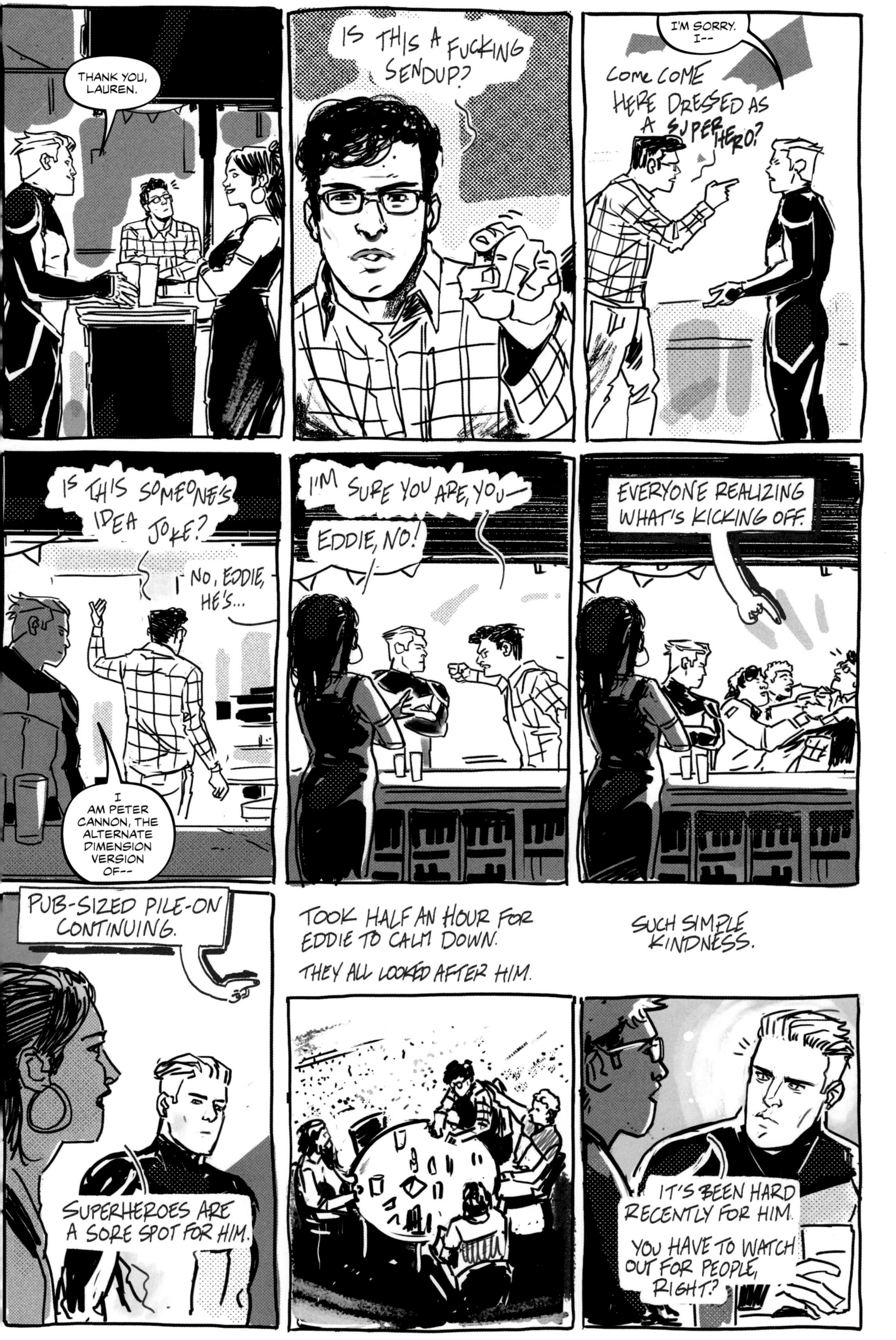
THANK YOU, LAUREN.
IS THIS A FUCKING SENDUP?
I'M SORRY. I--
COME COME HERE DRESSED AS A SUPERHERO?
IS THIS SOMEONE'S IDEA JOKE?
NO, EDDIE, HE'S...
I AM PETER CANNON, THE ALTERNATE DIMENSION VERSION OF--
I'M SURE YOU ARE, YOU--
EDDIE, NO!
EVERYONE REALIZING WHAT'S KICKING OFF.
PUB-SIZED PILE-ON CONTINUING.
SUPERHEROES ARE A SORE SPOT FOR HIM.
TOOK HALF AN HOUR FOR EDDIE TO CALM DOWN.
THEY ALL LOOKED AFTER HIM.
SUCH SIMPLE KINDNESS.
IT'S BEEN HARD RECENTLY FOR HIM.
YOU HAVE TO WATCH OUT FOR PEOPLE, RIGHT?

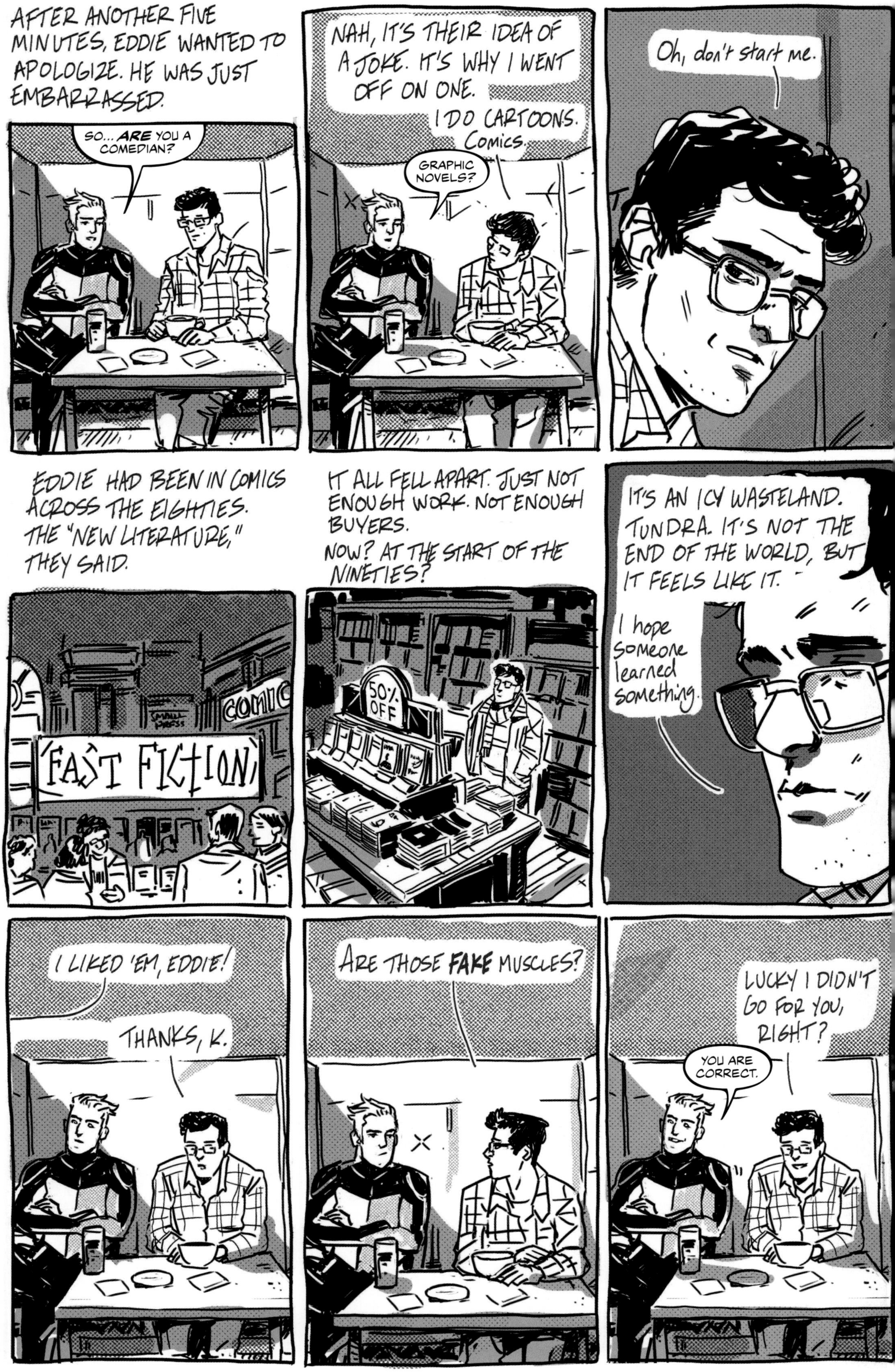
AFTER ANOTHER FIVE MINUTES, EDDIE WANTED TO APOLOGIZE. HE WAS JUST EMBARRASSED.
SO... **ARE** YOU A COMEDIAN?
NAH, IT'S THEIR IDEA OF A JOKE. IT'S WHY I WENT OFF ON ONE.
I DO CARTOONS. Comics.
GRAPHIC NOVELS?
Oh, don't start me.
EDDIE HAD BEEN IN COMICS ACROSS THE EIGHTIES. THE "NEW LITERATURE," THEY SAID.
COMIC
FAST FICTION
IT ALL FELL APART. JUST NOT ENOUGH WORK. NOT ENOUGH BUYERS.
NOW? AT THE START OF THE NINETIES?
50% OFF
IT'S AN ICY WASTELAND. TUNDRA. IT'S NOT THE END OF THE WORLD, BUT IT FEELS LIKE IT.
I hope someone learned something.
I LIKED 'EM, EDDIE!
THANKS, K.
ARE THOSE **FAKE** MUSCLES?
LUCKY I DIDN'T GO FOR YOU, RIGHT?
YOU ARE CORRECT.

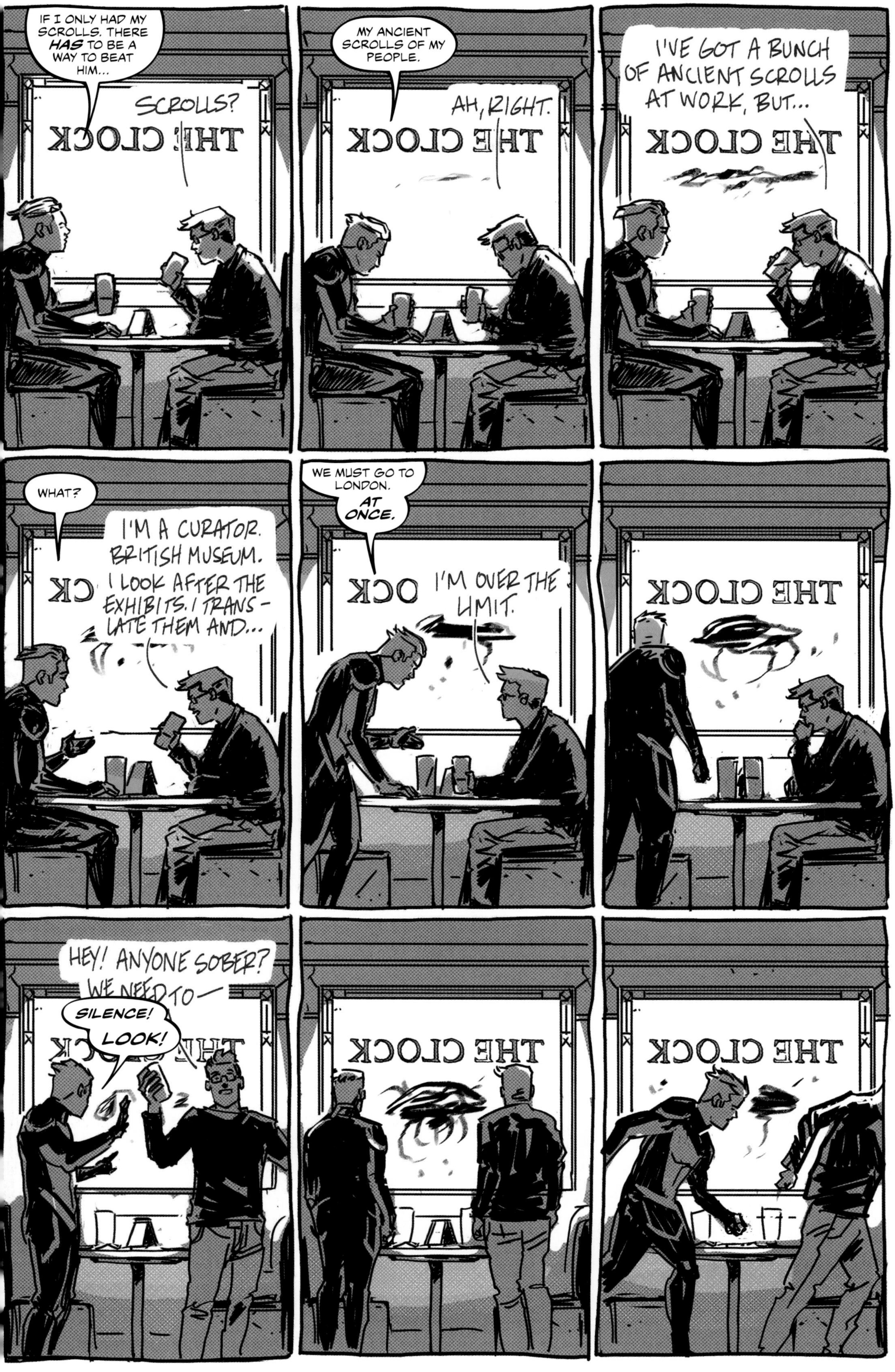
THE CLOCK
IF I ONLY HAD MY SCROLLS. THERE HAS TO BE A WAY TO BEAT HIM...
SCROLLS?
MY ANCIENT SCROLLS OF MY PEOPLE.
AH, RIGHT.
I'VE GOT A BUNCH OF ANCIENT SCROLLS AT WORK, BUT...
WHAT?
I'M A CURATOR. BRITISH MUSEUM. I LOOK AFTER THE EXHIBITS. I TRANSLATE THEM AND...
WE MUST GO TO LONDON. AT ONCE.
I'M OVER THE LIMIT.
HEY! ANYONE SOBER? WE NEED TO—
SILENCE!
LOOK!

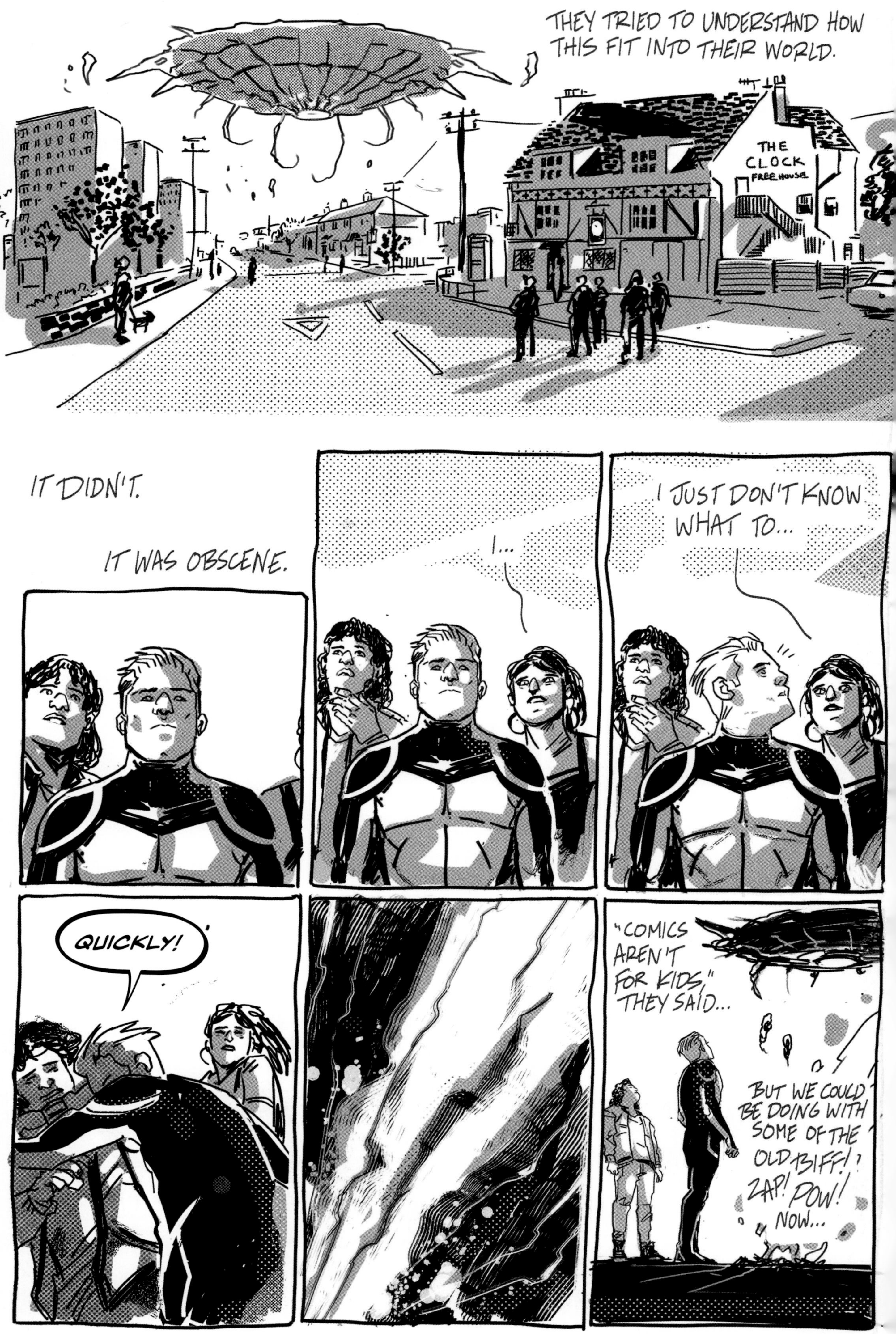
THEY TRIED TO UNDERSTAND HOW THIS FIT INTO THEIR WORLD.
THE CLOCK
FREE HOUSE
IT DIDN'T.
IT WAS OBSCENE.
I...
I JUST DON'T KNOW WHAT TO...
QUICKLY!
"COMICS AREN'T FOR KIDS," THEY SAID...
BUT WE COULD BE DOING WITH SOME OF THE OLD BIFF! ZAP! POW! NOW...

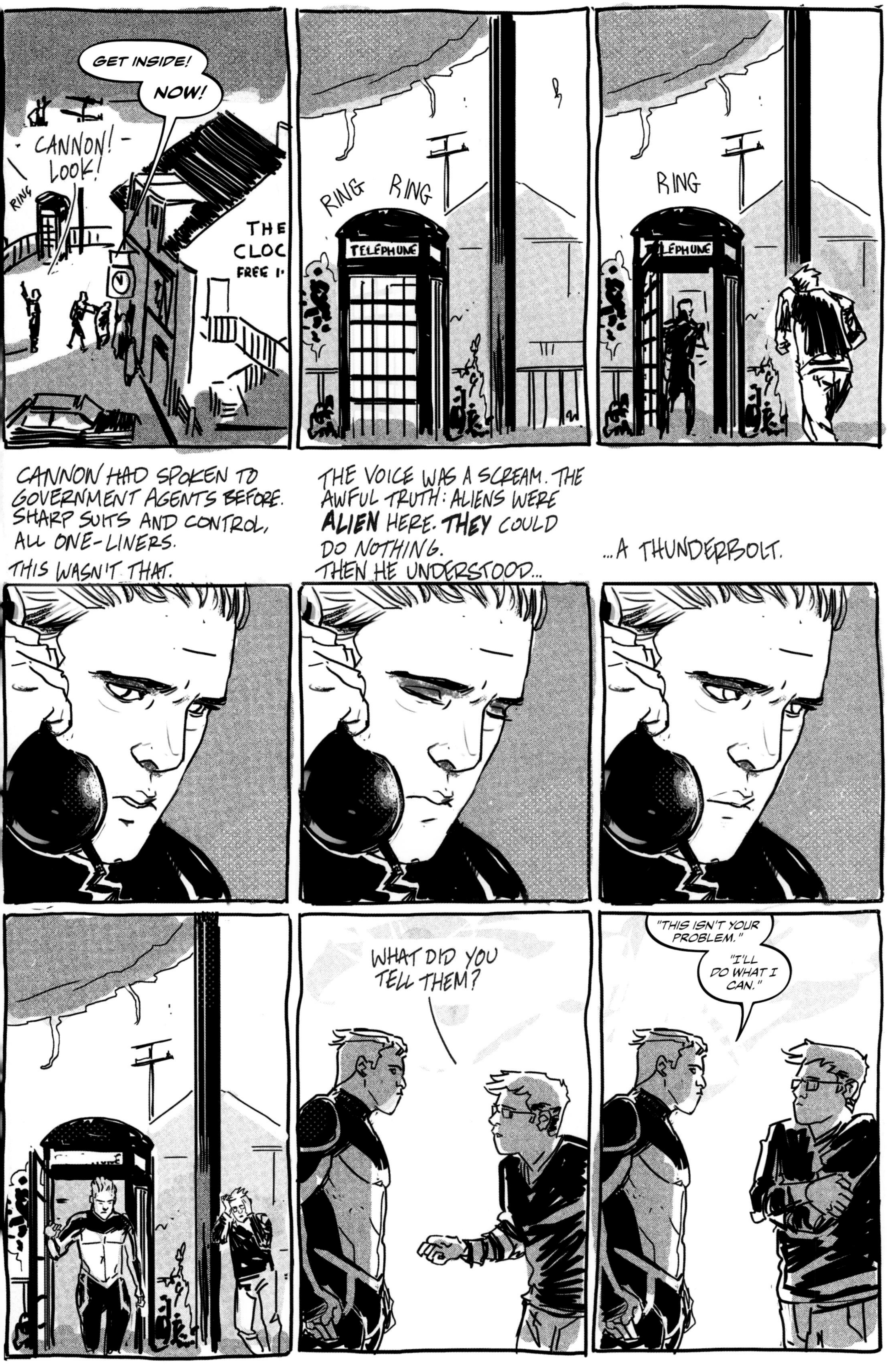
GET INSIDE!
NOW!
CANNON! LOOK!
RING
RING RING
TELEPHONE
RING
CANNON HAD SPOKEN TO GOVERNMENT AGENTS BEFORE. SHARP SUITS AND CONTROL, ALL ONE-LINERS.
THIS WASN'T THAT.
THE VOICE WAS A SCREAM. THE AWFUL TRUTH: ALIENS WERE **ALIEN** HERE. **THEY** COULD DO NOTHING.
THEN HE UNDERSTOOD...
...A THUNDERBOLT.
WHAT DID YOU TELL THEM?
"THIS ISN'T YOUR PROBLEM."
"I'LL DO WHAT I CAN."

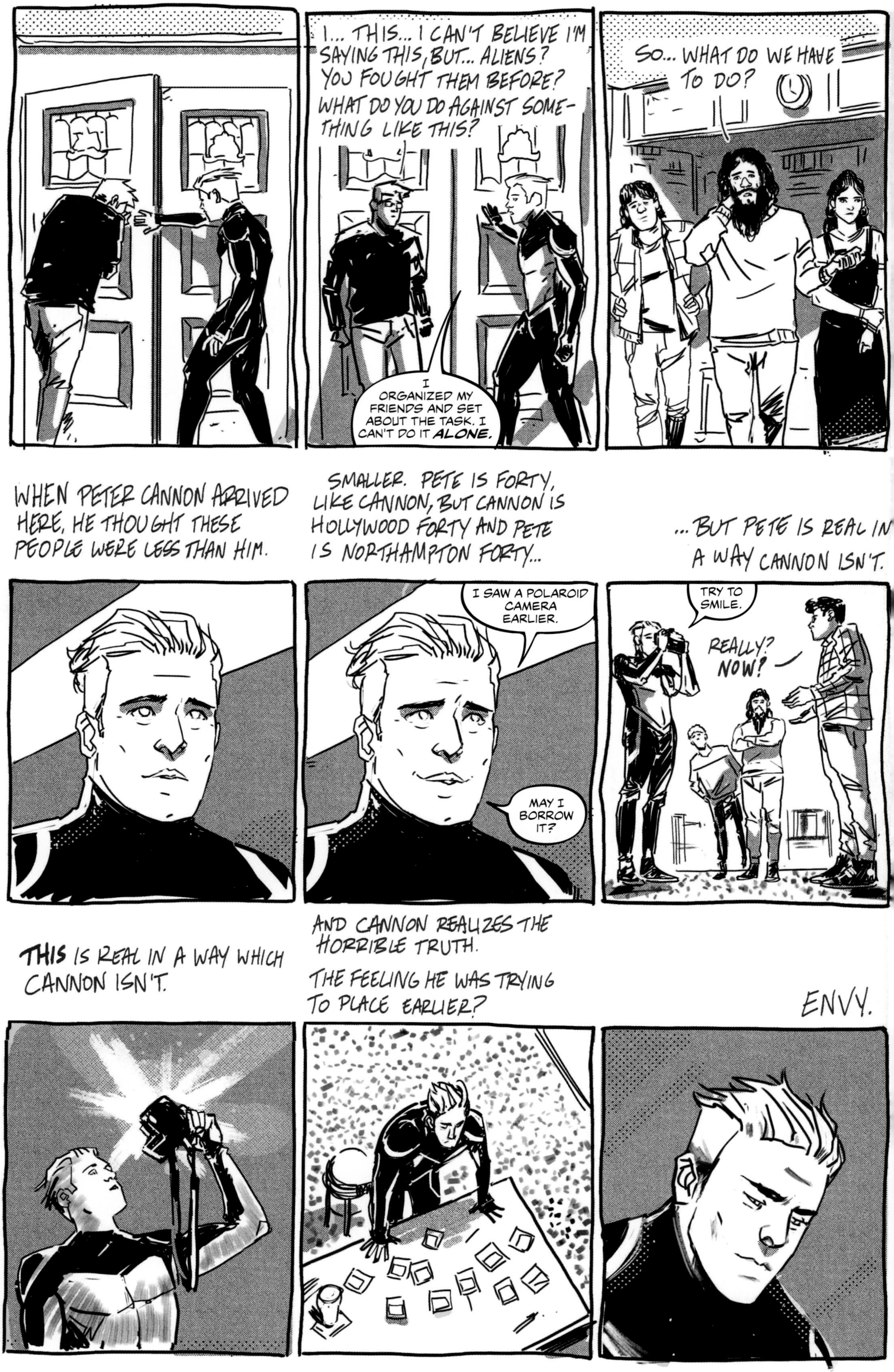

I... THIS... I CAN'T BELIEVE I'M SAYING THIS, BUT... ALIENS? YOU FOUGHT THEM BEFORE? WHAT DO YOU DO AGAINST SOMETHING LIKE THIS?
I ORGANIZED MY FRIENDS AND SET ABOUT THE TASK. I CAN'T DO IT ALONE.
SO... WHAT DO WE HAVE TO DO?
WHEN PETER CANNON ARRIVED HERE, HE THOUGHT THESE PEOPLE WERE LESS THAN HIM.
SMALLER. PETE IS FORTY, LIKE CANNON, BUT CANNON IS HOLLYWOOD FORTY AND PETE IS NORTHAMPTON FORTY...
I SAW A POLAROID CAMERA EARLIER.
MAY I BORROW IT?
...BUT PETE IS REAL IN A WAY CANNON ISN'T.
TRY TO SMILE.
REALLY? NOW?
THIS IS REAL IN A WAY WHICH CANNON ISN'T.
AND CANNON REALIZES THE HORRIBLE TRUTH.
THE FEELING HE WAS TRYING TO PLACE EARLIER?
ENVY.

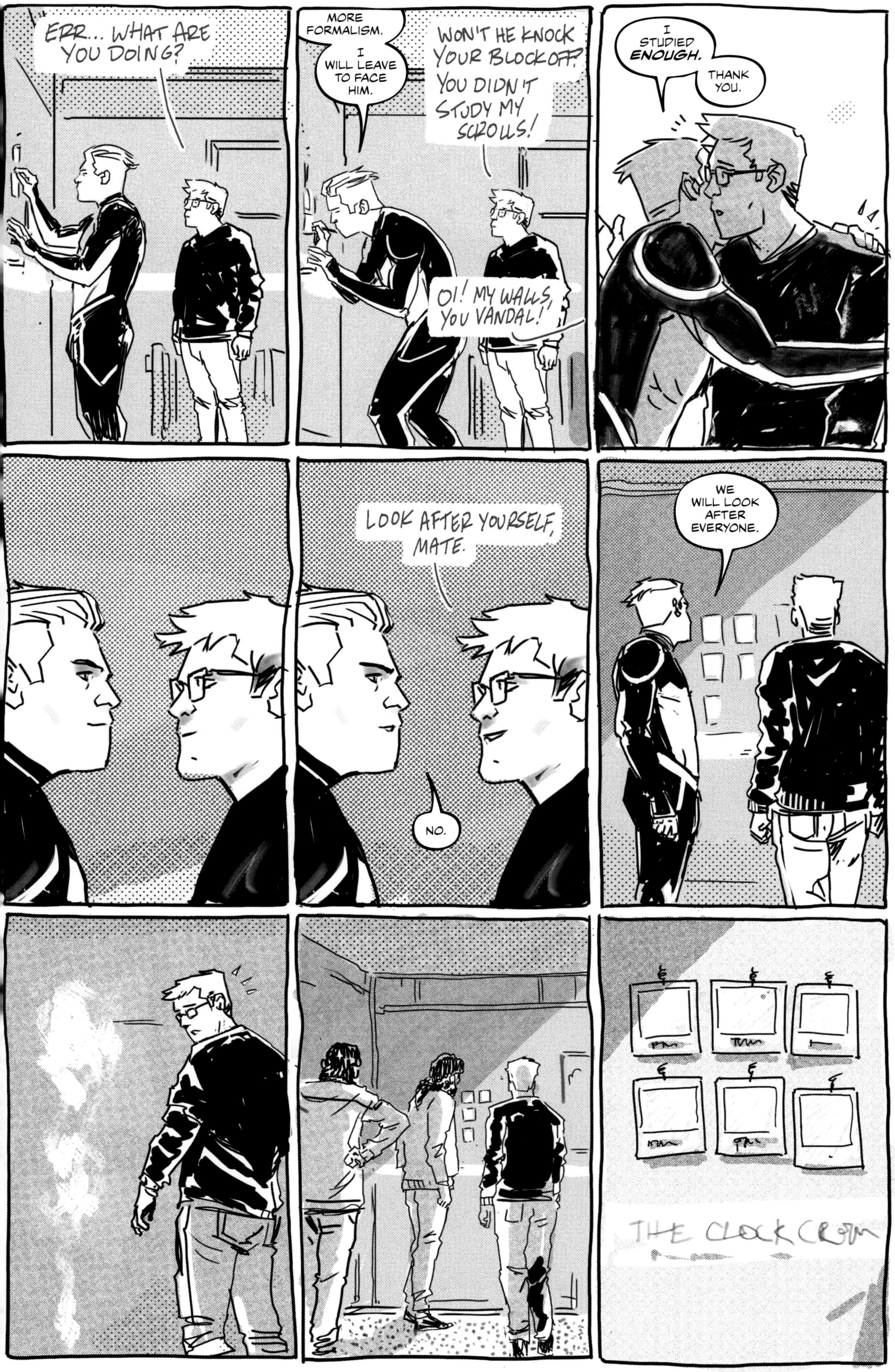
ERR... WHAT ARE YOU DOING?
MORE FORMALISM.
I WILL LEAVE TO FACE HIM.
WON'T HE KNOCK YOUR BLOCK OFF? YOU DIDN'T STUDY MY SCROLLS!
OI! MY WALLS, YOU VANDAL!
I STUDIED **ENOUGH.**
THANK YOU.
LOOK AFTER YOURSELF, MATE.
NO.
WE WILL LOOK AFTER EVERYONE.
THE CLOCK CROWN

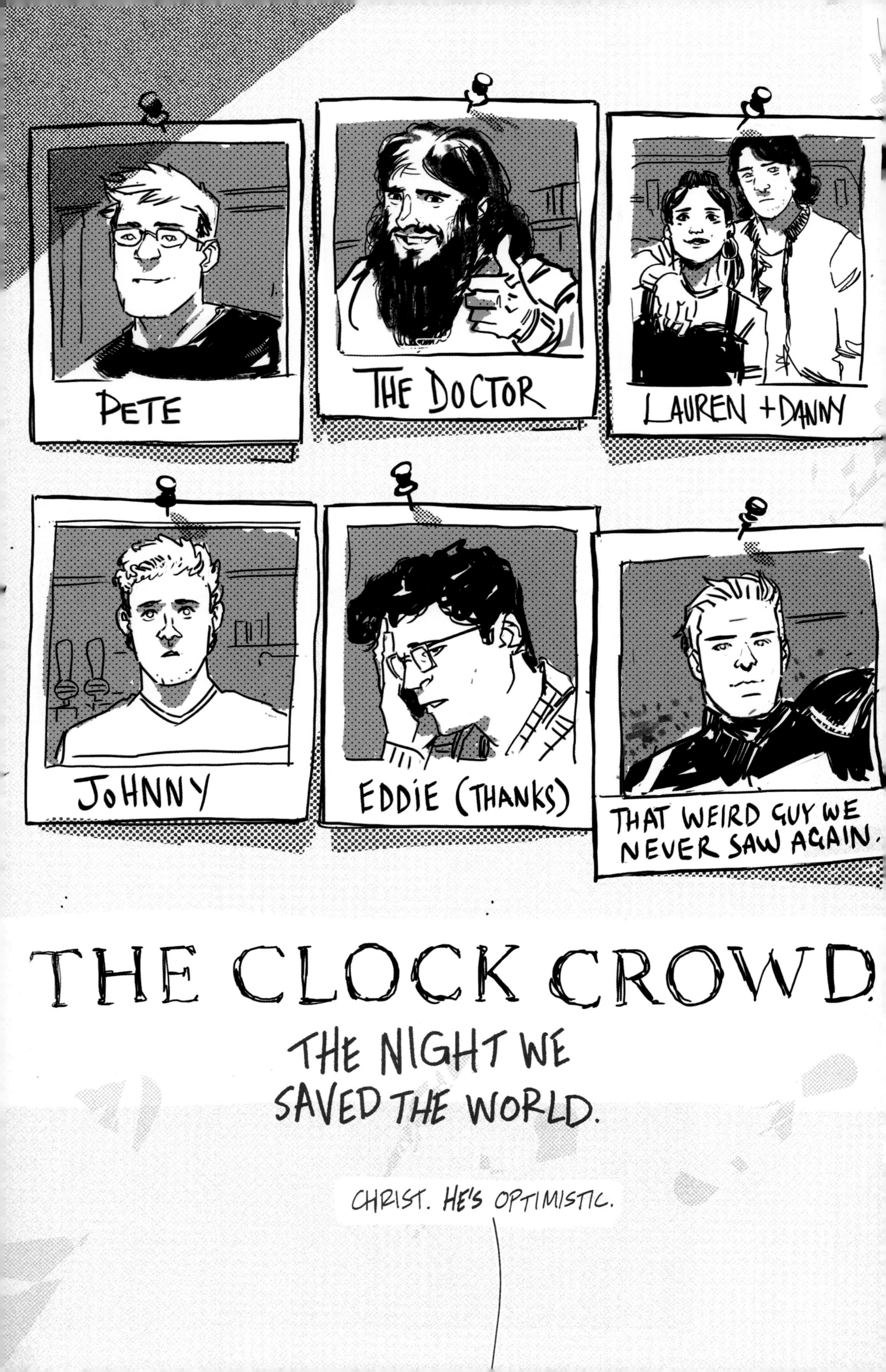
PETE
THE DOCTOR
LAUREN + DANNY
JOHNNY
EDDIE (THANKS)
THAT WEIRD GUY WE NEVER SAW AGAIN.
THE CLOCK CROWD
THE NIGHT WE SAVED THE WORLD.
CHRIST. HE'S OPTIMISTIC.

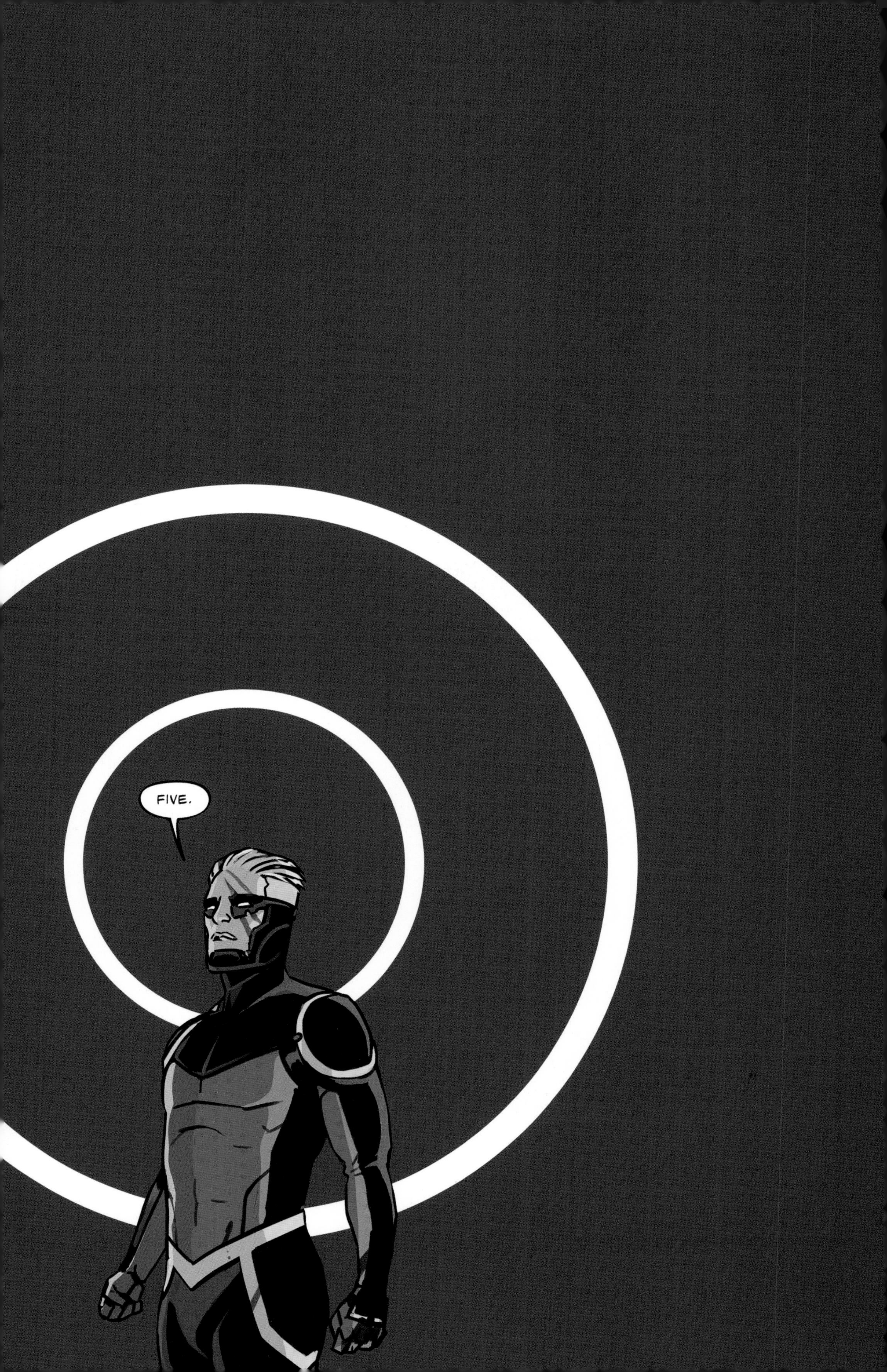
FIVE.

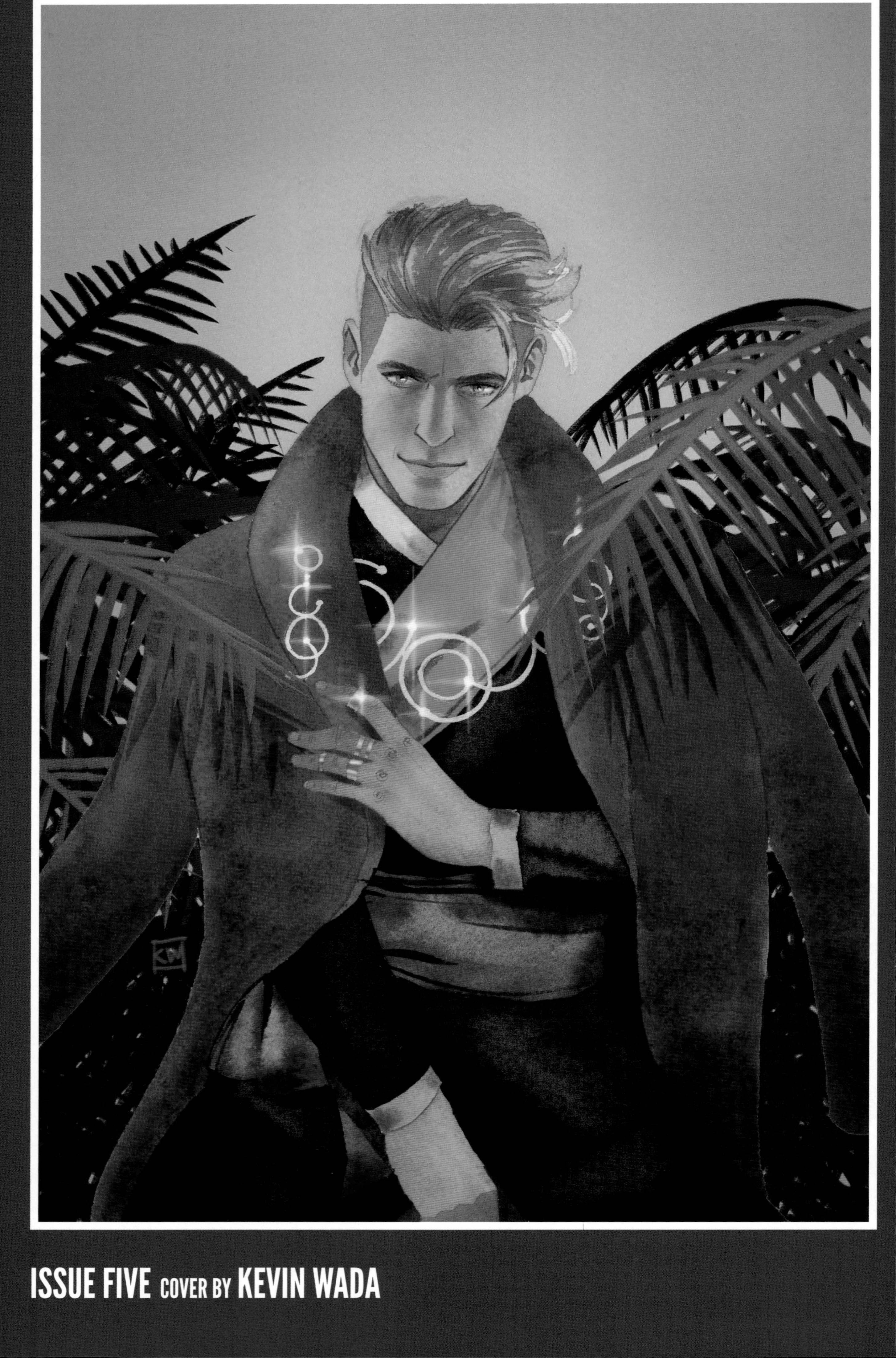

ISSUE FIVE COVER BY KEVIN WADA

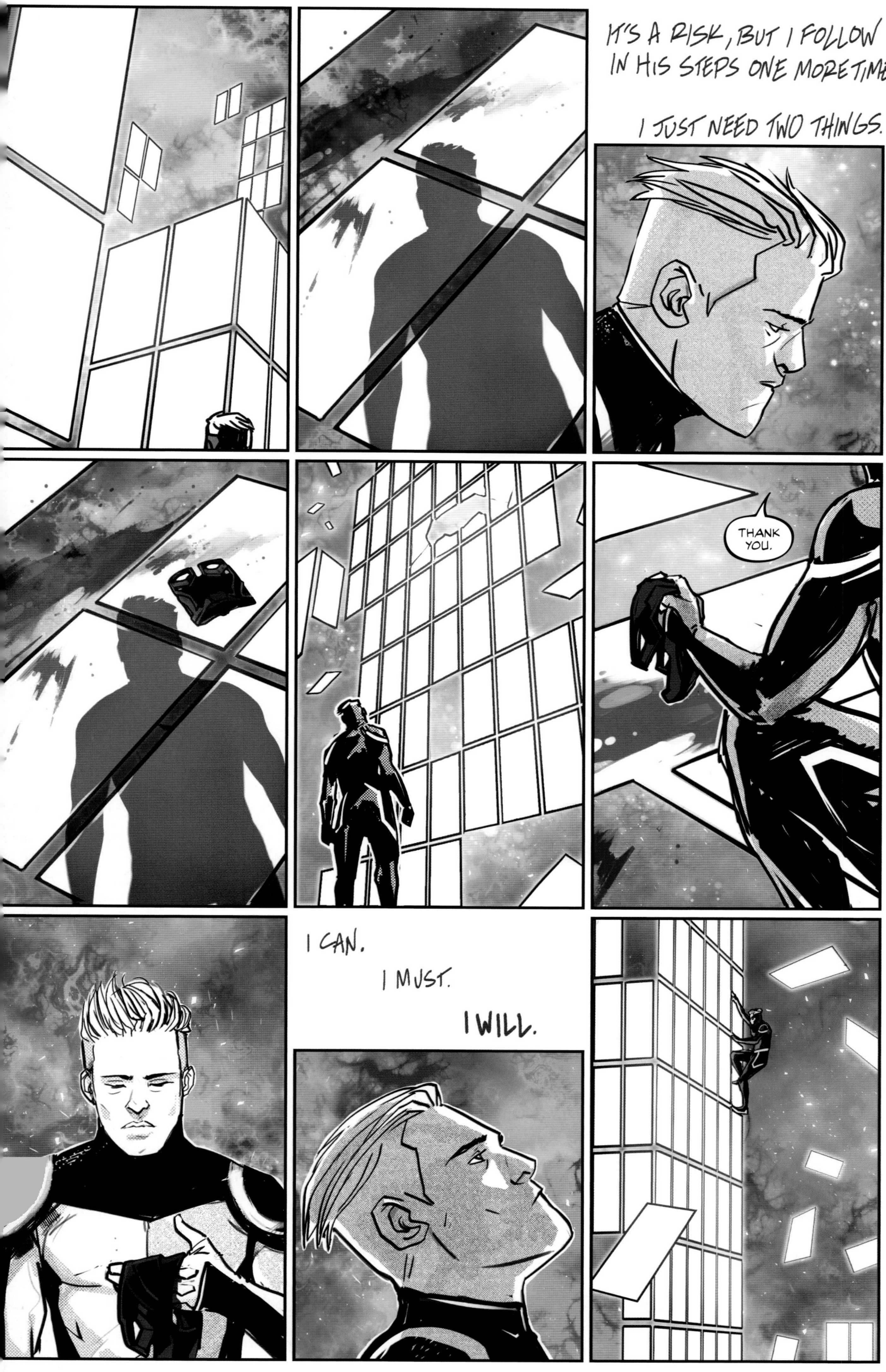

IT'S A RISK, BUT I FOLLOW IN HIS STEPS ONE MORE TIME.
I JUST NEED TWO THINGS.
THANK YOU.
I CAN.
I MUST.
I WILL.

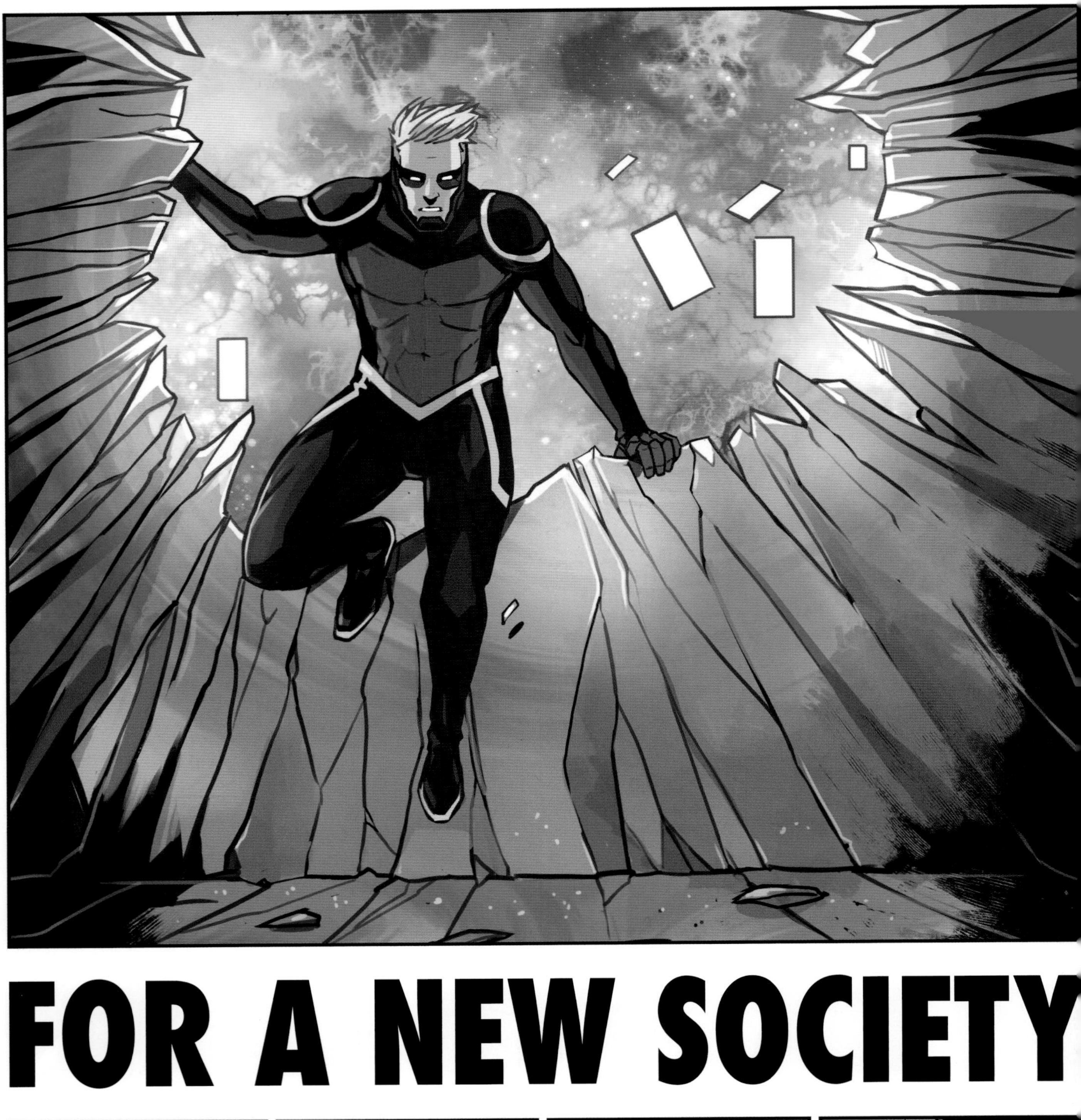

FOR A NEW SOCIETY

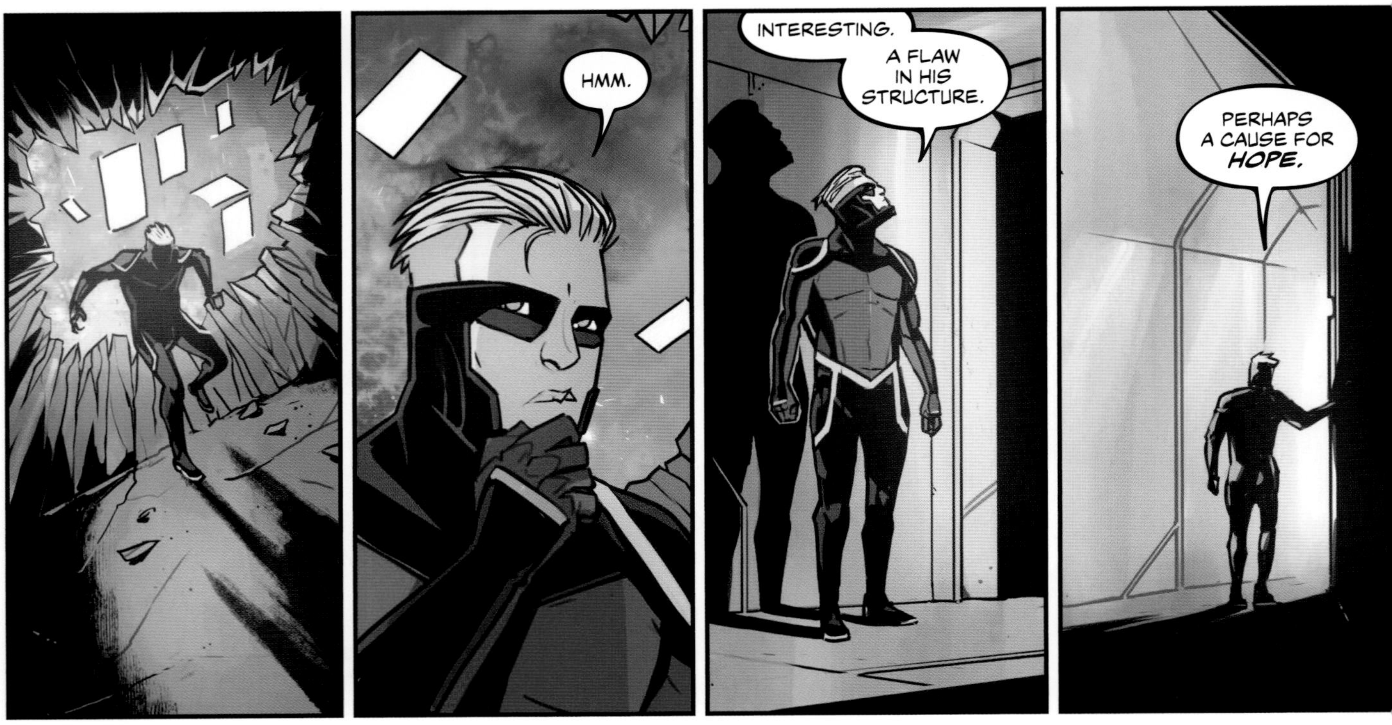
HMM.
INTERESTING.
A FLAW IN HIS STRUCTURE.
PERHAPS A CAUSE FOR *HOPE.*

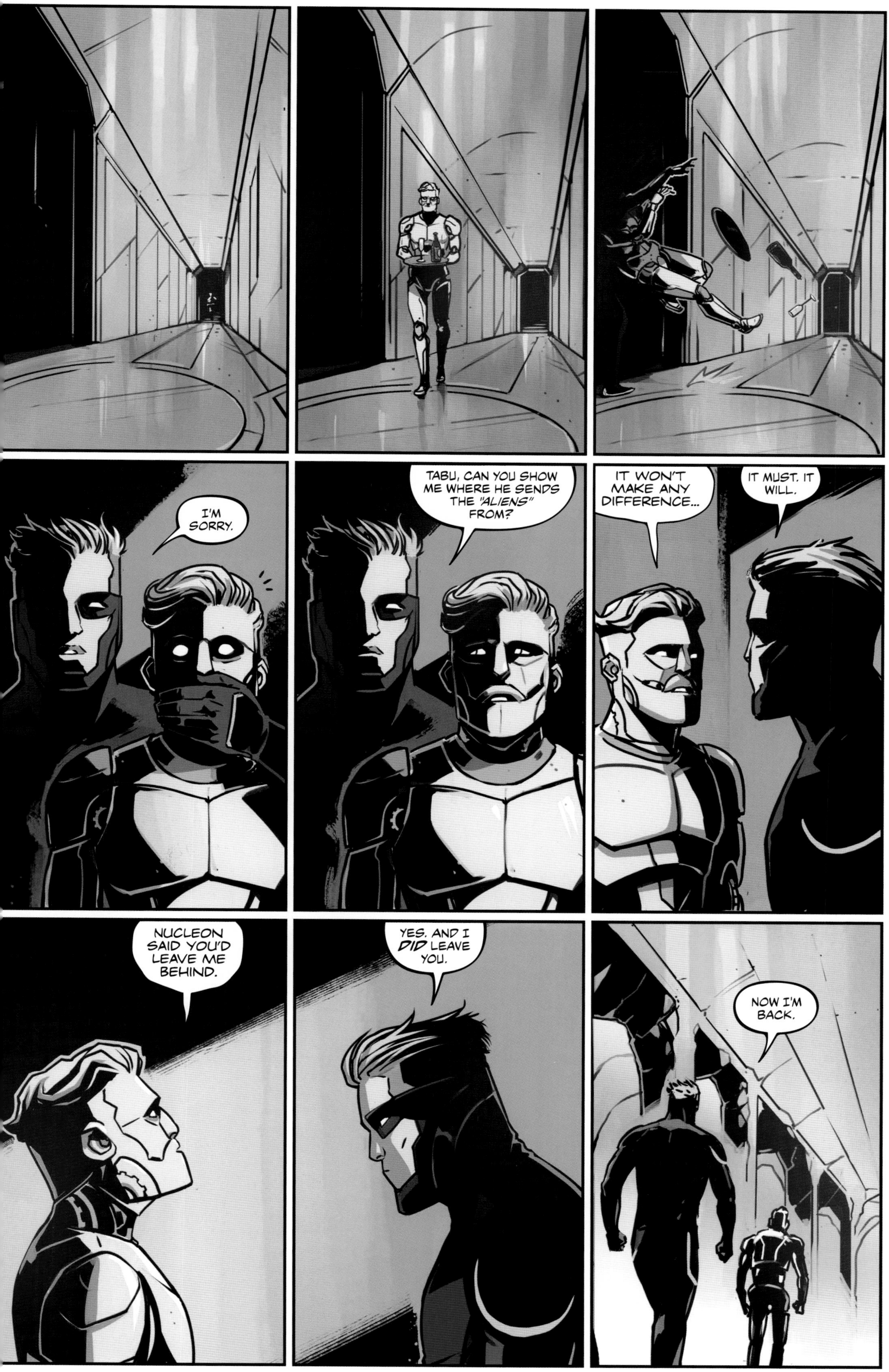
I'M SORRY.
TABU, CAN YOU SHOW ME WHERE HE SENDS THE "ALIENS" FROM?
IT WON'T MAKE ANY DIFFERENCE...
IT MUST. IT WILL.
NUCLEON SAID YOU'D LEAVE ME BEHIND.
YES. AND I DID LEAVE YOU.
NOW I'M BACK.

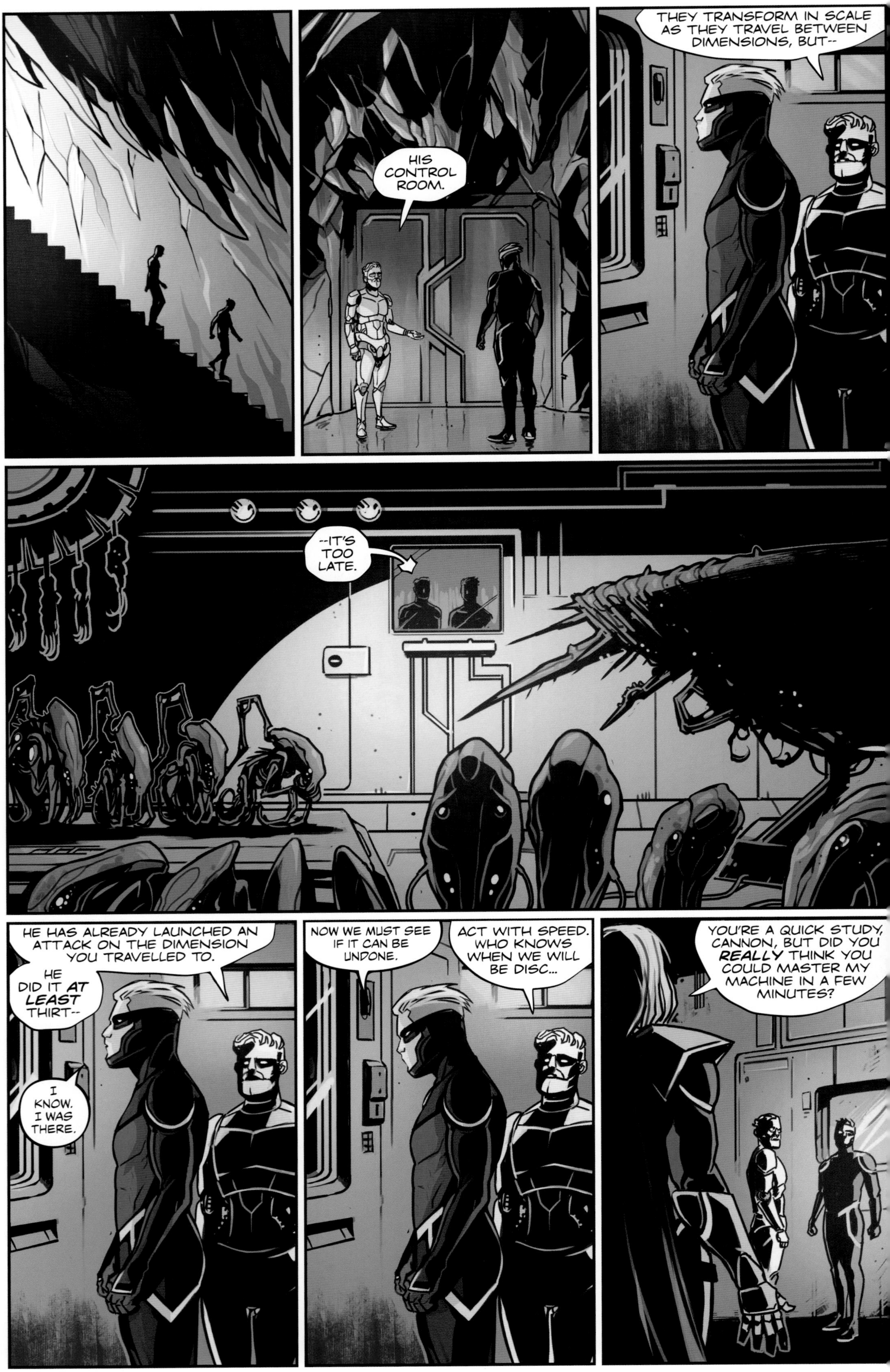
HIS CONTROL ROOM.
THEY TRANSFORM IN SCALE AS THEY TRAVEL BETWEEN DIMENSIONS, BUT--
--IT'S TOO LATE.
HE HAS ALREADY LAUNCHED AN ATTACK ON THE DIMENSION YOU TRAVELLED TO.
HE DID IT **AT LEAST** THIRT--
I KNOW. I WAS THERE.
NOW WE MUST SEE IF IT CAN BE UNDONE.
ACT WITH SPEED. WHO KNOWS WHEN WE WILL BE DISC...
YOU'RE A QUICK STUDY, CANNON, BUT DID YOU **REALLY** THINK YOU COULD MASTER MY MACHINE IN A FEW MINUTES?

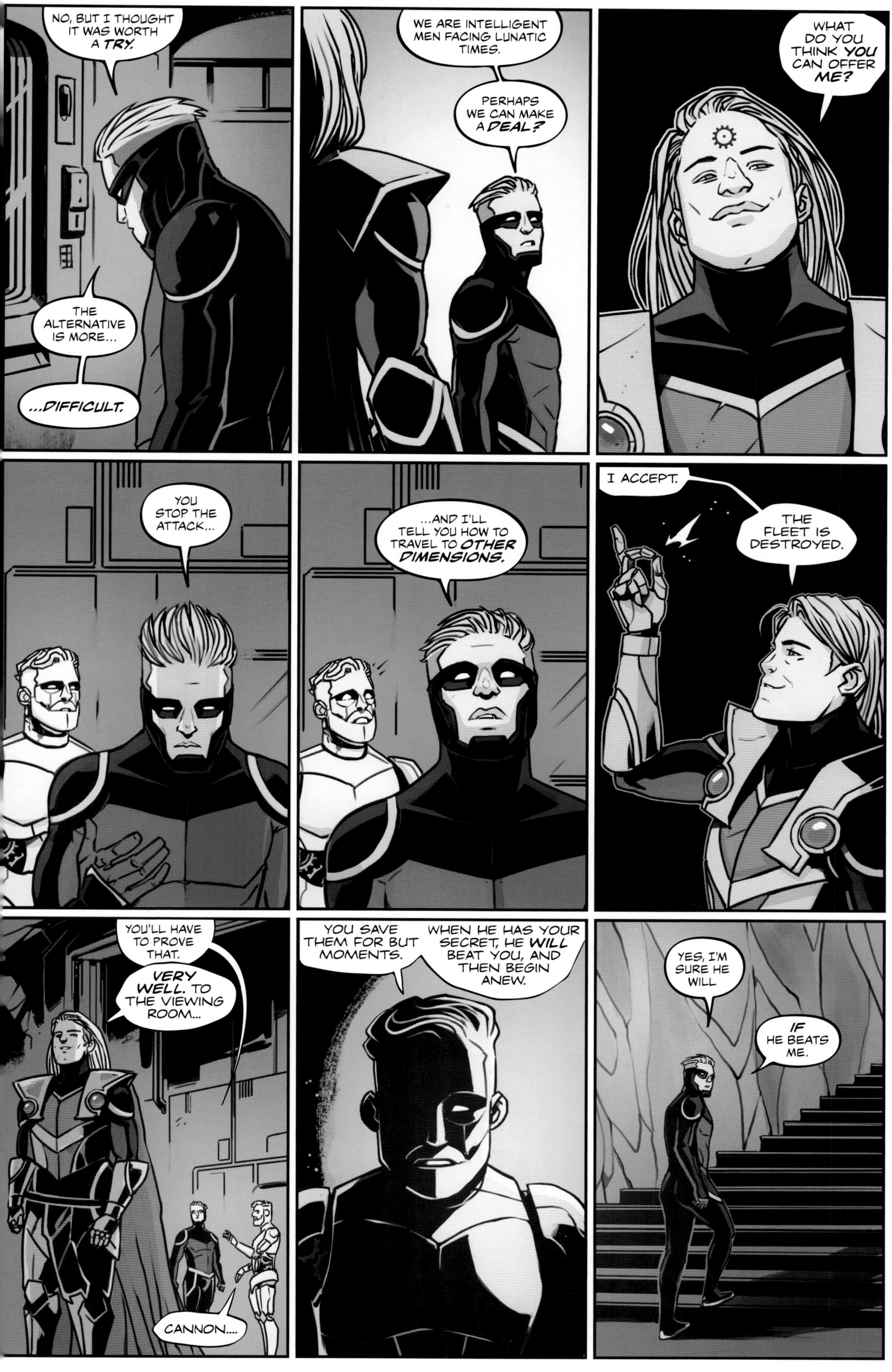
NO, BUT I THOUGHT IT WAS WORTH A TRY.
THE ALTERNATIVE IS MORE...
...DIFFICULT.
WE ARE INTELLIGENT MEN FACING LUNATIC TIMES.
PERHAPS WE CAN MAKE A DEAL?
WHAT DO YOU THINK YOU CAN OFFER ME?
YOU STOP THE ATTACK...
...AND I'LL TELL YOU HOW TO TRAVEL TO OTHER DIMENSIONS.
I ACCEPT.
THE FLEET IS DESTROYED.
YOU'LL HAVE TO PROVE THAT.
VERY WELL. TO THE VIEWING ROOM...
CANNON....
YOU SAVE THEM FOR BUT MOMENTS.
WHEN HE HAS YOUR SECRET, HE WILL BEAT YOU, AND THEN BEGIN ANEW.
YES, I'M SURE HE WILL
IF HE BEATS ME.

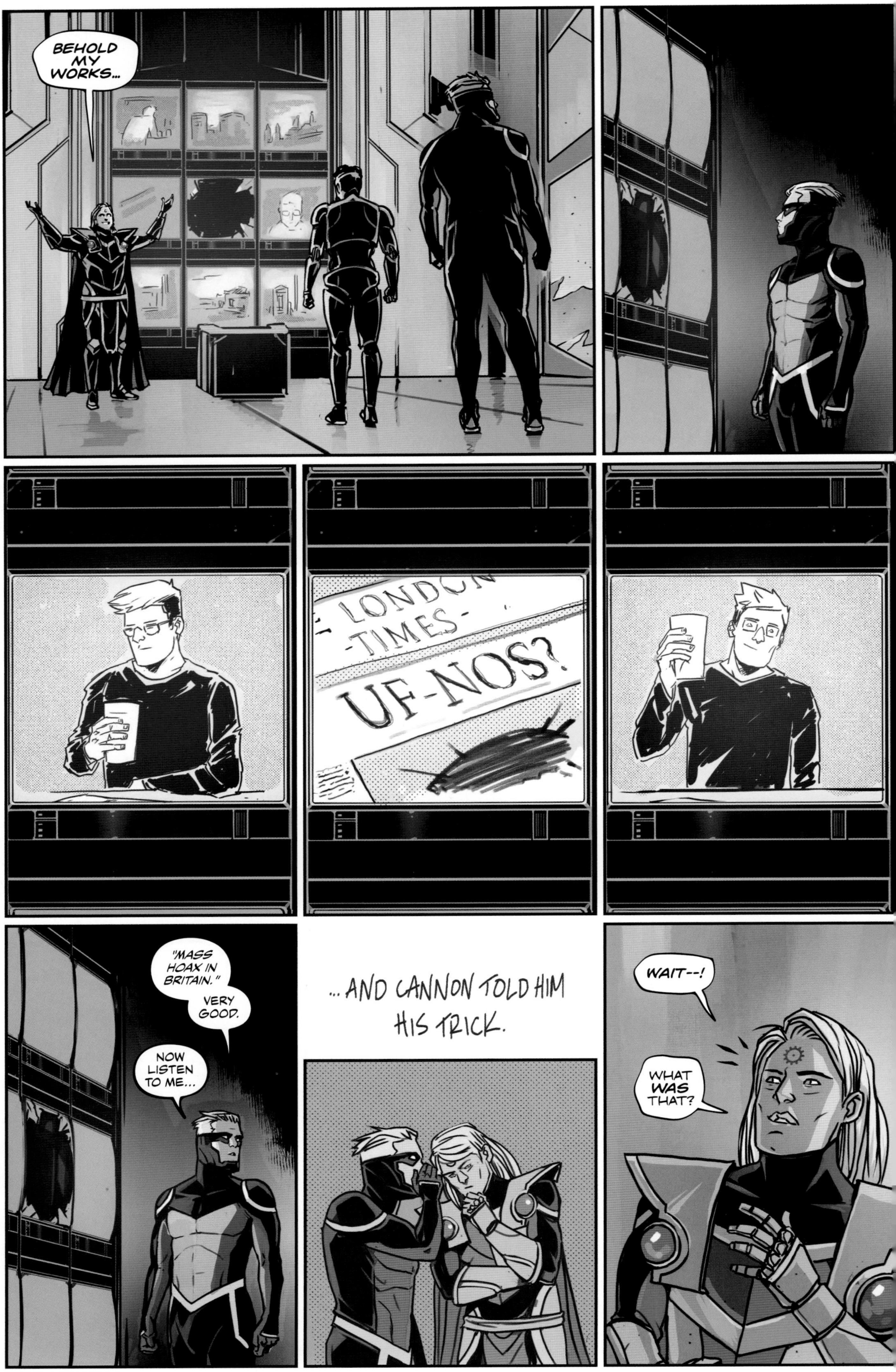
BEHOLD MY WORKS...
-LONDON-
-TIMES-
UF-NOS?
"MASS HOAX IN BRITAIN."
VERY GOOD.
NOW LISTEN TO ME...
...AND CANNON TOLD HIM HIS TRICK.
WAIT--!
WHAT WAS THAT?

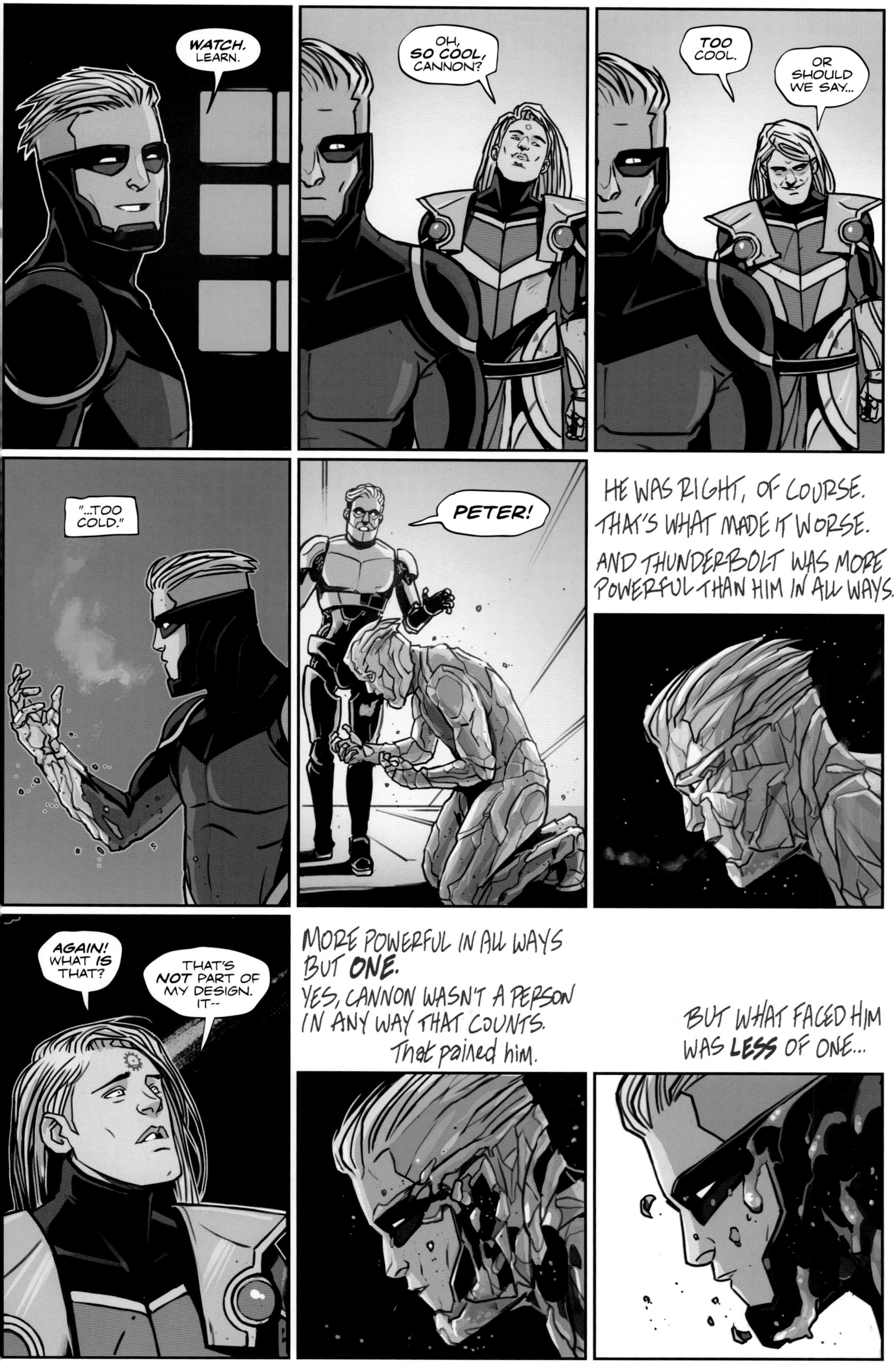
WATCH. LEARN.
OH, SO COOL, CANNON?
TOO COOL.
OR SHOULD WE SAY...
"...TOO COLD."
PETER!
HE WAS RIGHT, OF COURSE.
THAT'S WHAT MADE IT WORSE.
AND THUNDERBOLT WAS MORE POWERFUL THAN HIM IN ALL WAYS.
AGAIN! WHAT IS THAT?
THAT'S NOT PART OF MY DESIGN. IT--
MORE POWERFUL IN ALL WAYS BUT ONE.
YES, CANNON WASN'T A PERSON IN ANY WAY THAT COUNTS.
That pained him.
BUT WHAT FACED HIM WAS LESS OF ONE...

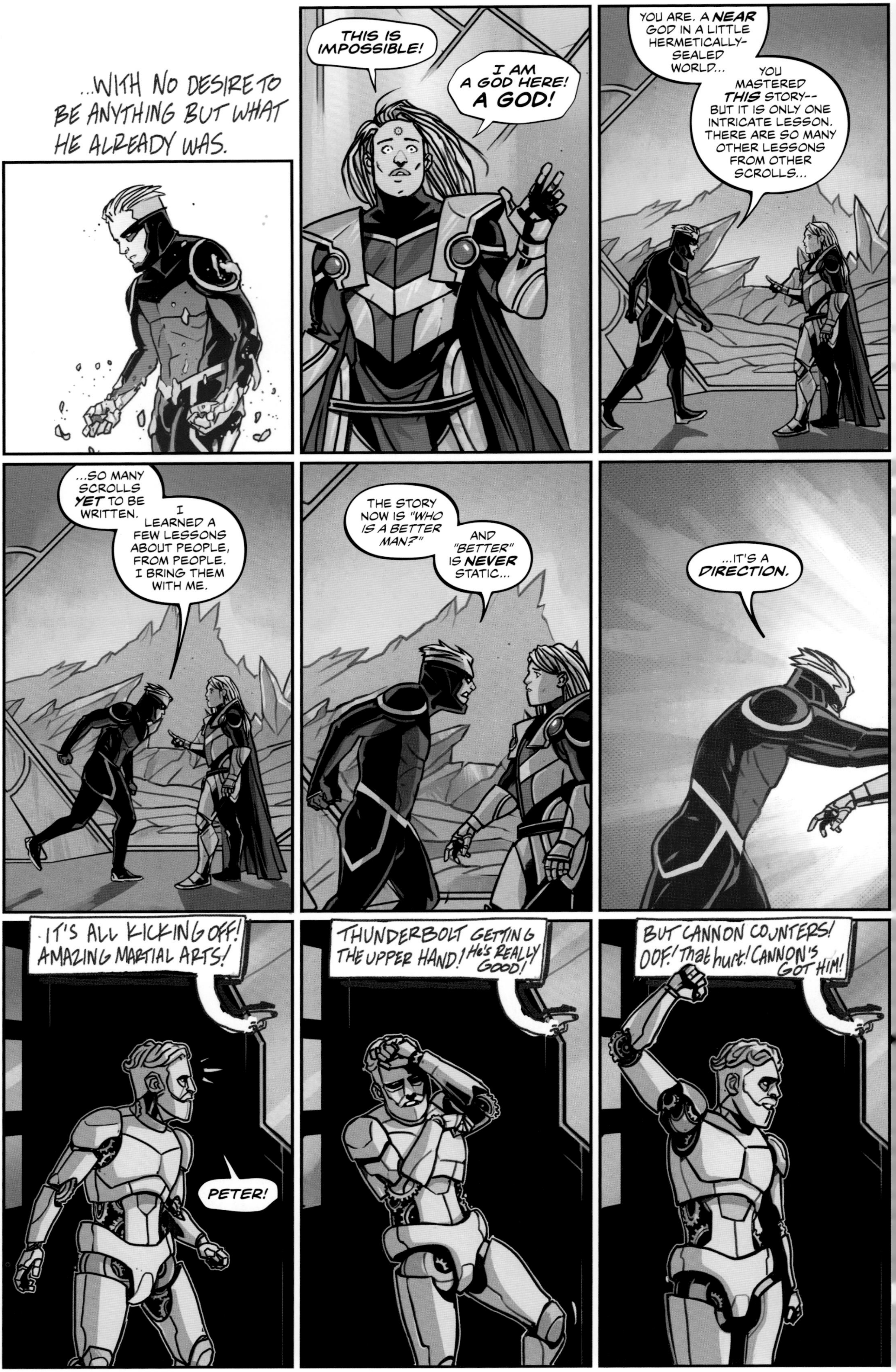
...WITH NO DESIRE TO BE ANYTHING BUT WHAT HE ALREADY WAS.
THIS IS IMPOSSIBLE!
I AM A GOD HERE! A GOD!
YOU ARE. A NEAR GOD IN A LITTLE HERMETICALLY-SEALED WORLD...
YOU MASTERED THIS STORY-- BUT IT IS ONLY ONE INTRICATE LESSON. THERE ARE SO MANY OTHER LESSONS FROM OTHER SCROLLS...
...SO MANY SCROLLS YET TO BE WRITTEN.
I LEARNED A FEW LESSONS ABOUT PEOPLE, FROM PEOPLE. I BRING THEM WITH ME.
THE STORY NOW IS "WHO IS A BETTER MAN?"
AND "BETTER" IS NEVER STATIC...
...IT'S A DIRECTION.
IT'S ALL KICKING OFF! AMAZING MARTIAL ARTS!
PETER!
THUNDERBOLT GETTING THE UPPER HAND! He's REALLY GOOD!
BUT CANNON COUNTERS! OOF! That hurt! CANNON'S GOT HIM!

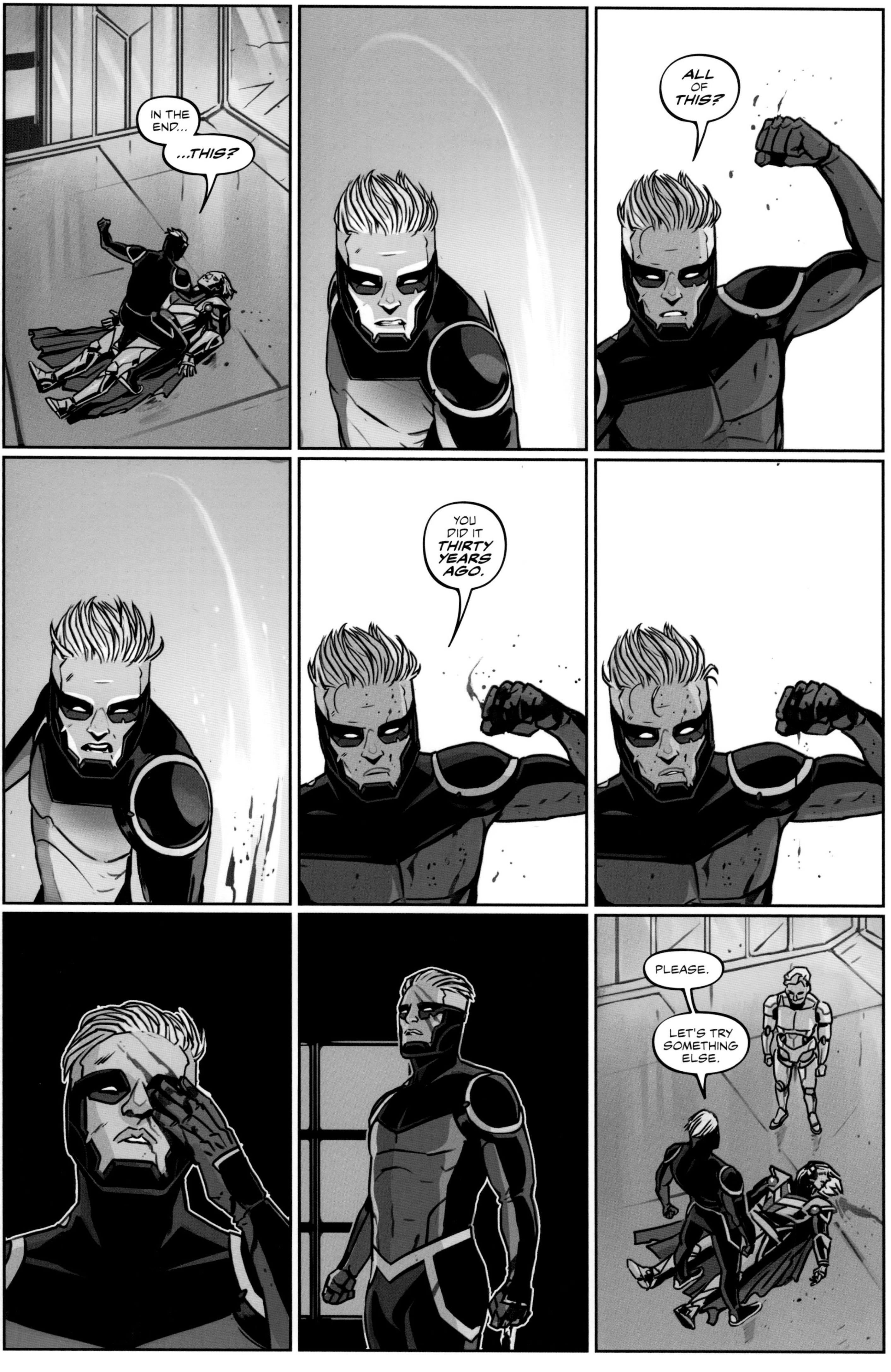
IN THE END...
...THIS?
ALL OF THIS?
YOU DID IT THIRTY YEARS AGO.
PLEASE.
LET'S TRY SOMETHING ELSE.

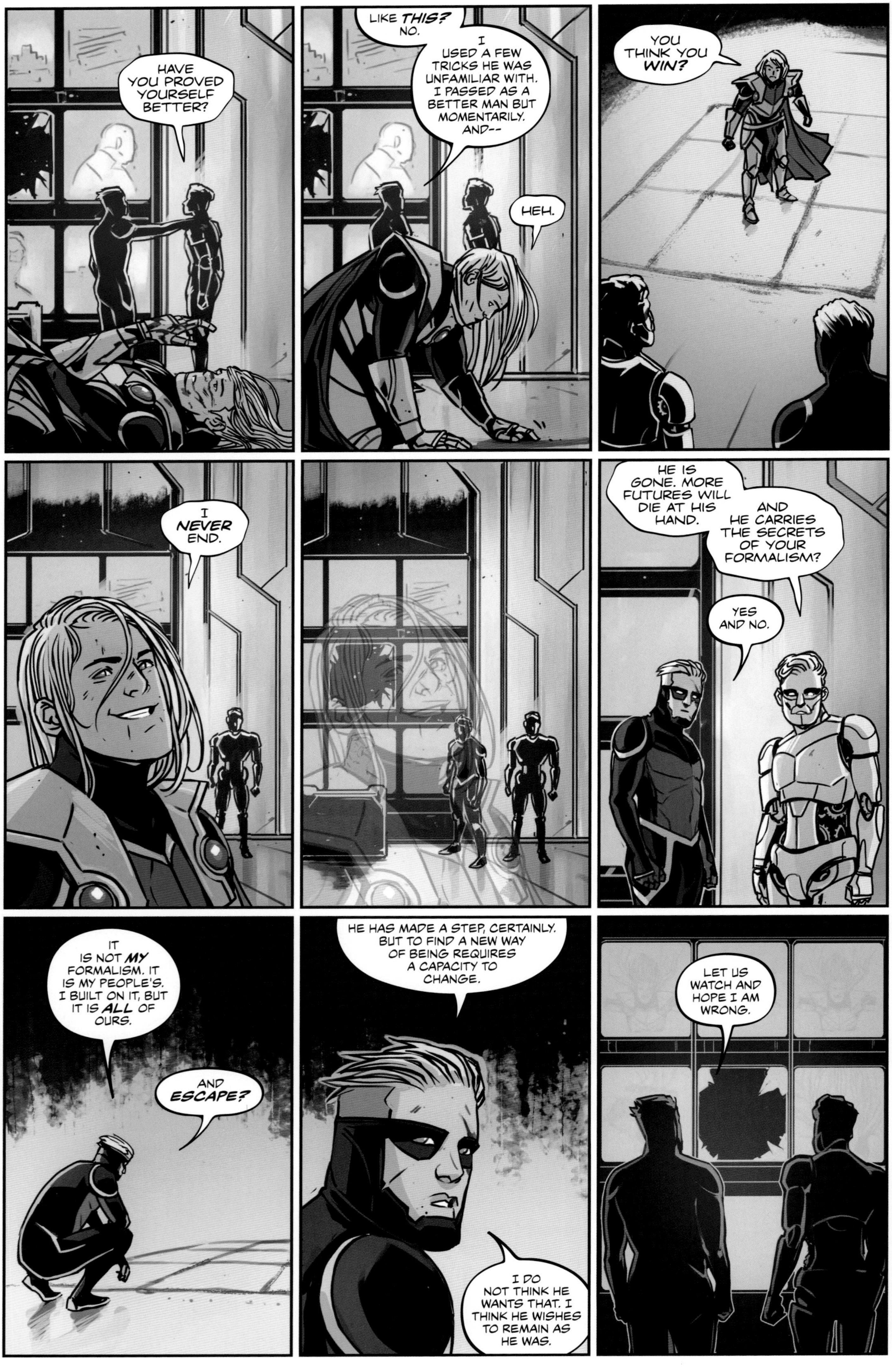
HAVE YOU PROVED YOURSELF BETTER?
LIKE THIS? NO.
I USED A FEW TRICKS HE WAS UNFAMILIAR WITH. I PASSED AS A BETTER MAN BUT MOMENTARILY. AND--
HEH.
YOU THINK YOU WIN?
I NEVER END.
HE IS GONE. MORE FUTURES WILL DIE AT HIS HAND.
AND HE CARRIES THE SECRETS OF YOUR FORMALISM?
YES AND NO.
IT IS NOT MY FORMALISM. IT IS MY PEOPLE'S. I BUILT ON IT, BUT IT IS ALL OF OURS.
AND ESCAPE?
HE HAS MADE A STEP, CERTAINLY. BUT TO FIND A NEW WAY OF BEING REQUIRES A CAPACITY TO CHANGE.
I DO NOT THINK HE WANTS THAT. I THINK HE WISHES TO REMAIN AS HE WAS.
LET US WATCH AND HOPE I AM WRONG.

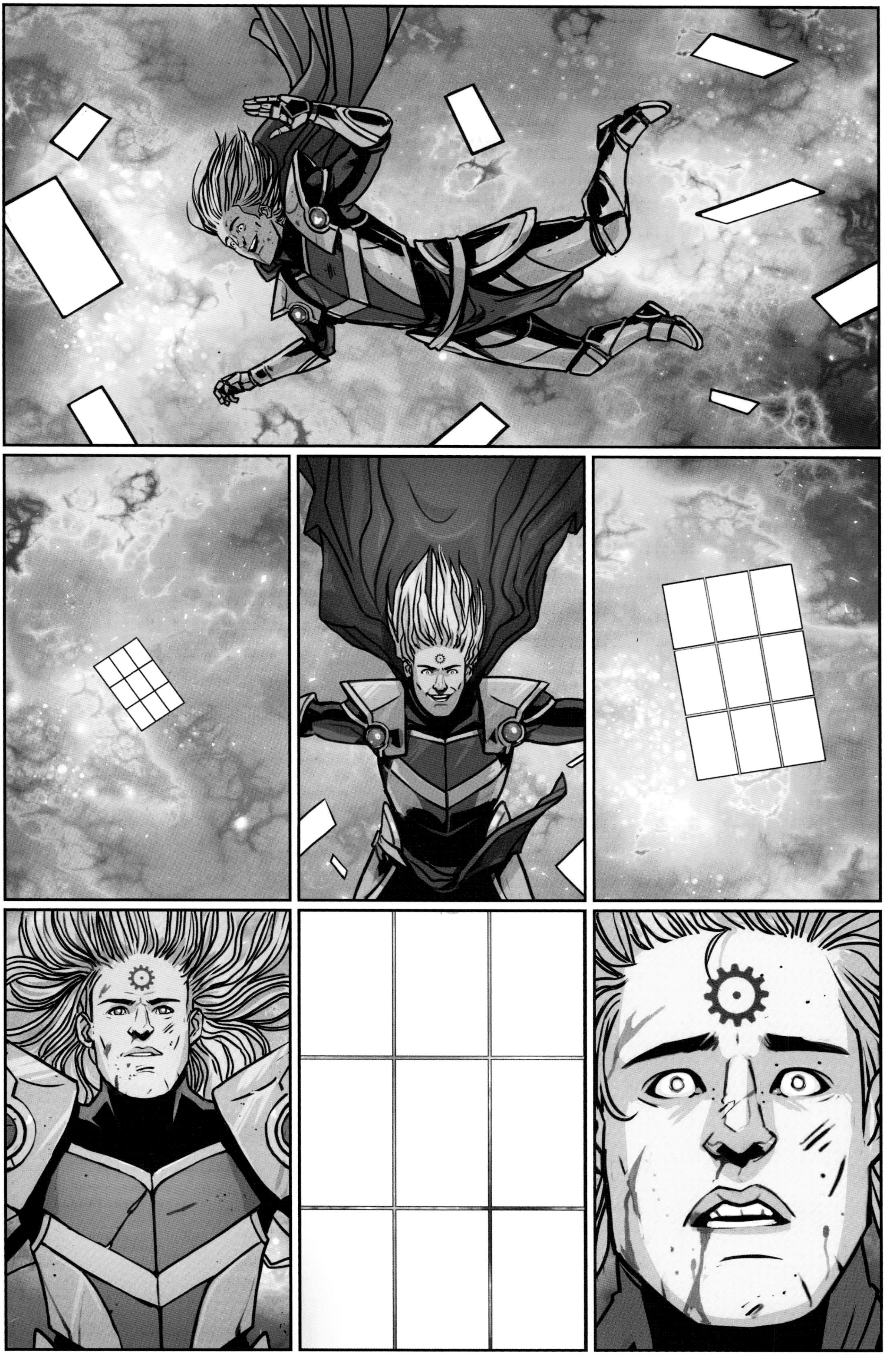

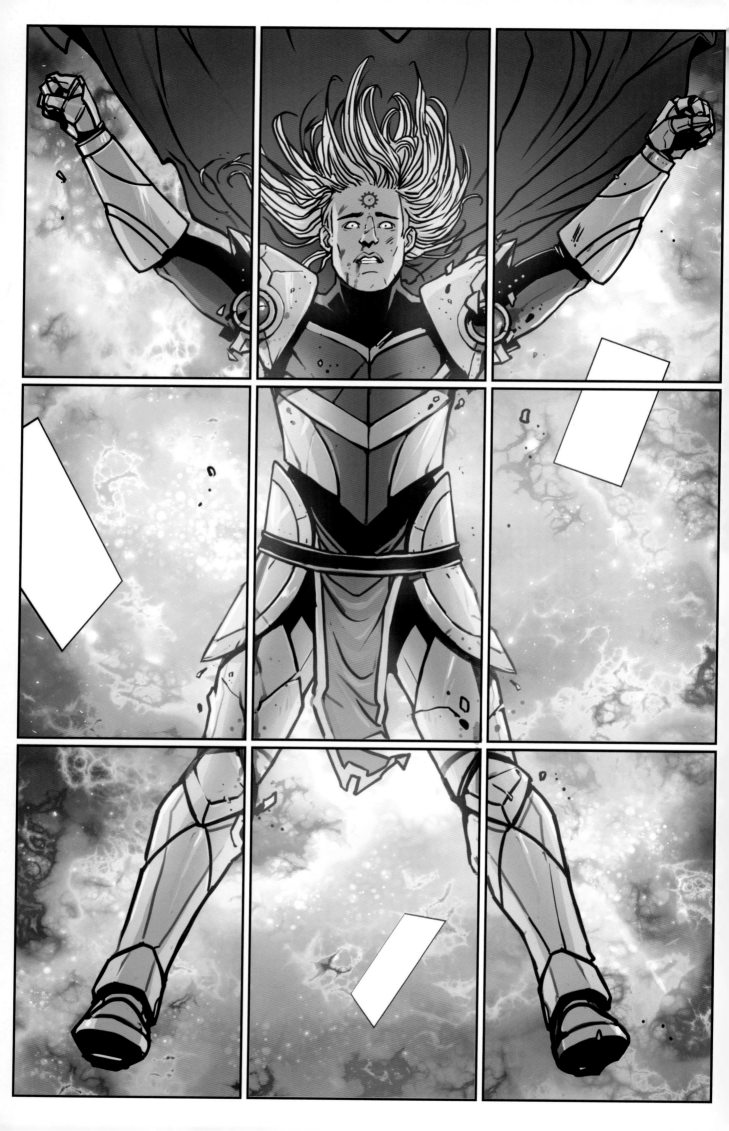

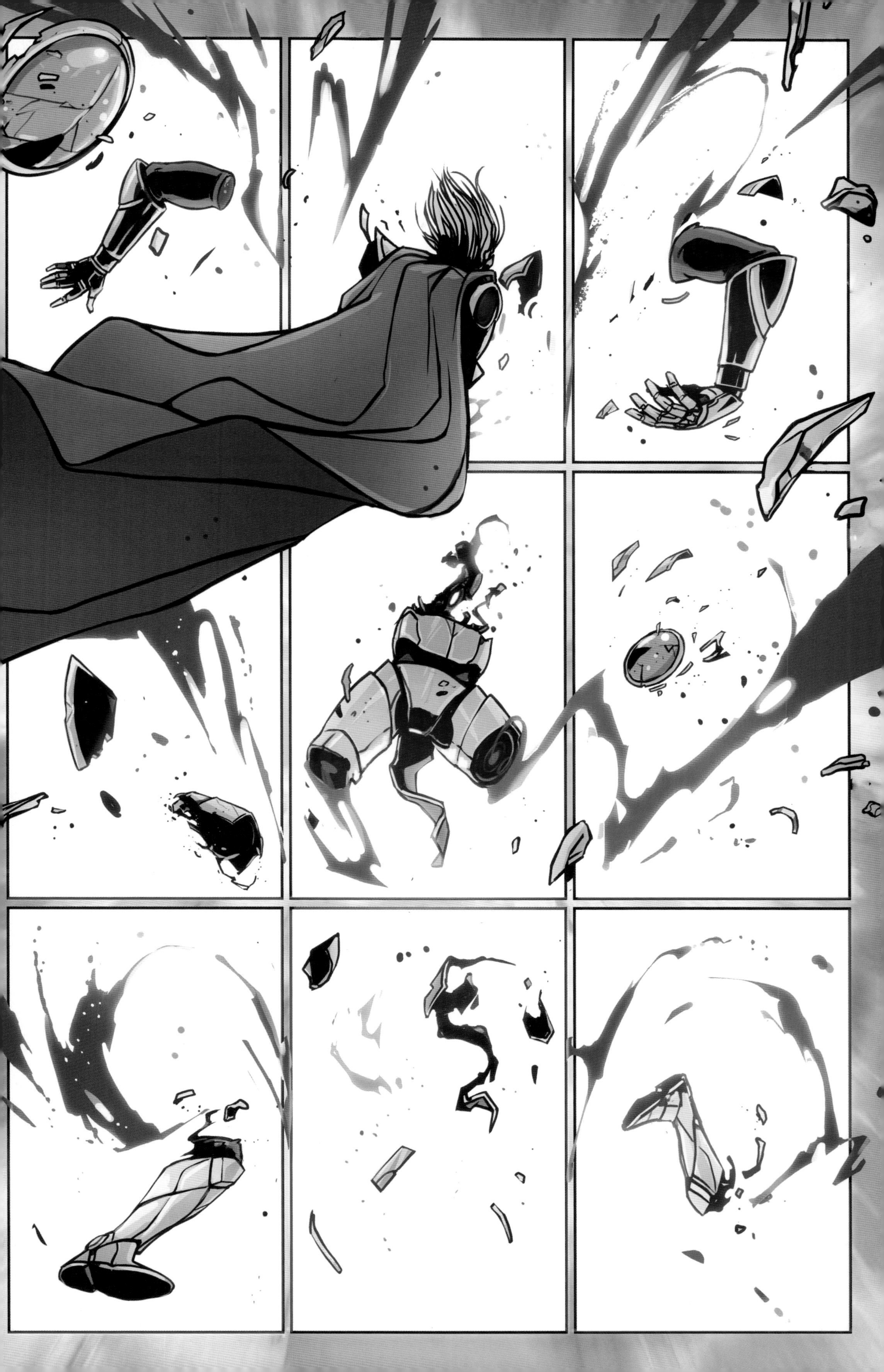

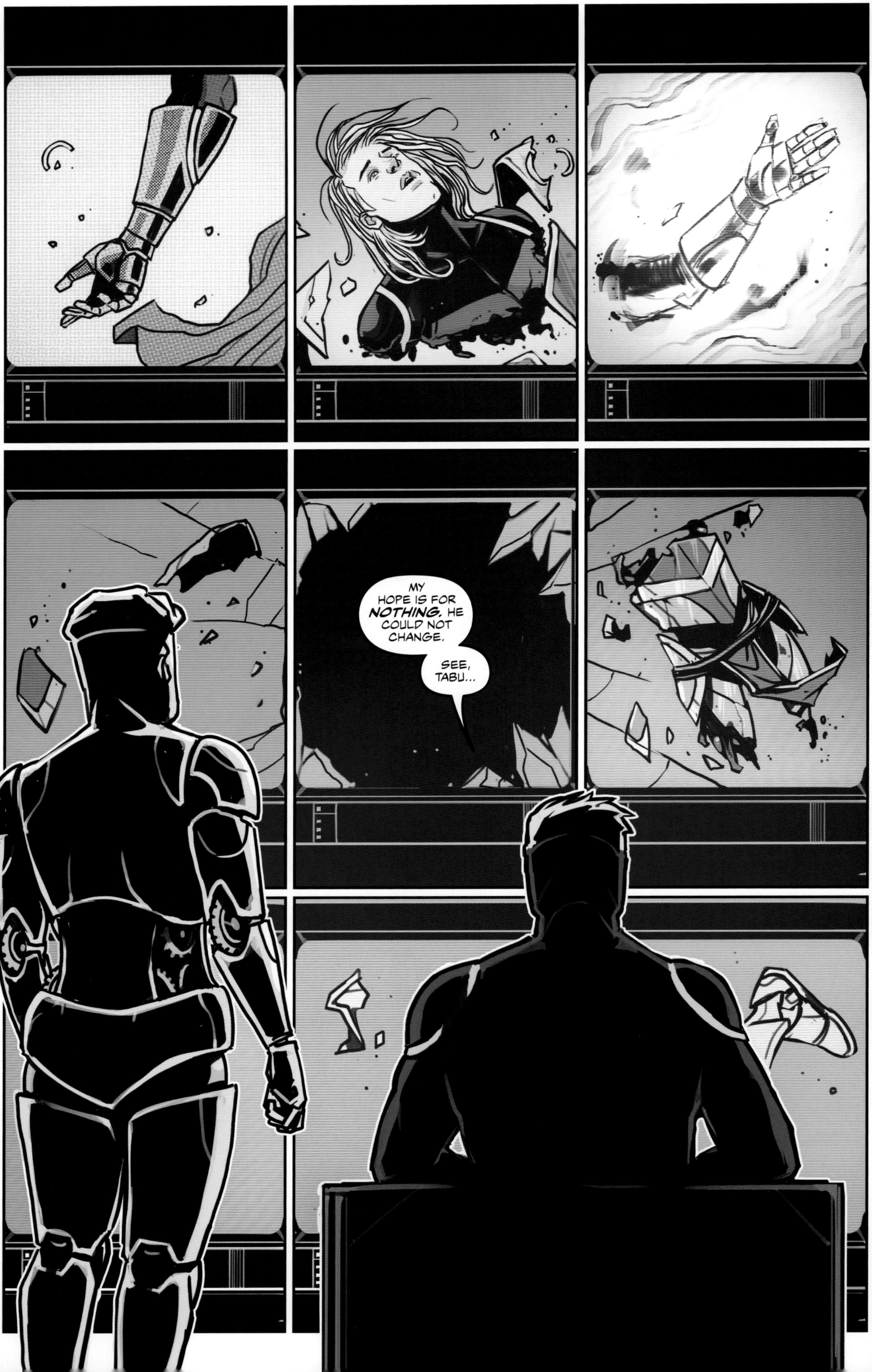
MY HOPE IS FOR NOTHING. HE COULD NOT CHANGE.
SEE, TABU...

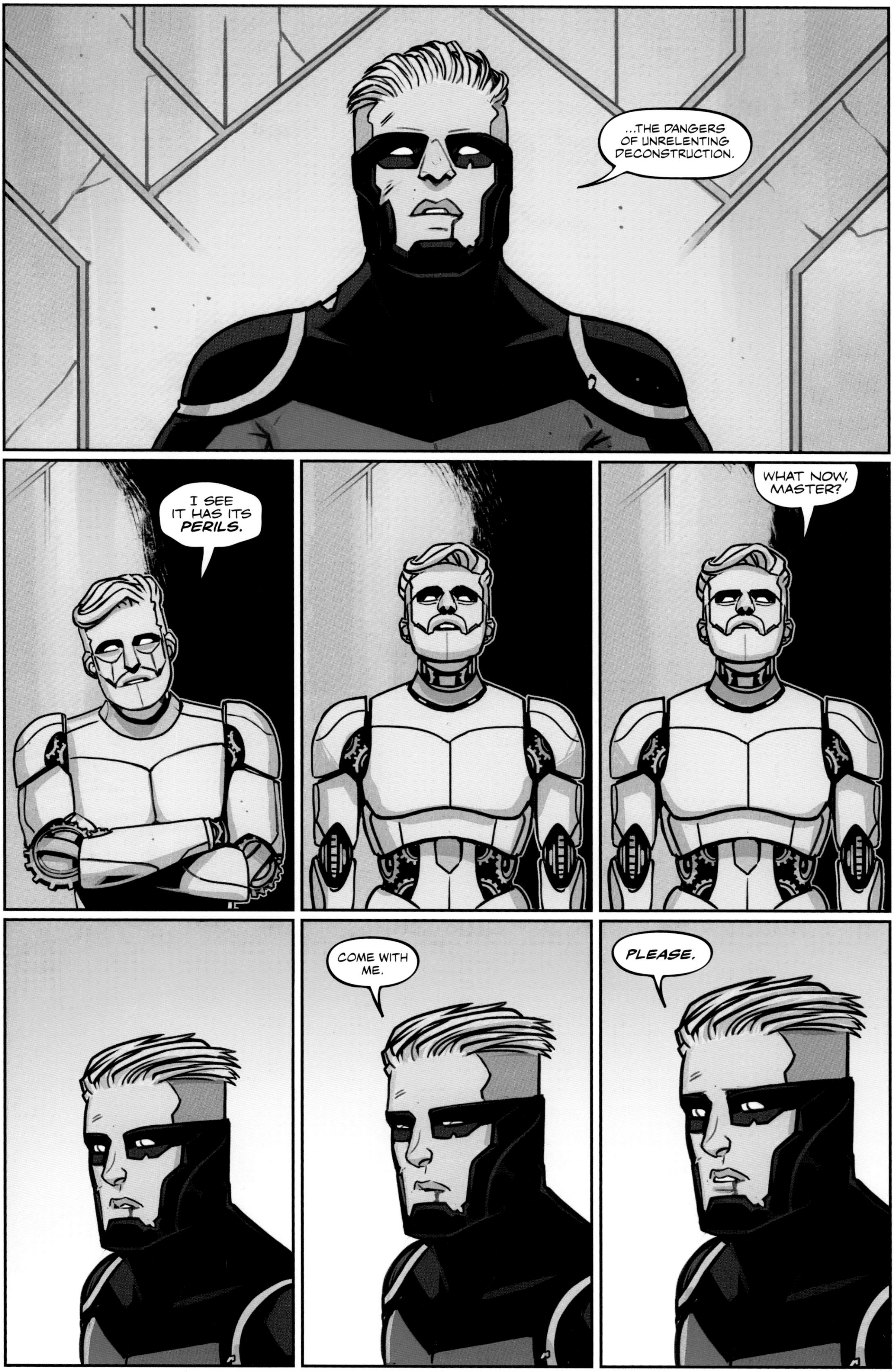
...THE DANGERS OF UNRELENTING DECONSTRUCTION.
I SEE IT HAS ITS *PERILS.*
WHAT NOW, MASTER?
COME WITH ME.
PLEASE.

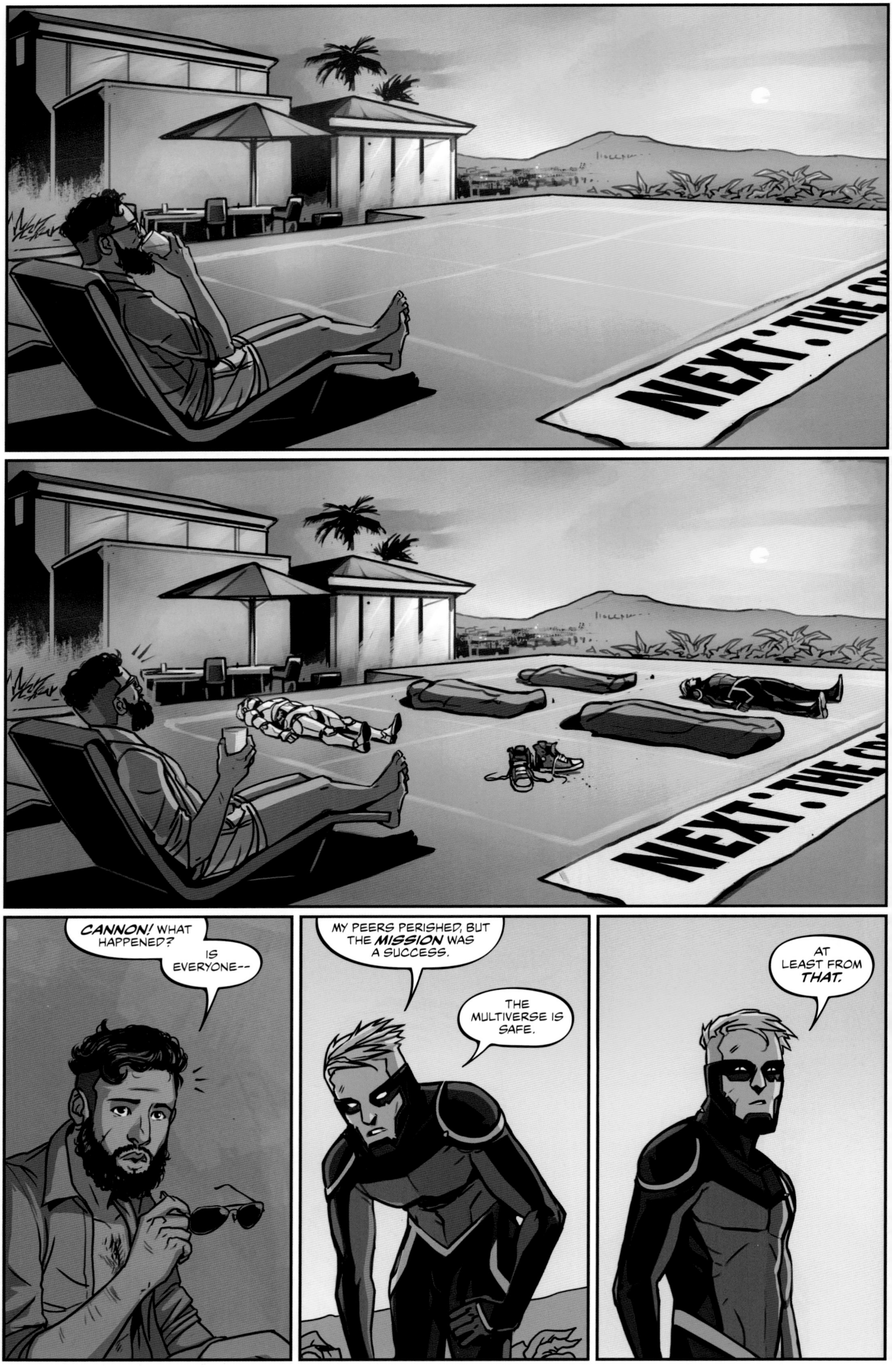
NEXT • THE CO
NEXT • THE CO
CANNON! WHAT HAPPENED?
IS EVERYONE--
MY PEERS PERISHED, BUT THE MISSION WAS A SUCCESS.
THE MULTIVERSE IS SAFE.
AT LEAST FROM THAT.

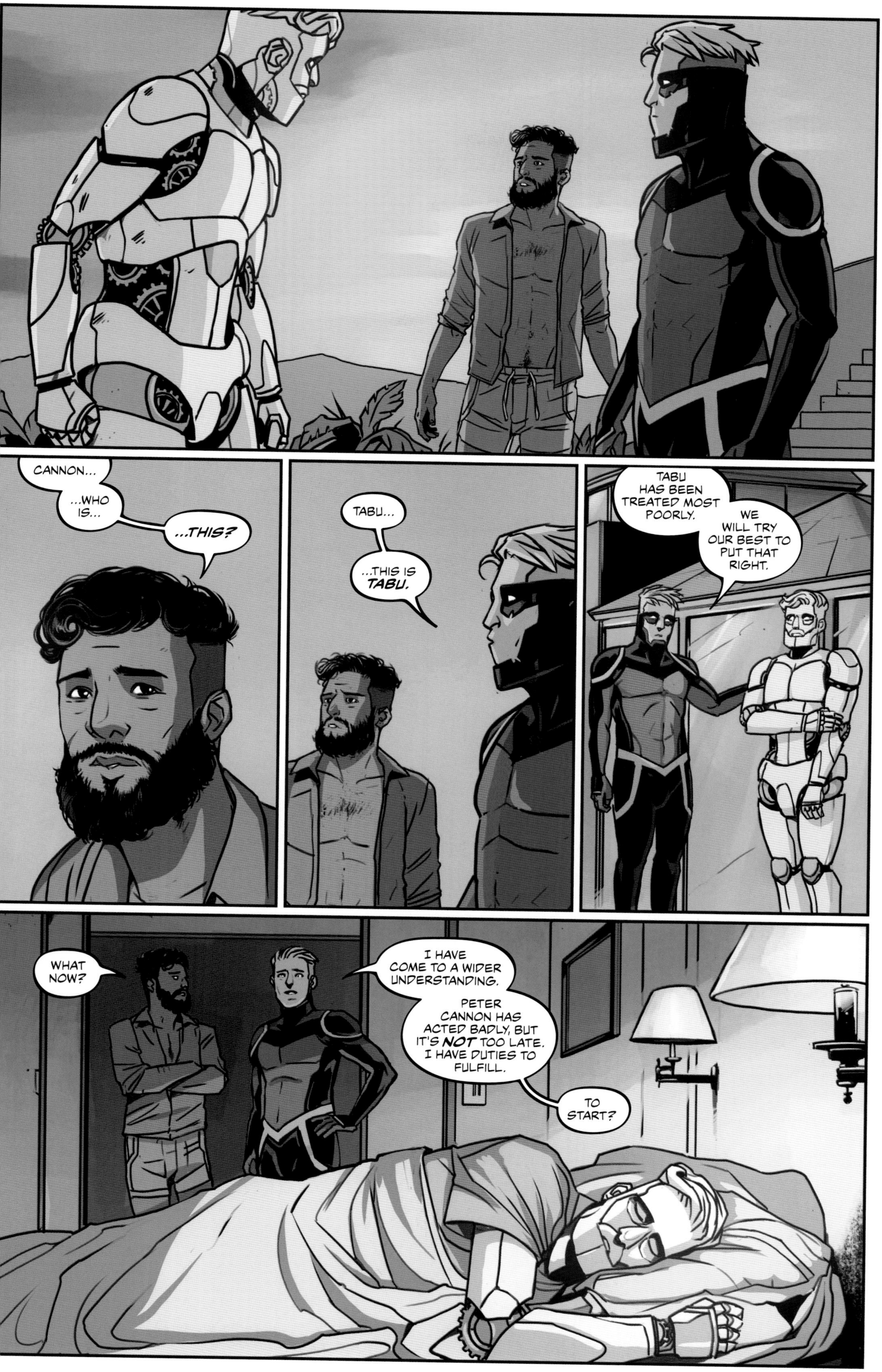
CANNON...
...WHO IS...
...THIS?
TABU...
...THIS IS TABU.
TABU HAS BEEN TREATED MOST POORLY.
WE WILL TRY OUR BEST TO PUT THAT RIGHT.
WHAT NOW?
I HAVE COME TO A WIDER UNDERSTANDING.
PETER CANNON HAS ACTED BADLY, BUT IT'S NOT TOO LATE. I HAVE DUTIES TO FULFILL.
TO START?

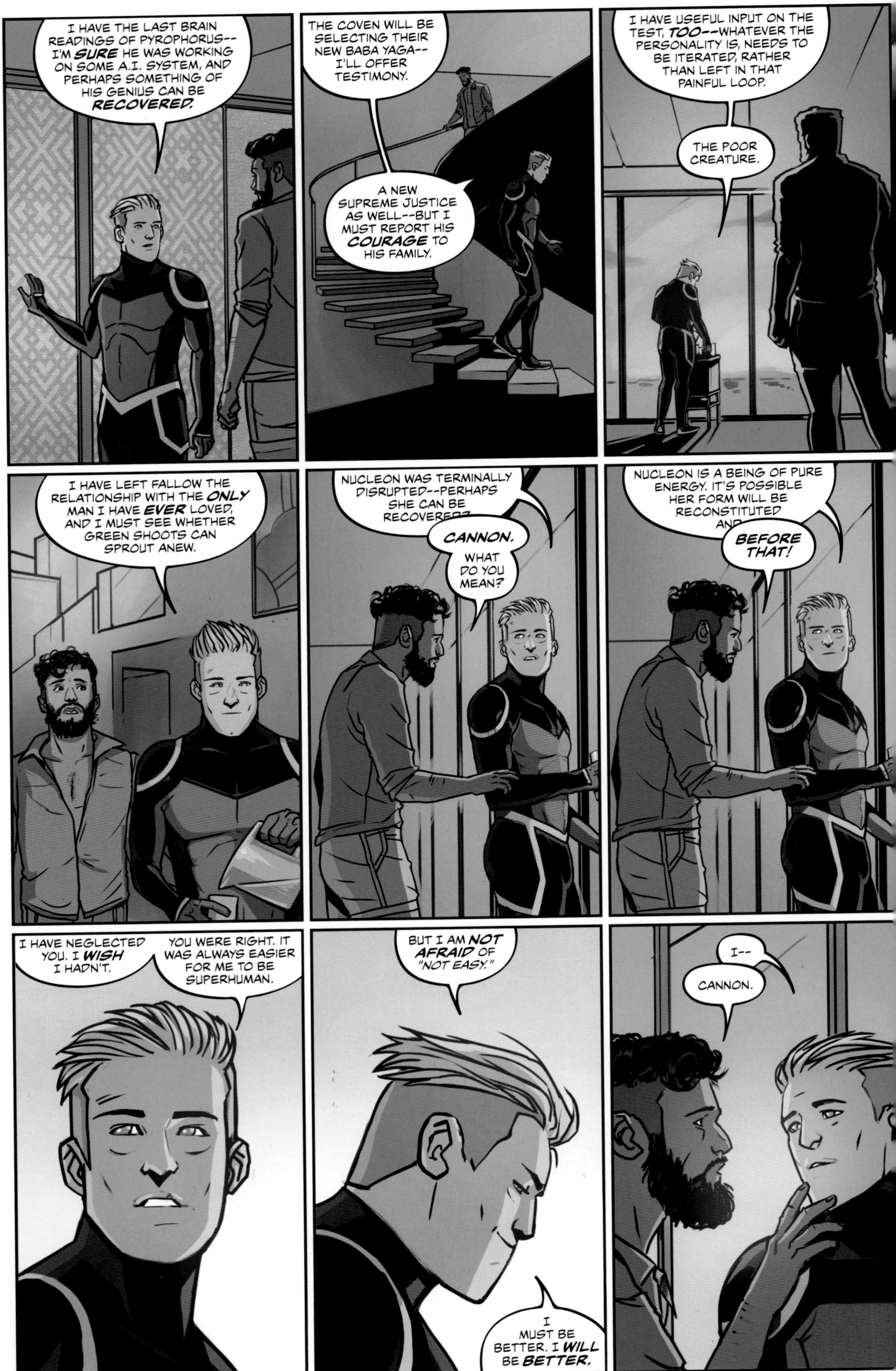
I HAVE THE LAST BRAIN READINGS OF PYROPHORUS-- I'M SURE HE WAS WORKING ON SOME A.I. SYSTEM, AND PERHAPS SOMETHING OF HIS GENIUS CAN BE RECOVERED.
THE COVEN WILL BE SELECTING THEIR NEW BABA YAGA-- I'LL OFFER TESTIMONY.
A NEW SUPREME JUSTICE AS WELL--BUT I MUST REPORT HIS COURAGE TO HIS FAMILY.
I HAVE USEFUL INPUT ON THE TEST, TOO--WHATEVER THE PERSONALITY IS, NEEDS TO BE ITERATED, RATHER THAN LEFT IN THAT PAINFUL LOOP.
THE POOR CREATURE.
I HAVE LEFT FALLOW THE RELATIONSHIP WITH THE ONLY MAN I HAVE EVER LOVED, AND I MUST SEE WHETHER GREEN SHOOTS CAN SPROUT ANEW.
NUCLEON WAS TERMINALLY DISRUPTED--PERHAPS SHE CAN BE
CANNON.
WHAT DO YOU MEAN?
NUCLEON IS A BEING OF PURE ENERGY. IT'S POSSIBLE HER FORM WILL BE RECONSTITUTED
BEFORE THAT!
I HAVE NEGLECTED YOU. I WISH I HADN'T.
YOU WERE RIGHT. IT WAS ALWAYS EASIER FOR ME TO BE SUPERHUMAN.
BUT I AM NOT AFRAID OF "NOT EASY."
I MUST BE BETTER. I WILL BE BETTER.
I--
CANNON.

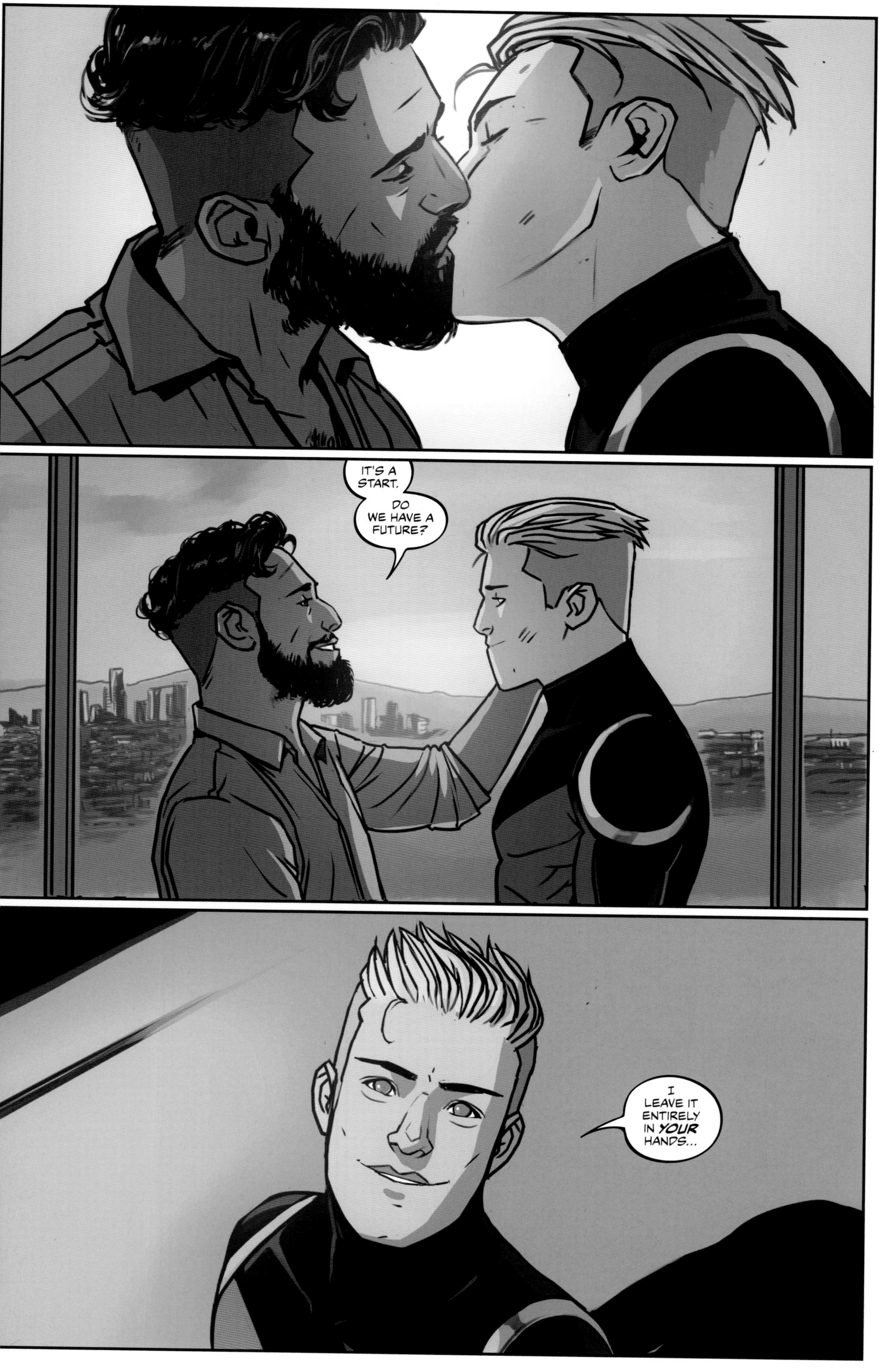
IT'S A START.
DO WE HAVE A FUTURE?
I LEAVE IT ENTIRELY IN *YOUR* HANDS...

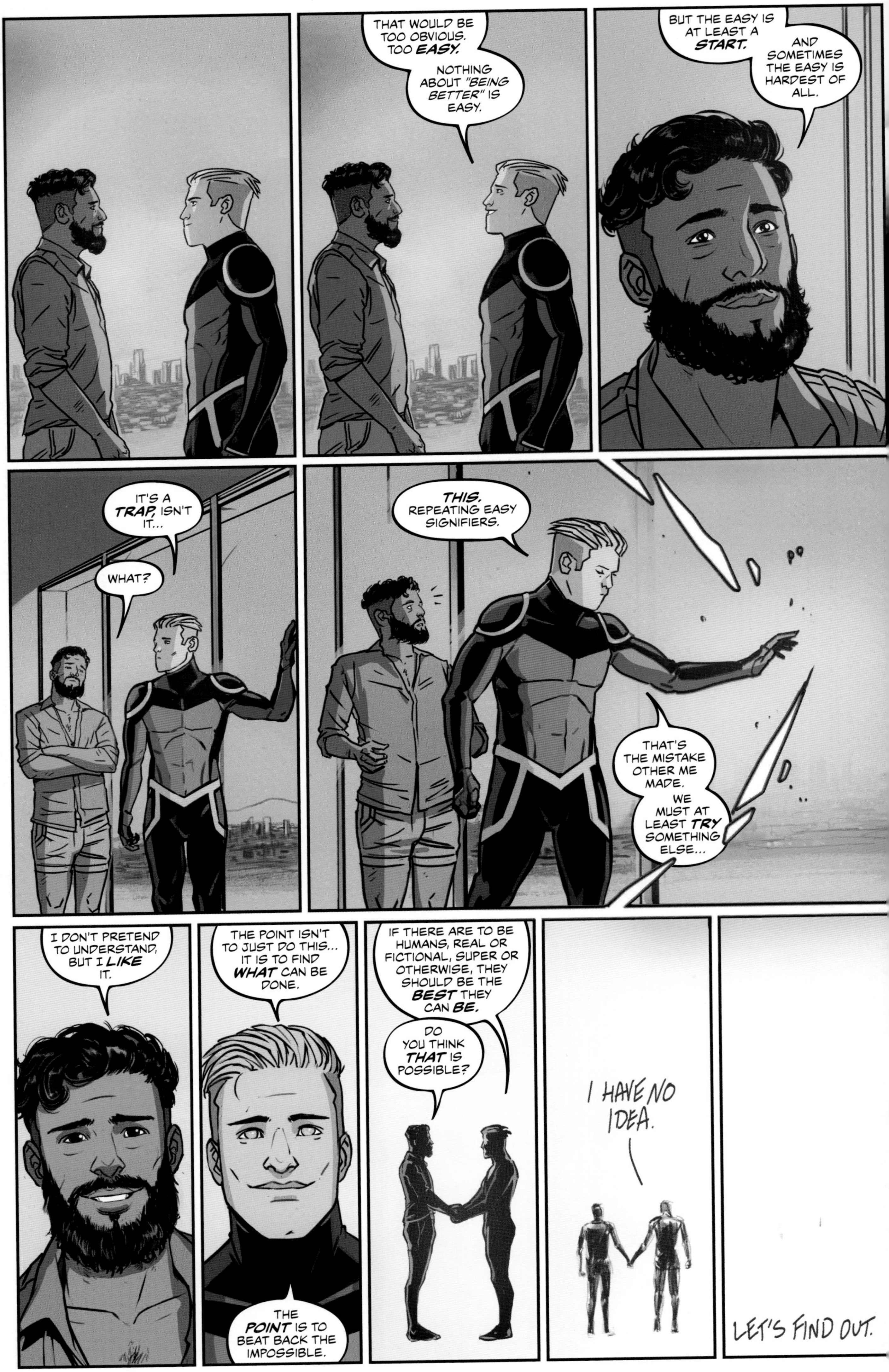
THAT WOULD BE TOO OBVIOUS. TOO EASY.
NOTHING ABOUT "BEING BETTER" IS EASY.
BUT THE EASY IS AT LEAST A START.
AND SOMETIMES THE EASY IS HARDEST OF ALL.
IT'S A TRAP, ISN'T IT...
WHAT?
THIS. REPEATING EASY SIGNIFIERS.
THAT'S THE MISTAKE OTHER ME MADE.
WE MUST AT LEAST TRY SOMETHING ELSE...
I DON'T PRETEND TO UNDERSTAND, BUT I LIKE IT.
THE POINT ISN'T TO JUST DO THIS... IT IS TO FIND WHAT CAN BE DONE.
THE POINT IS TO BEAT BACK THE IMPOSSIBLE.
IF THERE ARE TO BE HUMANS, REAL OR FICTIONAL, SUPER OR OTHERWISE, THEY SHOULD BE THE BEST THEY CAN BE.
DO YOU THINK THAT IS POSSIBLE?
I HAVE NO IDEA.
LET'S FIND OUT.

BONUS
MATERIALS

BEHIND THE SCENES
WITH KIERON GILLEN

CHARACTER DESIGNS & SKETCHES
BY CASPAR WIJNGAARD

W hat follows is Kieron's (only very slightly tweaked) formal pitch and outline for the series, offering a unique insight into both his creative process and glimpses of threads and themes that ultimately evolved into the (considerably different) story you have just read.

PETER CANNON: THUNDERBOLT

Our Peter Cannon is akin to the Peter Cannon in the original Charlton comics, but aged a decade or two. He's in his late thirties, early forties. Yes, like Ozymandias.
His origin remains mostly the same - his parents sacrificed themselves to help fight the Black Plague from wiping out the village. Due to giving the largest sacrifice, that means that he is the one who becomes their civilisation's equivalent of Iron Fist, coming into the possession of The Ancient Scrolls. This is the source of his powers, unlocking the 90% extra potential of the human spirit. This gives him great strength, agility, willpower - and also some strange moments where he can even control reality, though he has only ever rarely used that.
(The famous, particularly weird Dragon episode.)
He thinks he understands everything in the scrolls, or at least all that he needs to understand.
There is a significant tweak however - the civilisation that he guards is dead. Yes, his family sacrificed itself, but this wonderful place still died. He and his manservant Tabu (another outsider, taken in by this mystical civilisation) are the sole survivors. This means that Peter Cannon, for all his arrogance, has a humble streak. He knows he is only as he is due to the generosity of a better civilisation, who are now dead. He's already an archeologist in the Charlton books, and this part plays into that - he's trying to make sure as much of his culture as possible remains alive.
(Perhaps we'll come back to his traditional villain The Hooded One another time, but he's likely not in this story. I'd say he's a survivor too, and I'd likely avoid writing "sole survivor" when telling the above to leave room for it.)
 It especially gives him a reason to be bitter against the modern world – if they helped more, maybe this wonderful martial arts kingdom would have lived? If humanity did not save Peter Cannon's civilisation, why should he save theirs?
Because make no doubt about it - Peter Cannon fucking hates us. In all his original comics he basically tries to avoid helping humanity, only really getting involved when Tabu pushes him hard enough.
As far as I see it, this is the sort of thing Peter Cannon would think...

"I should stop bank robbers? Banks themselves steal from everyone. They act criminally, then steal from governments to remain solvent. Society itself is crime. You should be grateful I don't do anything about it."

He's not just the smartest guy in the room. He's the smartest guy on earth. And he hates Earth.
Worth stressing: I plan to make him fun. He is very Sherlock Holmes. Superior, but absolutely compelling to watch. In the original comics, he used to speak in this very macho American '60s male stereotype, which I'm reading as his attempts to "pass" in modern society. He learned it off the TV. I suspect he only does it in front of his peers, and when he's alone with Tabu, he returns to the Sherlockian mode.
"Pass" is a loaded word. When he's forced to be in public, he plays the macho American hero. In private, he becomes who he is. Peter Cannon is gay - or perhaps bisexual, though having basically done a book full of bisexual characters makes me loathe to repeat myself. The only reason I would is if I re-read the original comics and find an interaction which I can't read as a half--closeted gay guy. I don't plan to make a huge deal of it, but him and Tabu were lovers. Worth noting the past tense. It's a long time ago now, they're still friends - Tabu is still his confidante - but the inability to sustain a romantic relation-ship is also a symbol of Peter Cannon's distance from humanity. Even the only other person who's shared his background is still too far away.
It's also really interesting that there's a dichotomy - Peter Cannon wants to be isolated archeologist Peter Cannon, while Tabu constantly urges him to be more heroic saviour Thunderbolt. This dynamic has been going on for twenty years, and he is no closer to being Thunderbolt full-time than he ever was.
In other words, our Peter Cannon is a highly reluctant hero. The civilisation is not worth saving. He mainly lives his life;

researching, his own battles, helping people according to his own moral code.
This drives his peers absolutely fucking batshit. They know how good he is, and nine times out of ten he just won't help.

PETER CANNON'S HOME DIMENSION

He lives in a fairly standard superhero world. As in, superheroes' presence has not significantly changed Earth's history. There is a top-level superhero team who Peter Cannon is abstractly a member of. Abstractly. Worth noting: while the other heroes will be powerful, they're secondary – in fact, compared to Peter Cannon, they're kind of chumps. For all their abilities, if Peter Cannon is Sherlock Holmes then they're all Watson.
Our other heroes fight to keep the status quo. The difference is that rather than the current political situation, it's a few years in the future, and things have gone to shit. There's a growing second cold war, America deeply divided with serious talk of a second Civil War, the collapse of the EU leading to real talk of a land war in Europe. It's bad. The superheroes all know it's bad, but feel impotent.

ANALOGUES

This is a story with a bunch of analogues in it. They'll have names in the story, but for the sake of this document, most will be listed as their analogue name and the world they come from.
The exception are the three main Peter Cannons.
Our hero will be referred to as Cannon.
Our villain will be referred to as Thunderbolt - though the temptation to call him "Peter Canon" due to his reality control skills is strong.
When we meet him, our "real world" Peter Cannon will just be called Peter.

WATCHING NOTHING BUT THE WATCHMEN

In the first version of the outline, I was saying I was going to have to populate them with superheroes. I played with various options, including the Project Superpowers one, but ended up with something which I think is more fun, and on theme, and especially useful as I'm primarily writing an update of the Charlton Thunderbolt.
The team are analogues of the Watchmen (and the original Charlton heroes).
However, we are unlikely to realise that until the end of the first episode (and likely during the second one.) When we meet them, we will think we're doing Avengers analogues. I am still playing with doing JLA analogues - I don't want to make the analogues that interesting, and JLA-analogues are common as muck, when Avengers ones are a little rarer. If I do analogues of the Avengers, it immediately raises an eyebrow. That said, if the subtext of the story is about how Watchmen's tone infected the entire genre, the story being about a DC-analogue-character fucking with a Marvel-analogue-universe makes some sense.
I'm still working on the characters, and likely will want to get Caspar's visual influence in here, but this is basically who I think they'll come across as. I'd likely gender switch a bunch as well.
This set of analogues exist in both Thunderbolt's and Cannon's universes. They twist according to the world they're in, so they're not 1:1 but they're recognisably the same person. The version in Thunderbolt's universe will skew a little darker, the ones in Cannon's universe will skew a little lighter - not least because we will want to root for them.

Captain Atom/Doctor Manhattan – Atomic Bomb-created hero? Hulk. I was playing with Phoenix ("Children of the Atom") but Hulk is more pure Avengers. A Radioactive powerhouse, who spends most of his time inside a sealed vault with its energies running cities and unleashed only when absolutely needed.
Blue Beetle/Nite Owl – Iron Man, but an Iron Man who read Adrian Tchaikovsky's Children of Time. Hell, maybe he wrote it

in our universe. Insect-obsessive Adrian Tchaikovsky as Iron Man.

The Question/Rorschach - Imagine a Deadpool, but with his scars moving over his body. Probably some Moon Knight in there as well due to the psychosis. Taking the role of the extreme loner. People will likely see Wolverine as well. And Batman. People sure do like their extreme loners. I suspect I'll update him as an Internet Conspiracy Freak.

Nightshade/Silk Spectre – Is the hardest one to square the two characters. Nightshade has darkness powers, while Silk Spectre has no powers whatsoever. So for the former, it may end up being a Cloak and Dagger who is a single person, but for the latter is straight Black Widow. Only when actually writing this do I think we can absolutely merge the two. Despite the characters never being that, "Cloak and Dagger" is a name which suggests espionage. So Mystic Eastern Bloc Spy? That could be spun. Baba Yaga meets Modesty Blaise.

Peacemaker/Comedian – I'm not sure we need to go much further than "Neocon Captain America". Do you know the James Bond fan theory? That James Bond isn't his name - it's a job title, and it's basically whoever's being Britain's Blunt Instrument? I'd like to do that, but with superpowers. There's one man who takes the job of Captain America, and it's been like that since the war. The War of Independence. Whoever wields the saber has this power, and it's a role that's given by the government for life (ala Supreme Justices). In Thunderbolt's dimension, the last died recently. The current government selected this one. Which Captain America do you think Trump would pick? It's this guy. In Cannon's dimension, the previous one is still alive, but aware he won't be Captain America for long, and worries about who will be next…

Peter Cannon, Thunderbolt – In terms of this team, is viewed as a cross between Thor (thunderbolt, geddit?) and Doctor Strange. He's the otherworldly one, in both worlds.

FORMALISM

When Peter Cannon (in all his forms) enters the story, we enter the nine- panel grid. The opening of the story is in splashes (which I think I'll be able to do in three pages) until Peter becomes viewpoint… and then we're in that Nine-Panel Grid. We'll be modifying the nine-panel grid as we go along, ala Watchmen, merging panels, etc. I wonder whether it may be best to "signal" the grid is still there, by having indentations in the panel borders where the grid would be. Making it as oppressive and visible as possible. As the story eventually builds towards an abandonment of the nine-panel grid, fermenting level of unease seems like a good idea.

However, before we abandon the grid entirely, as Cannon learns more about the nature of his powers from The Ancient Scrolls, we start to push the nine-panel grids in way it's rarely touched. I'll be looking at this before I start writing, but The Tale Of One Bad Rat by Brian Talbot takes a different approach to the nine-panel grid. He doesn't just use the grid, but uses the gutters, and every other part of the meta-structure to create much more flexibility. As said, I need to study this (see - the "Learn his powers from ancient scrolls!") but I think this would be a useful way to show Cannon's growth, before the nine-panel is abandoned entirely.

FIVE OR SIX ISSUES?

I've written this up for Five issues, though I suspect there's enough material for it to work into six. Ending issue 3 with arriving in the Mundane Universe, having four as all set on the mundane universe, with Cannon getting his head together and interacting with this world and the invasion of the Mundane World happening at the end of 4. That basically means that if it's six issues, issue 4 is the Training Montage plus down-to-earth humanity. It would give Cannon more time to come, to have more time to get in touch with his humanity as well.

That said, as this is primarily nine-panel grids, it will be dense. I've never written a fully nine-panel grid comic so may be surprised how quickly I burn through material.

ISSUE ONE

We open with our superteam coming to Cannon asking for help due to a disaster. A world-scale Authority-scale alien invasion of monstrous bugs from another dimension. As this is a threat to the species rather than civilisation,
After some pushing of Cannon's button and a quick physical threat that Cannon overcomes almost instantly (via fancy 9-panel grid martial arts), he agrees to help. This is an unprecedented threat. Of course he'll help. He may not like the civilisation, but he's fond of the species.
(We get our basic beats of Cannon in here - his background, the hint of the real background - or possibly just the reveals, but most importantly, the ancient scrolls. The ancient scrolls are where he got the knowledge of his power from.)
Rest of the issue is dealing with the invasion, done in a disaster move style. This is actually a mode of comics that disappeared in the early '00s for obvious, understandable and correct reasons, but I think it taking-superhero-carnage seriously is due a revival. The attack is stopped, and then we go to the Justice-League-esque meeting to decide what to do next. This has scared all the governments. The UN are making plans to try and form a planetary defence force. There's a flicker of optimism after a time of growing international discord...
Cannon returns to his mansion, in contemplation. Tabu is happy – both at the chance of peace, and that his beloved Thunderbolt got involved in earth politics. Cannon isn't. He's worried.
He's worried because he realises what is happening. This is not a genuine attack. This is a hoax in order to provoke this positive response.
Tabu is shocked. Who would do this? Who would think of such a thing? Cannon explains that he, Cannon, would. He had thought of it, and dismissed it as immoral. I would never do this, and no-one else on this planet has the capacity of imagination and talent to achieve it. Tabu is confused. What does that mean?

"I suspect these are the actions of another Peter Cannon from another dimension."

Hard cut to the next dimension over.

A fortress in a wilderness we instantly think is ice, but realise is actually diamond. We get a voice-over, impressed. "Ah yes. Of course you'd work it out". We reveal on a figure sitting in front of a series of dimensional viewing portals, arranged like two nine-panel grid pages facing one another, like the famous shot from Watchmen...

...and we flip, to reveal who it is. Thunderbolt essentially, an Ozymandias who gained the powers of Doctor Manhattan.

But the symbol in the middle of his forehead. It's not an atomic symbol.

It's a clock face.

(I mentioned the Hidden One earlier. It may be fun to put some of the design elements of The Hidden One into Thunderbolt. Effectively in this story, Peter Cannon is his own Hidden One, if you see what I mean.)

ISSUE TWO

Cannon explains the situation to his peers, and there's the ethical debate - there's at least a flicker of a "Well... is it so bad if it brings peace?" to it, before it's abandoned. They don't need to reveal that Thunderbolt did it... but they need to ensure he can't do it again. They also have no idea what he'd do next.
Cannon also touches on how he knows this, talking of his own reality control abilities, and how he's always shied away from them. There is much in the scrolls, and much I have interpreted... in a limited fashion. Whether this is positive or negative is up in the air.

But what to do about it? They're under attack from another dimension. Who can travel between dimensions?
Cannon notes he will try to see if it can be done.
"Can you do it?"
"I can do it. I must do it. I will do it."
He starts his research of the scrolls. So much he didn't know, or see until now. All reality as a perfect clock. a designed mechanism...
Eventually, Cannon gathers the team and makes the attempt. They all know this is dangerous...
We go into a dimension travel sequence. I have the image of the multiverse here - and it's each dimension as a clock, and they interlink. They travel between them. I feel we may not actually do this bit in a nine-panel grid. This is a moment of... something else. Perhaps a foreshadowing of where he ends up going. But we see these dimensions, each embodied by a clock... and the ones they travel are almost all dead. Something killed them.
They land in Thunderbolt's dimension, and we explore it. I see it as bleak - we get the potted histories of what happened here. The heroes all died. Multiple invasions from aliens, each trying to provoke a peace. A small nuclear war. Eventually we get peace - but only because Thunderbolt has become a quasi-benevolent dictator of a broken world. "Quasi" being the word - because by the time he tapped (what he believes) is the ultimate secret of the scrolls, he also discovered other worlds, and started trying to bring peace to there as well. As we saw earlier, he has mostly failed... but he believes he's getting better. Thunderbolt always thought he was the smartest man in the world... but when he discovered there were other worlds, he felt himself the smartest in all of them, and should guide them all. What matters if billions die in his experiments if he can save hundreds of billions?
(I was playing with having Thunderbolt having faced off against the Manhattan/Hulk analogue in this world and stole his powers, which is what gives him the upgrade, which makes it a 1:1 Watchmen riff... but I think keeping everything connected to the Scrolls makes it cleaner.)
(I'm also planning with this having happened some time ago. As in, over thirty years. Thunderbolt has been working on variations of his plan for all this time - by implication, turning Thunderbolt into a metaphor for creators who've been picking over Watchmen's bones for the last thirty-two years. Clearly, this beat is particularly meta if played badly, but does set up a meta punchline in the final episode. I'll write it in the pitch, even though I suspect we'll abandon for "this is just too much" reasons. Or maybe not. It's pretty funny.)
We build towards our heroes going to face Thunderbolt in the diamond fortress. We either end with the facing off, and the admission of Thunderbolt's crimes, or with Thunderbolt killing our Rorschach analogue. "I never get bored of doing that."

In short: this is the Horrible Alternative Reality issue, and we lean into it.

ISSUE THREE

The battle against Thunderbolt. It goes poorly. This is a big set-piece and the majority of the issue.
There is one note of hope: Thunderbolt doesn't know how they managed to get here. He can't go to other dimensions himself. For all that Thunderbolt thinks he knows everything, he clearly doesn't.
With all the rest of his team killed, Cannon tries to escape via the only way he can. He throws himself, without preparation, between dimensions.
He's disorientated, falling backwards through a window. He falls to the street, floors below, only his skills meaning he can slow his fall at all...
We realise that this panel layout is 100% the opening of Watchmen. Us panning down to the bloody form of Cannon, lying in the street.
A man steps in to help him. It's Peter, an entirely normal historian. "Why did you fall out of the window while cosplaying?"
He gets Cannon, who's delirious, to hospital. We realise he's in a world where there's no superheroes. Peter has a similar origin - my parents died when they were off helping a distant isolated civilization. Years later, the sole survivor - this dimension's Tabu - brought Peter these scrolls which he's been studying.
He's introduced to a therapist friend of Peter - a Doctor Kovacs (Er... he won't be that, but for the pitch). Kovacs was inspired

by a story of a brutal murder to see if there's any way to help disturbed people. "You're not trapped in here with me. I'm not trapped in here with you. We're trapped in here with each other... which means we have to help each other." Yes, I'm suggesting a Rorschach who thinks the best way to help people is with kindness and understanding rather than finger snapping.   I suspect I'll work in as many other analogues as I can. Expect more of this if it goes to six issues.

Cannon is trying to explain the danger of the situation - which they clearly don't believe, which is why the mental health professional is here - when something adds weight to his story.

The Aliens start invading this entirely mundane reality.

ISSUE FOUR

Mundane Reality, under attack. Goes badly. It's very Independence Day.

Cannon helps as best he can, but he has no resources. He is put in contact with world leaders... and they are generally not useful. This is not a world where any of this superhero stuff happens. There is now powered individuals. They think it's a trick. This is going to accelerate into war. In other words, Thunderbolt has misjudged this one again - trying to stop Cannon, he has presumed this one would also have powered beings or experience with aliens. He acted too quickly. He has the powers of a god, but not the foresight.

Cannon is also obviously blamed for it and taken into custody. He escapes and finds his way back to Peter. He needs to have a look at the Ancient Scrolls of this dimension. Peter says they won't be the same. I don't have powers, and I've been studying it all my life.

They get to Peter's office and find the papers. They are the same.

Now, dovetailing to all of this, we see a lot of Peter. And by this point we realise something about him? Peter's interpretations of the scrolls have made him a hero to so many of the people his life has touched. He's a respected teacher. We likely get people who helped Peter step forward to help Cannon and Peter, just because of what Peter did for them.

The lessons of humanity he learned in there has helped so many people. These are also the lessons that Cannon never learned.

At which point, we also get the idea of interpretation of the ancient scrolls. All the Peter Cannons we've met have loved the scrolls, in their different ways. They've all taken different lessons from it. Yes, Thunderbolt has extrapolated incredible power from the scrolls... but he's missed the stuff that's natural to Peter even more than Cannon has.

Now, we've talked about the theme of the story - it's not "Peter Cannon should be any of these things" but "Peter Cannon can be many things." I have always had an annoyance at comics which argue for an aesthetic preference, even if I love them. Kingdom Come's eye-roll at the Image generation. Flex Mentallo's (amazing) line of "only a bitter little adolescent boy could confuse realism with pessimism." I mean, stop stacking the deck. Saying comics can only be light or dark is just saying comics should be smaller - just a smaller you like. I'm in the Comics Can Be Anything corner - and if I have to pick a side, it's the Comics Should Be New corner. I don't care if it's down or up. Give me the new.

So, that's subtext and where we're building. We have this canon text which these three men have interpreted in three different ways. What are we all missing? What else could we doing?

It's around here that Peter Cannon is starting to push it. We start getting modifications on the nine-panel grid, in the manner of One Bad Rat.

We end the issue with Cannon leaving Peter, who is going to try and stop Thunderbolt before he sends another wave of aliens through. Peter doesn't get it - Cannon's never liked civilisation. Why right everything for this one? Because Cannon has finally got it. He hates civilisation. But civilisation is full of people, and all people are important, as Peter and his friends has shown.

And so, Peter Cannon goes to fight god.

(Okay - I'm doing handwaving in the above, and I swear, I will be more subtle when I write it. It's likely I'll push some of Cannon's realisation of humanity's worth - yes, very much a parallel to Watchmen's Doctor Manhattan's on Mars beat - into next issue, and leave it a little enigmatic here. We only really want the emotional arc to explicitly end next issue... but Cannon's moment of truth is this issue, even if the reader doesn't 100% get it, they see that something's changed in Cannon)

ISSUE FIVE

While I suspect we'll have a little of Cannon sabotaging alien machines before Thunderbolt finds him, but really?
This is Cannon versus Thunderbolt, round two.
A formalist show-piece, shall we say. The fundamental axis is that Thunderbolt can't quite believe it. He simply is more powerful than Cannon.
Thunderbolt appears to be right. Cannon is pushed back and back, and there's about to be a kill blow. It misses. It missed by a half-inch, because Cannon's using a modified nine-panel grid, which uses the gutters. As we set up in the first issue, where Cannon wins a fight against his peers by being able to use the nine-panel grid, here Cannon does something that Thunderbolt cannot even comprehend.
Cannon takes him down, slowly, intricately, beautifully. We're using the modified grid to make the martial arts fight between the two of them become fascinating kinetic. This will be an absolute showcase for Caspar, our version of the Matrix fights.
We head towards the final victory, and Thunderbolt just can't believe it. Where does it say in the text you can do this?
"It doesn't," says Cannon, carrying on, "The scrolls say so much, but they also are about what they don't say. They show a better way of being. It is to be interpreted and built upon. You can't just recapitulate it."

Cannon gestures to the machinery and the god works and the maps of the universes and everything.
"This?"
Punch.
"All of this?"
Punch.
"You did it thirty years ago!"

Thunderbolt corpses, and Cannon makes a decision. He goes home.

We likely end with Peter, back in his dimension, finding a letter Cannon wrote him before leaving, which explains his turn of heart towards humanity. He returns home to his dimension, where he's now the only hero. He apologises for being the man he was for Tabu, and (as the letter is explaining the importance of humanity) says that he wants to help people.
He's the smartest man in the world - and any man that smart knows a world is more than enough to care about. He has no experience in caring, but he'd like to try.
What comes next? They don't know. That's the entire point. Every day, we remake the world. We all get to make our own Canon.

//end//

The ensuing pages pull the curtain back on the character design process, as recounted by series artist Caspar Wijngaard. Some truly odd directions were considered—how Caspar avoided those pitfalls is entertaining, to say the least.

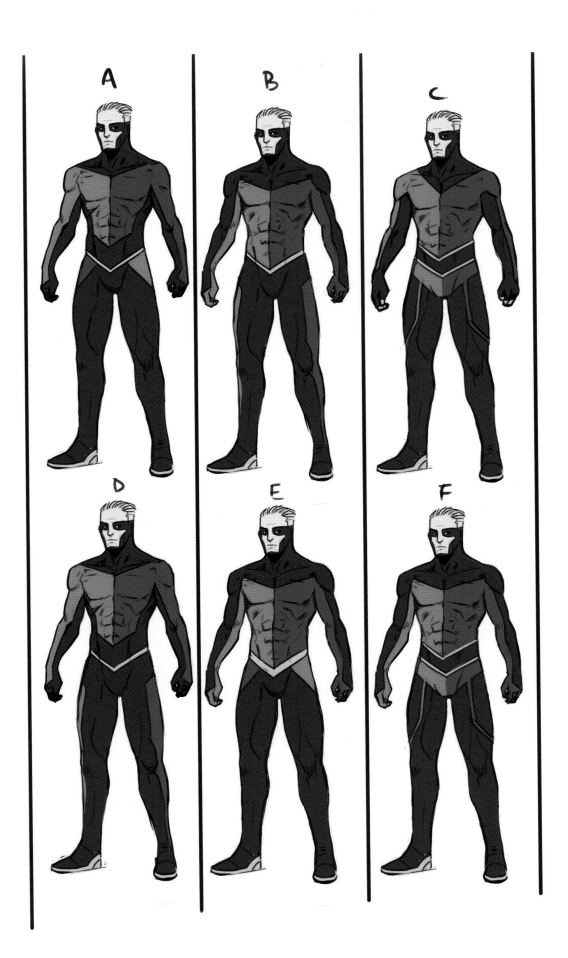

Peter Cannon

I wanted Pete's suit to pay homage to his previous designs, using the Alex Ross suit as a foundation and reworking it to feel familiar to the Pete Morisi original. Adding yellow was really important to me—the red/blue sections of the costume always felt a little offbeat, I wanted there to be elements that appeared more intentional and held the design together. As for Peter himself, I wanted ours to appear beautiful but hurt; I began using references of a very young Rutger Hauer as a starting point and developed his look from there.

Thunderbolt

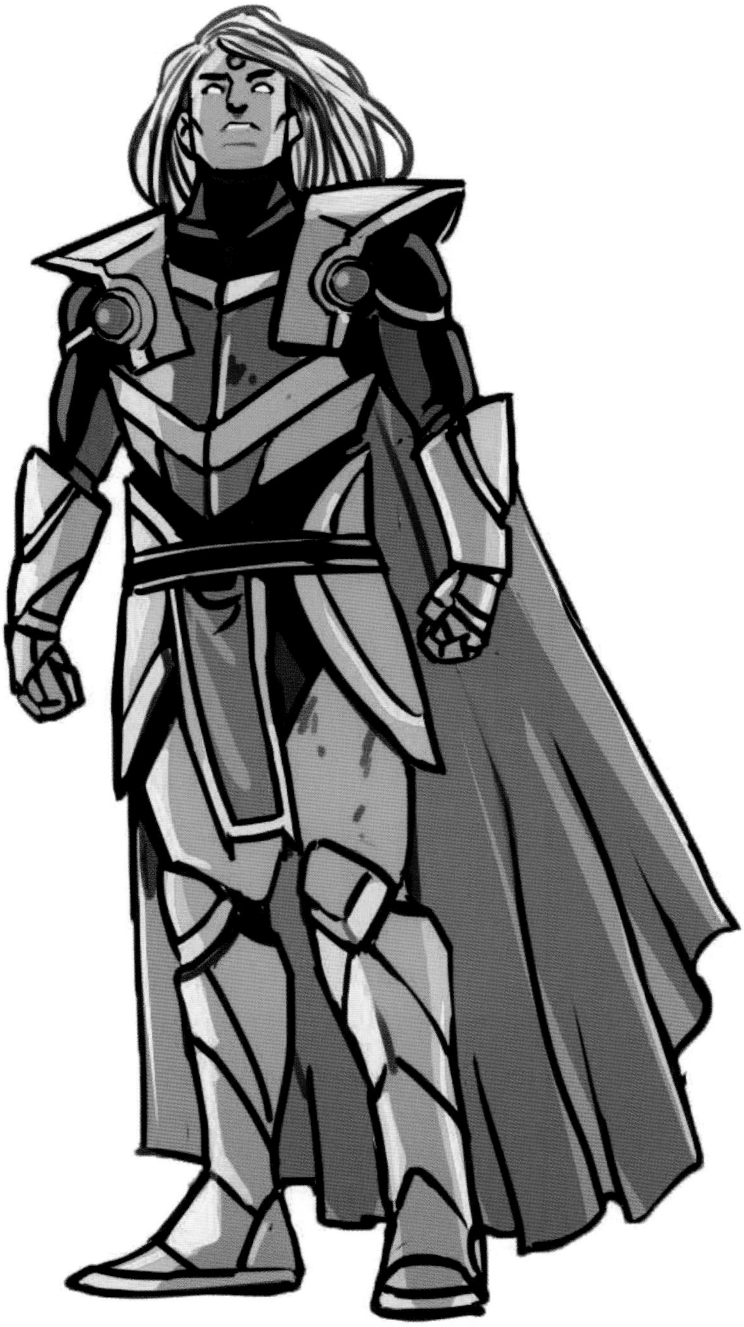

Pete's tragic dimensional alternate.
I actually drew his design straight onto the page, Kieron suggested he echo the Egyptian golden flair of another (cough) billionaire with an extraordinarily high IQ.

Personally, his design has all the workings of a JRPG villain. Handsome with angelic locks, technically baffling armour, long monologues and a flare for mass destruction. Underneath the armour is Peter Cannon's costume, a little haunting reminder of his past self.

The Heroes

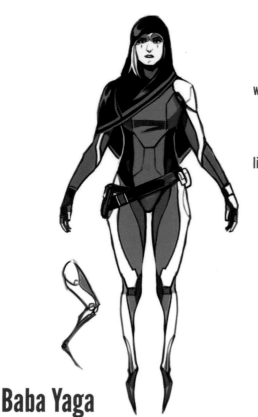

Baba Yaga

Our supernatural Russian Assassin. Her name is derived from the Slavic folklore character, a forest dwelling witch who traverses on large chicken legs. While supernatural in her abilities, I really wanted our Baba to retain something from her namesake. I floated the idea of her possibly operating a large chicken-legged mech, but quickly favoured her adorning switchblade-like prosthetics limbs that she would use to great effect in combat. Delighted with this idea, Kieron sent me a link to ballerinas dancing on blades.

Pyrophorus

Another wealthy genius playing superhero. The design is based on the Pyrophorus Fire Beetle, the helmet and visor matching that of its shell. The design was rooted in anime, I mean who wouldn't want a cool looking mech suit? My original pass was a chromatic dark blue but Kieron pointed out that because he's based on fire beetles, a flame theme would be more appropriate. He was right.

Supreme Justice

The mythical embodiment of the USA, Kieron suggested he is one in a line of many predecessors to the role, which spans back to the founding of America. The original costume would have resembled that of an outfit worn during the American Revolution. It has been refined over the centuries with each successor, but still retains several design elements.

There was a brief discussion of him wielding a sword, being an old calvary man, and then the idea of a gavel came up based on a joke about the justice system while seriously considering a hammer of justice, but I really like the idea of him thinking with his fists.

The Test

Test is our totally radical, pouch-wearing, energy drink-guzzling, movie-quipping antihero based on '90s comic analogs. This guy just owned you while dying his hair on a livestream. He's part Zero Cool, aka Crash Override aka part real life FPS shooter complete with gun hands. Get real.

I adore this design, it's so simplistic and daft. I loved how the team was held together by a towering yellow hazmat suit, with this incredibly powerful glowing beauty hidden underneath this unremarkable PVC chrysalis

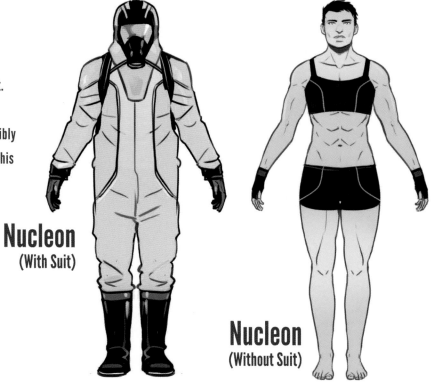

Nucleon
(With Suit)

Nucleon
(Without Suit)

Tabu

Kieron said, "Do you know Dream Daddy?" Caspar said "yes." The rest is history.

Cover Sketches

A

B

C

D

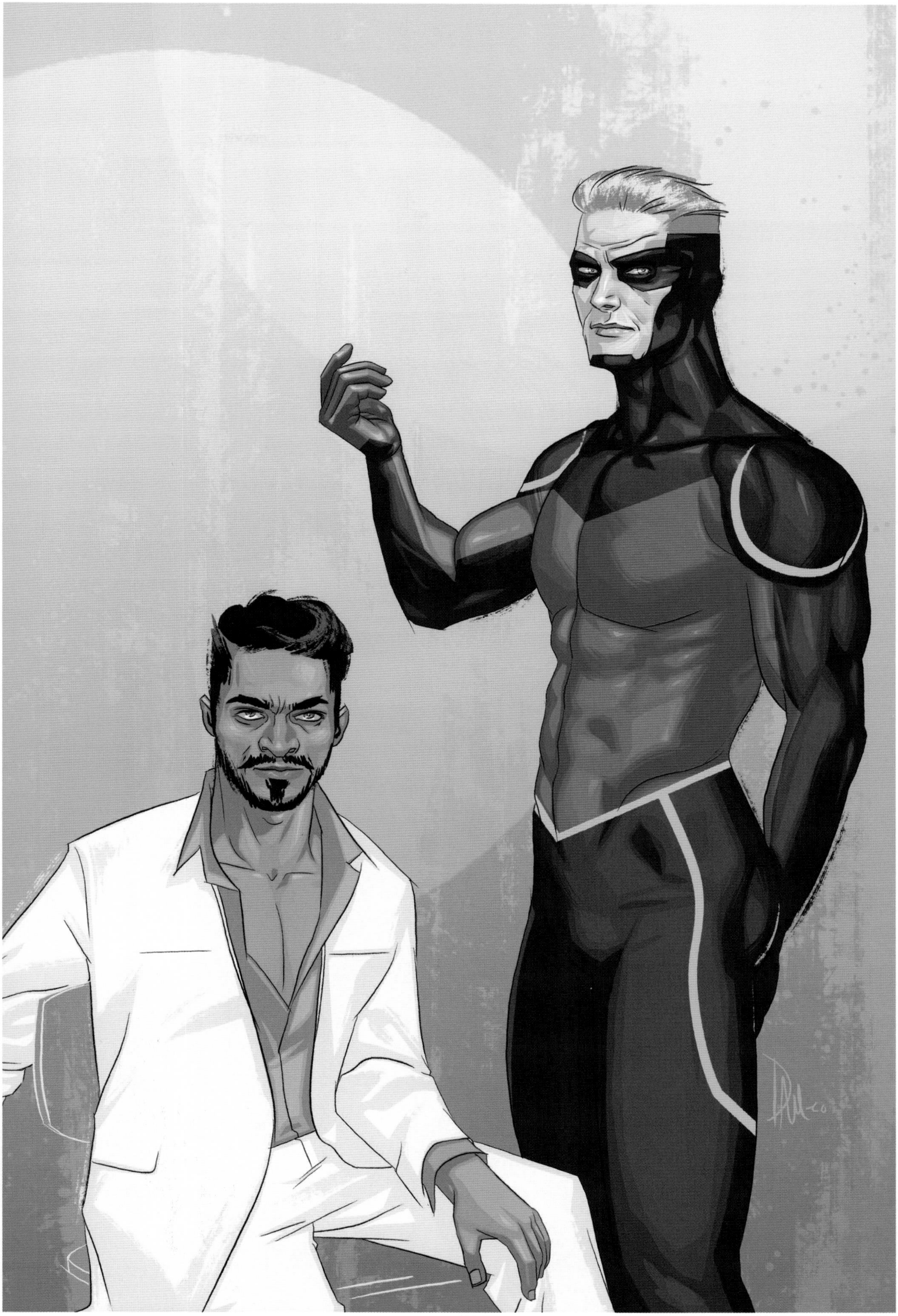

ISSUE ONE VARIANT COVER BY DAVE McCAIG

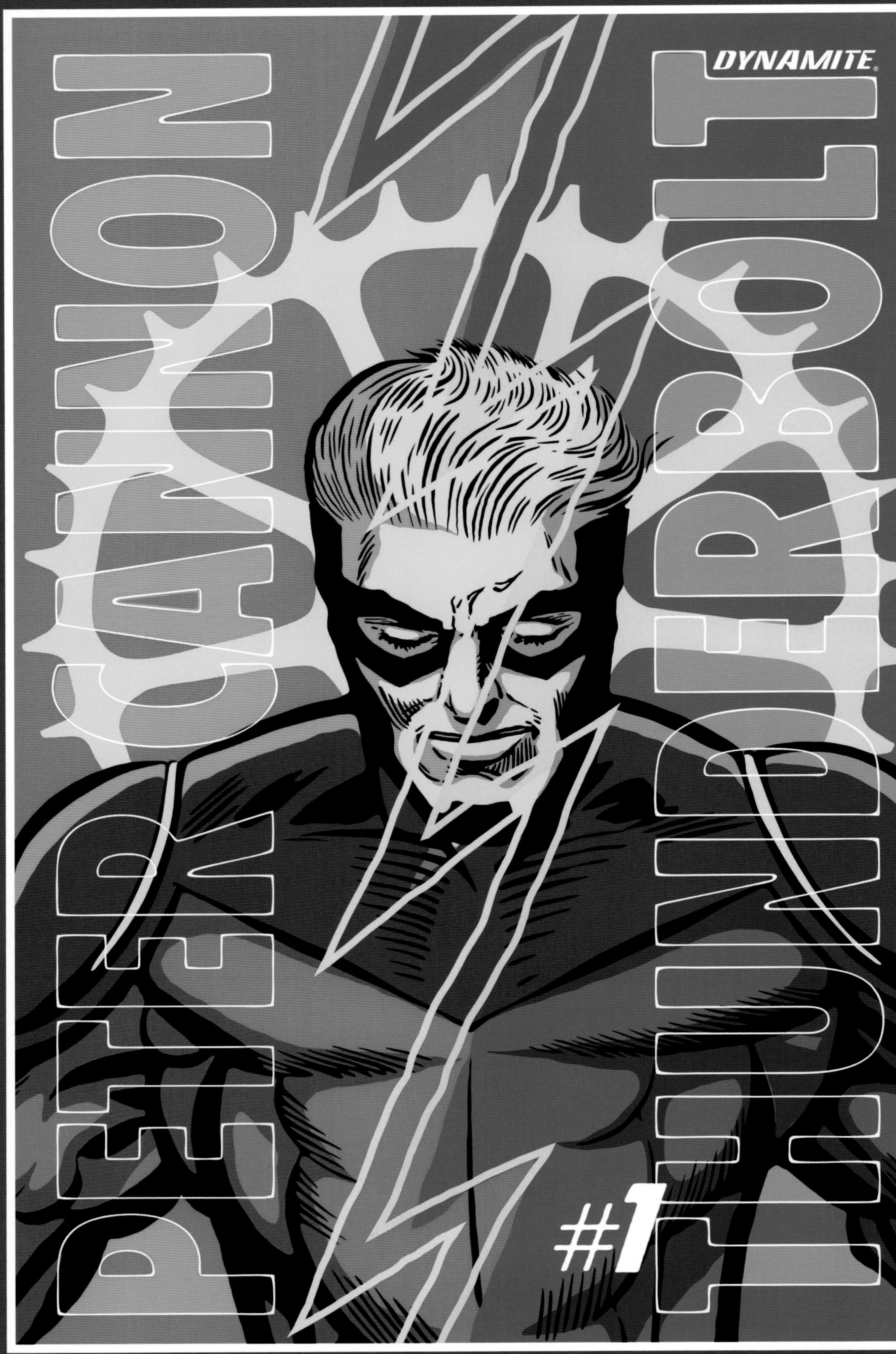
DYNAMITE
PETER CANNON
THUNDERBOLT
#1

ISSUE ONE VARIANT COVER BY BUTCHER BILLY

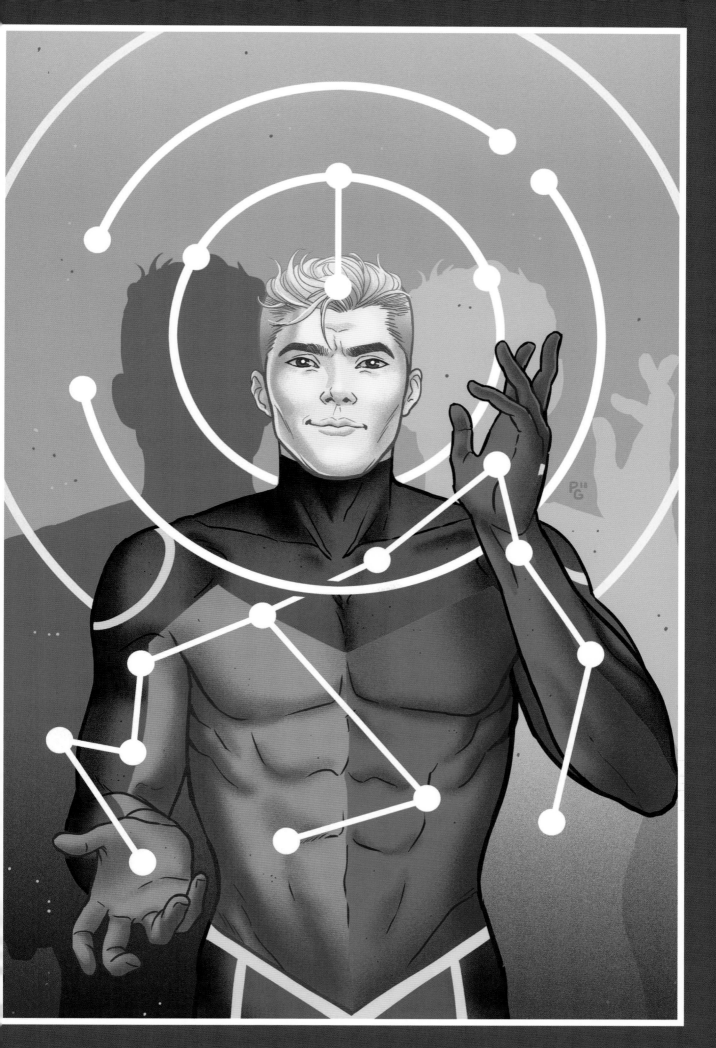

ISSUE ONE VARIANT COVER BY PAULINA GANUCHEAU

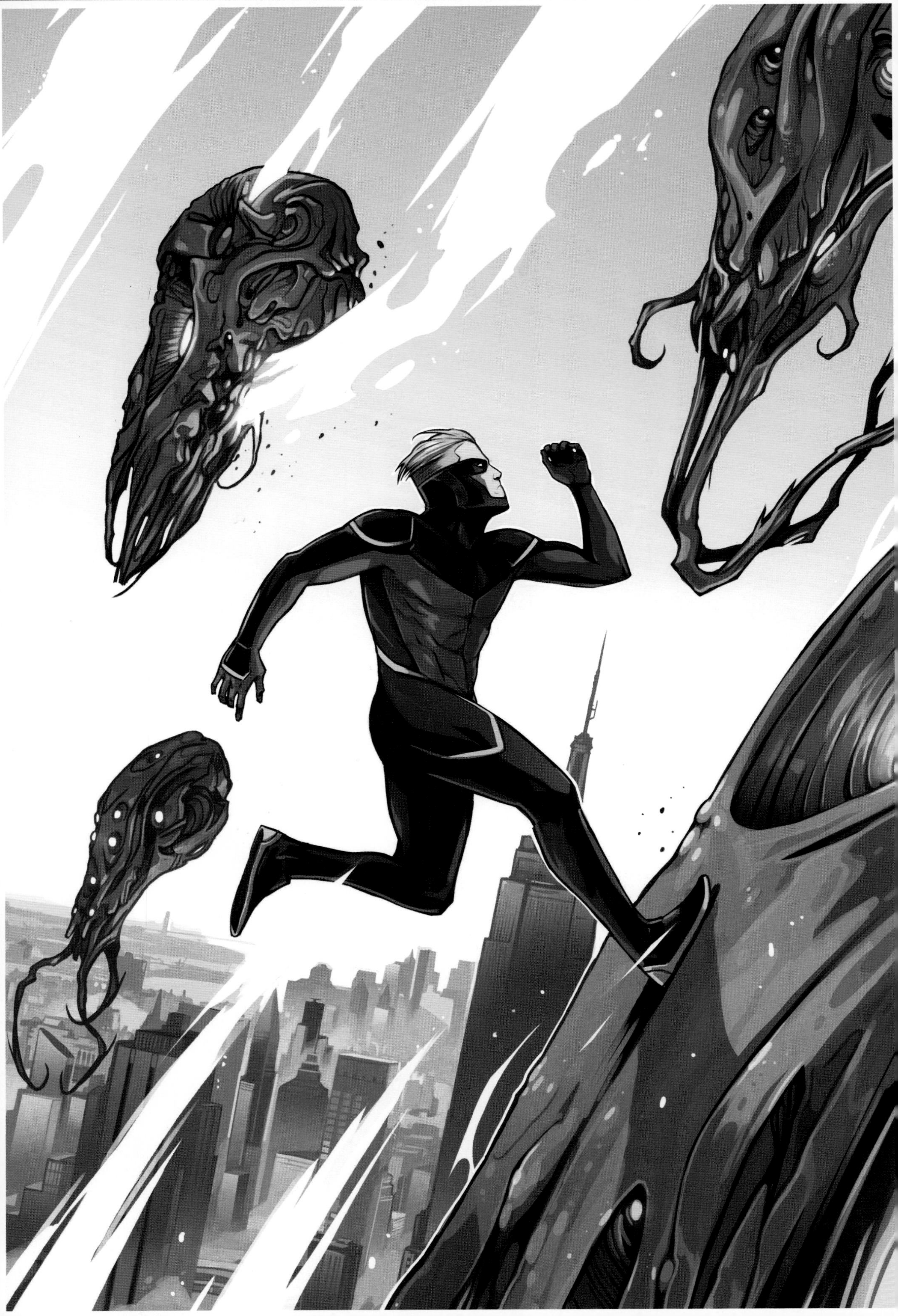

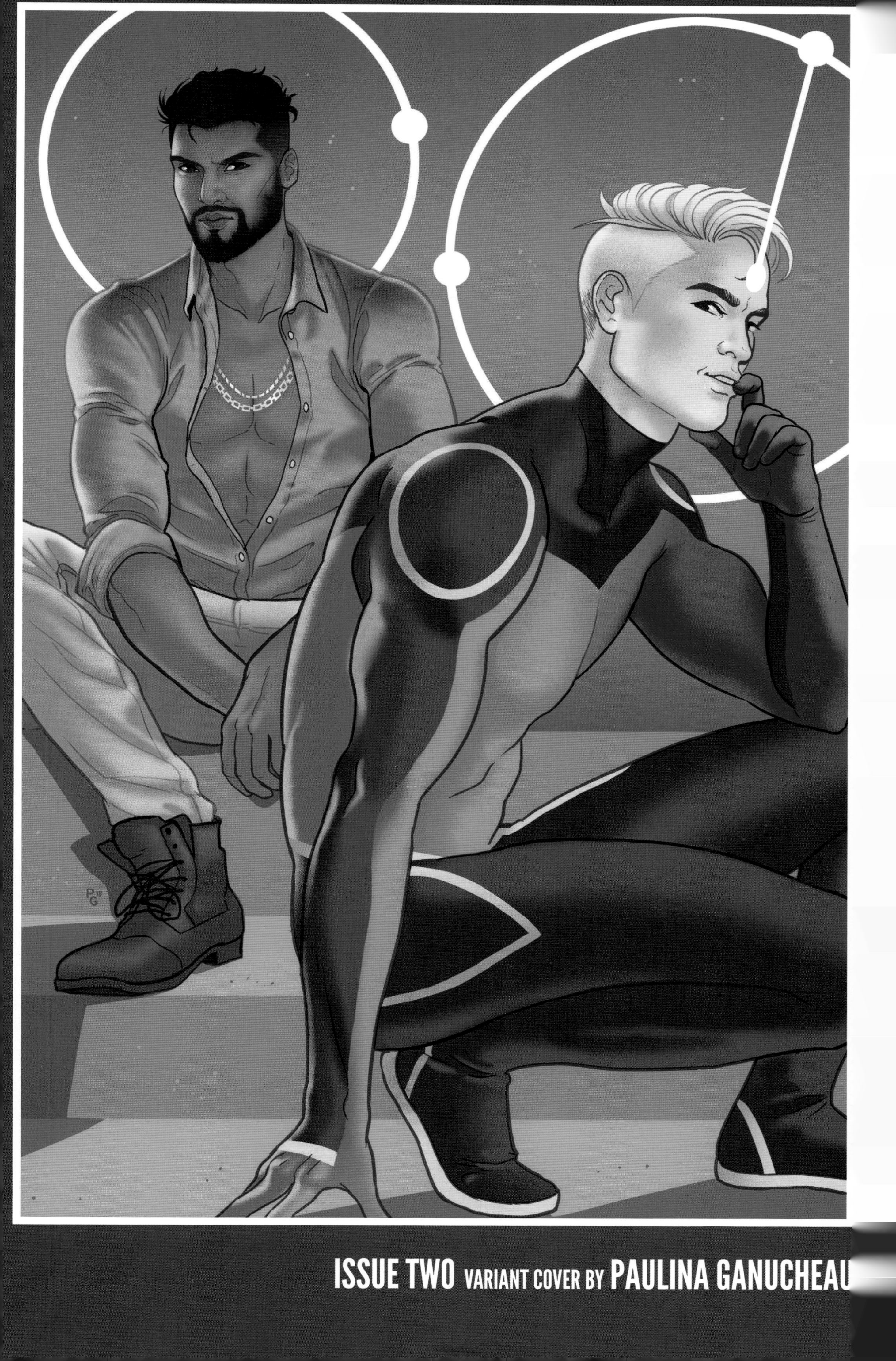
PG 18

ISSUE TWO VARIANT COVER BY PAULINA GANUCHEAU

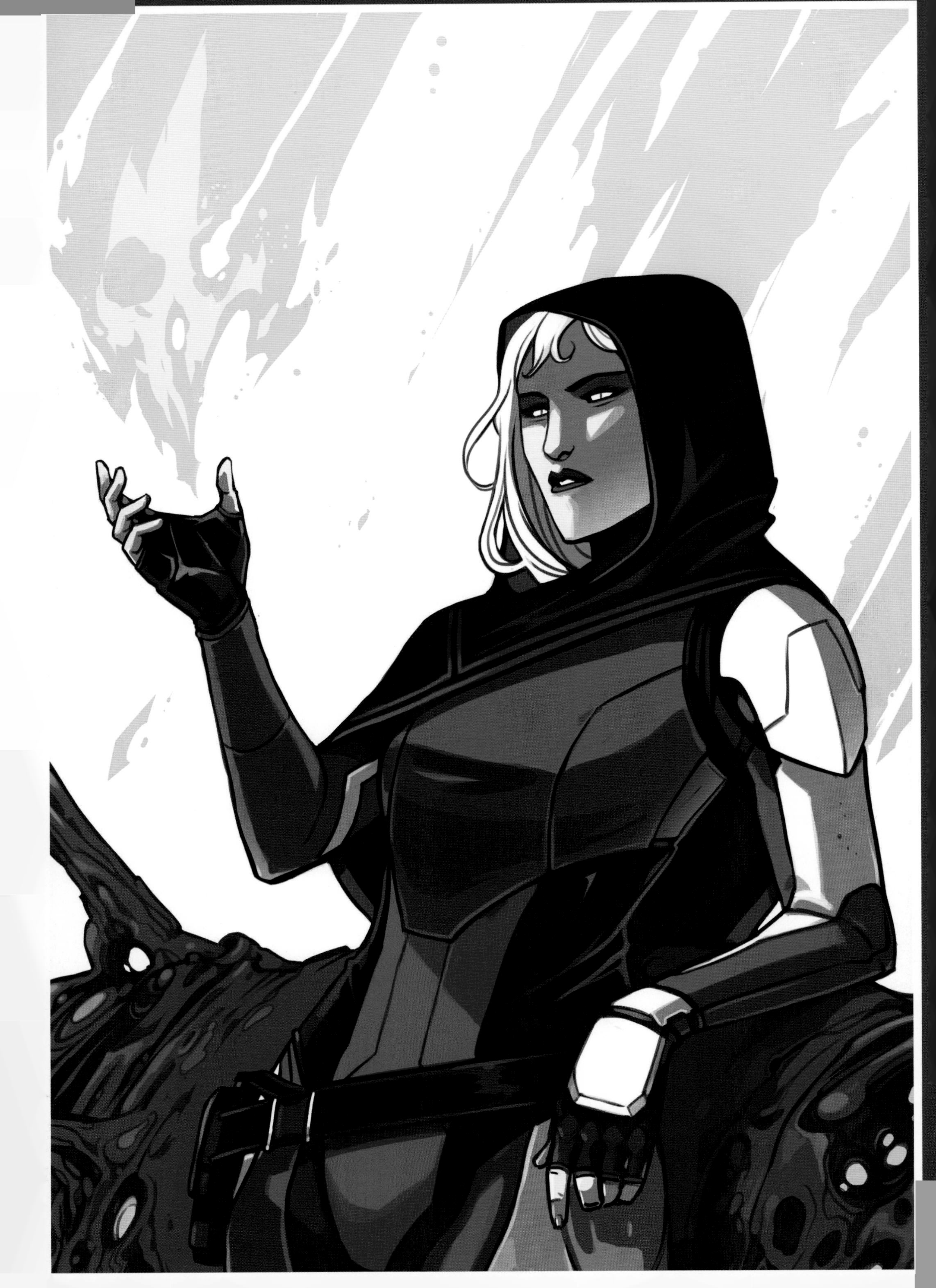

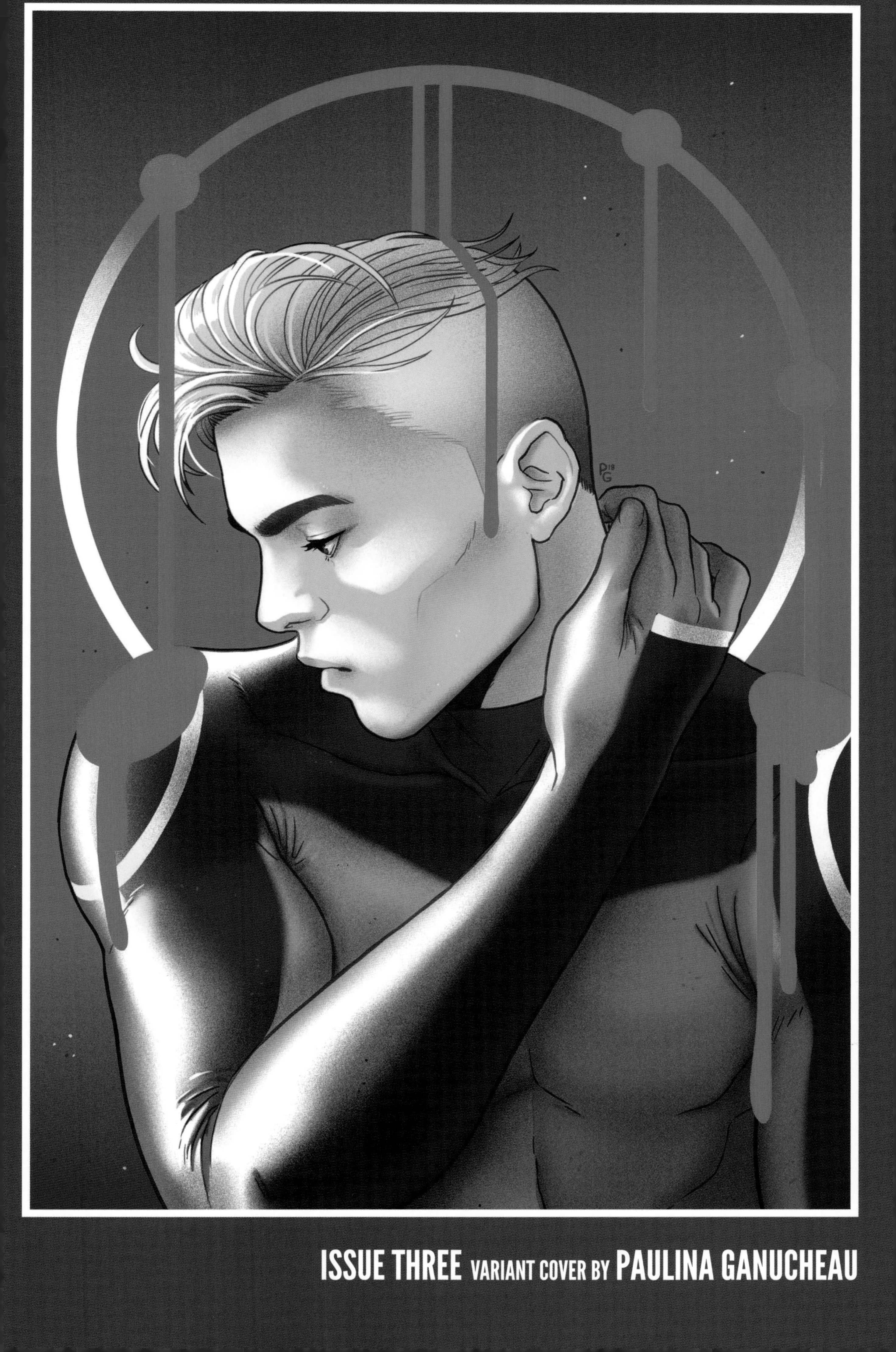

ISSUE THREE VARIANT COVER BY PAULINA GANUCHEAU

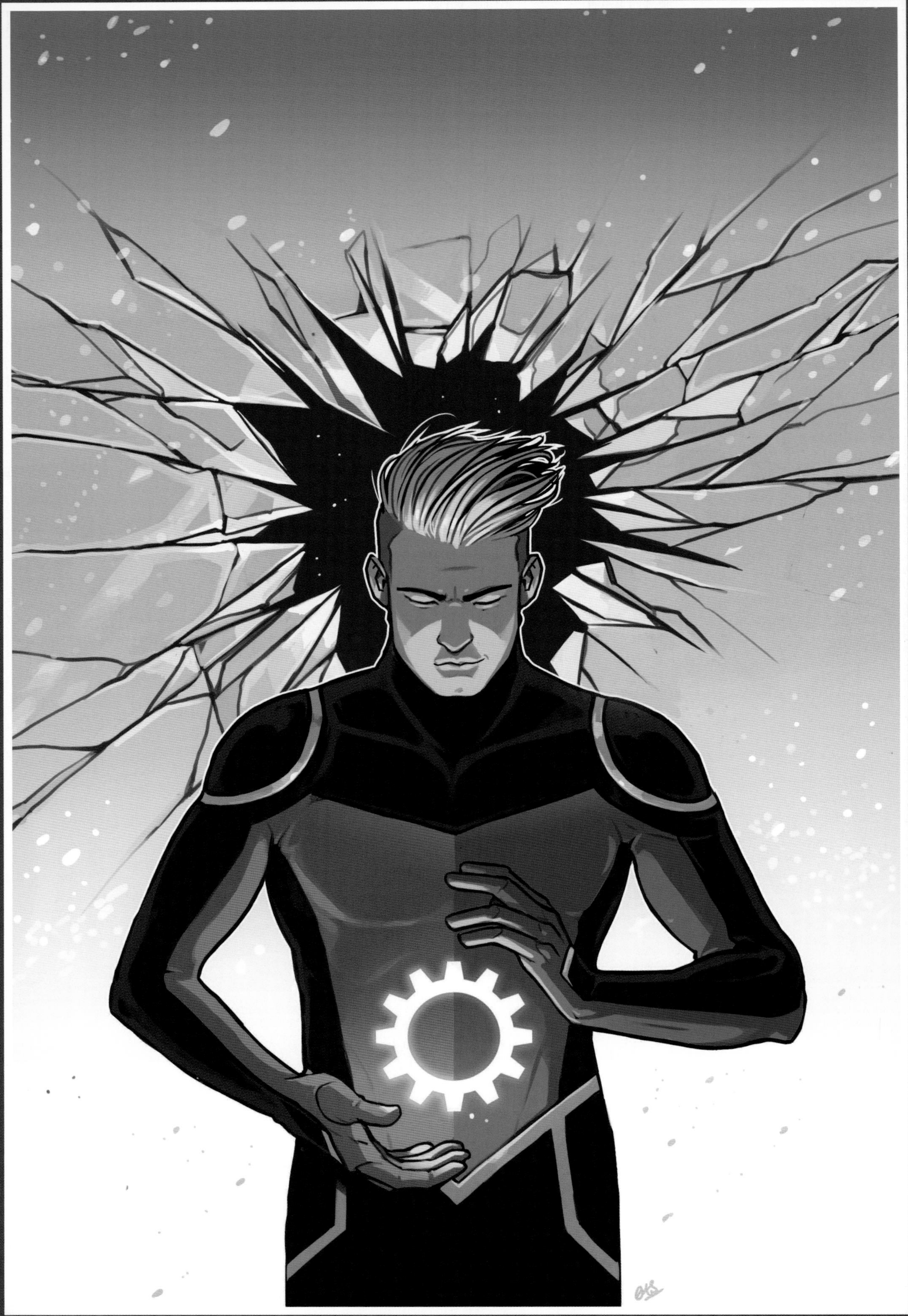

ISSUE THREE VARIANT COVER BY CASPAR WIJNGAARD

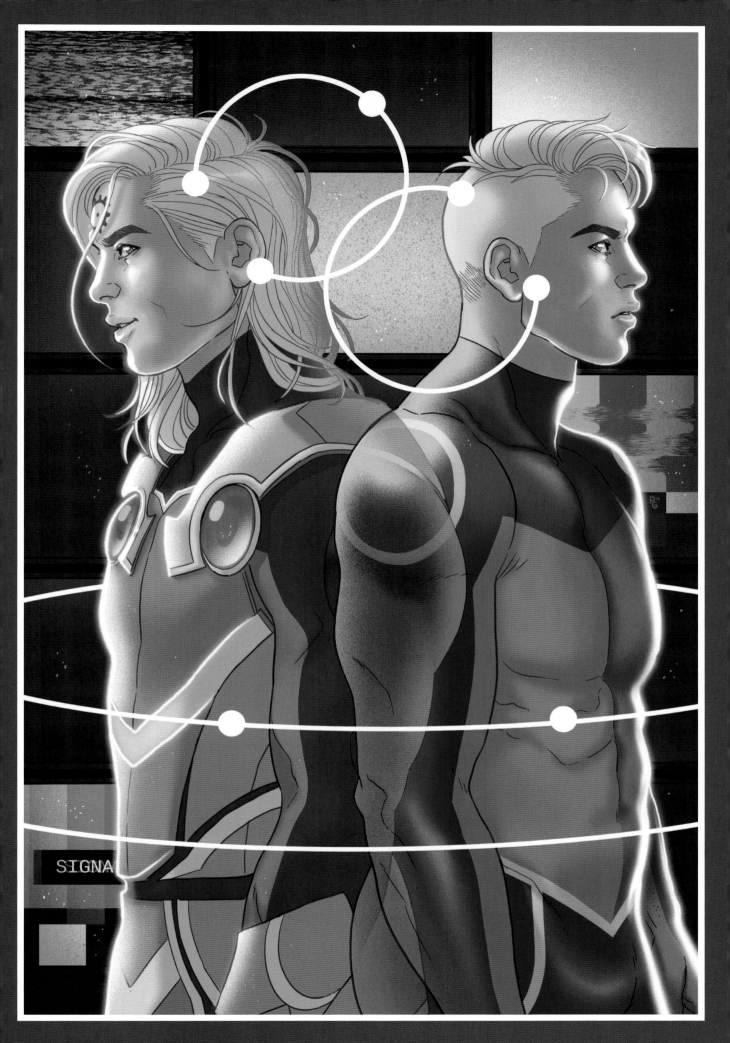

ISSUE FOUR VARIANT COVER BY PAULINA GANUCHEAU

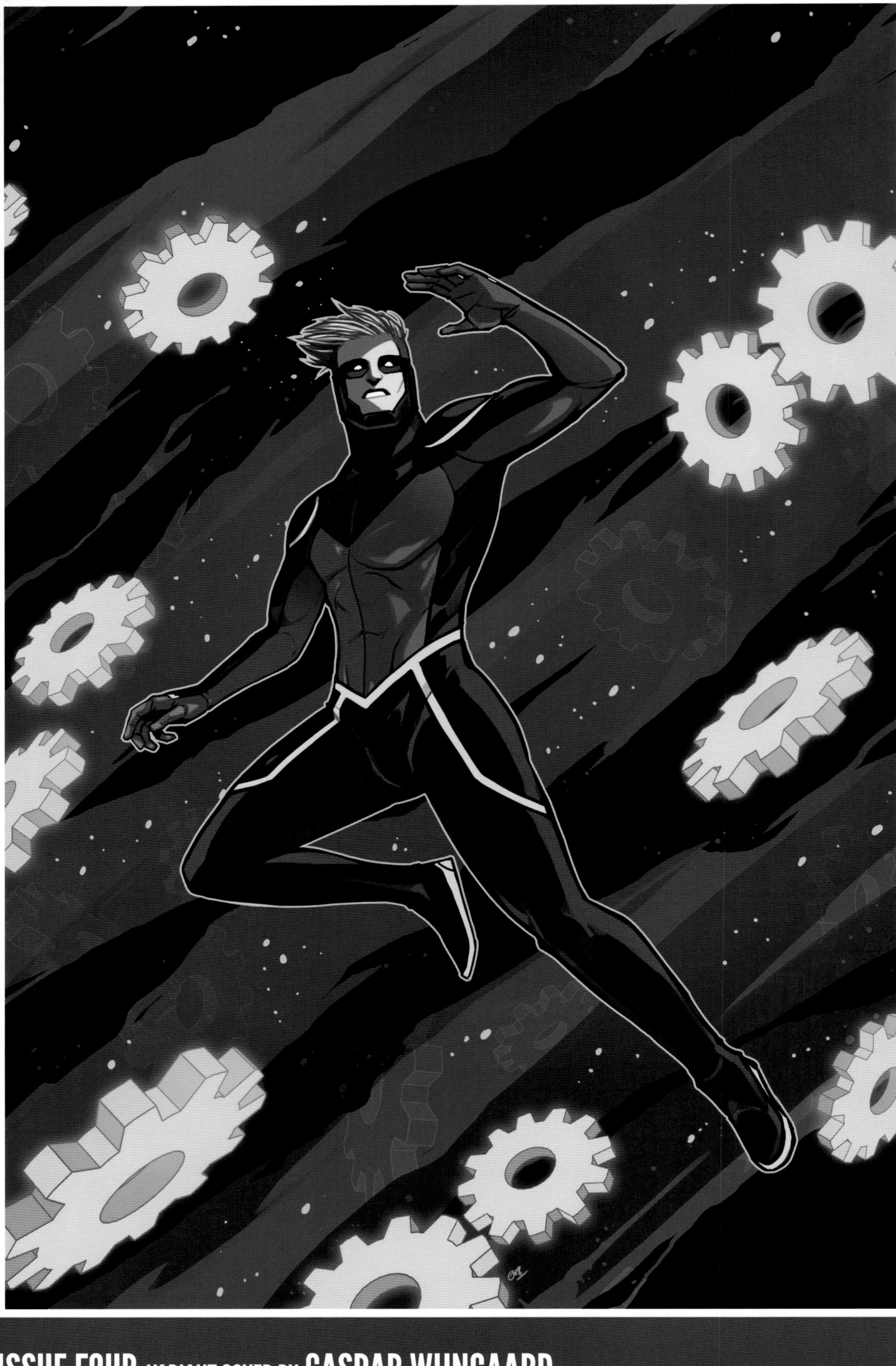

ISSUE FOUR VARIANT COVER BY CASPAR WIJNGAARD

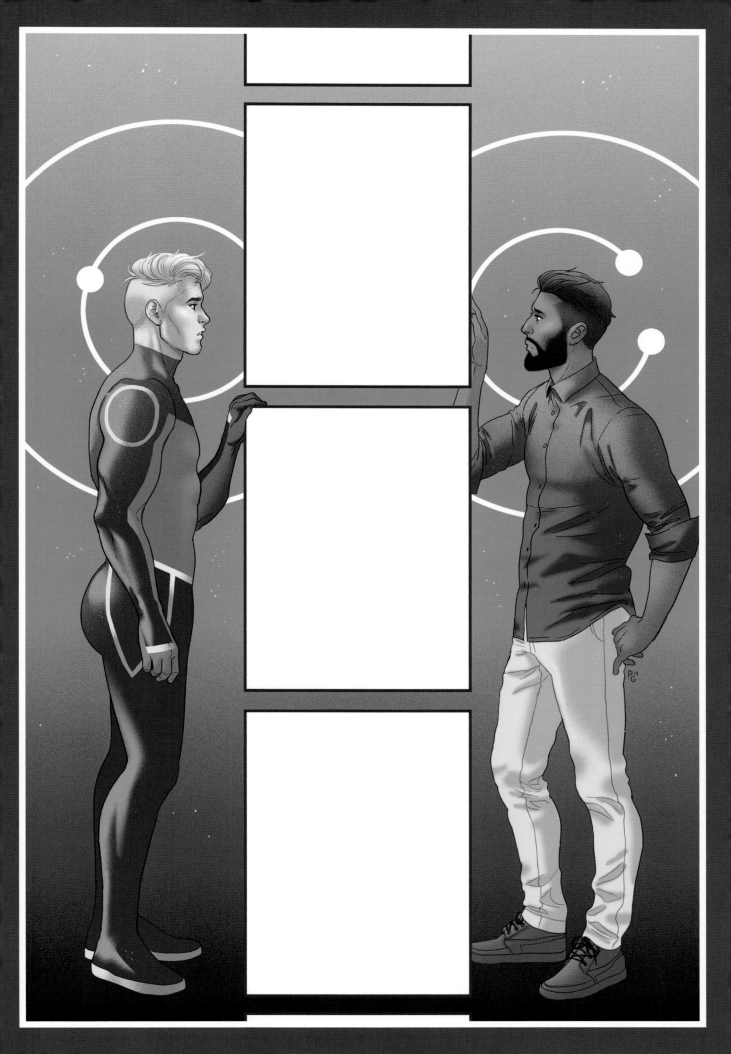

ISSUE FIVE VARIANT COVER BY PAULINA GANUCHEAU

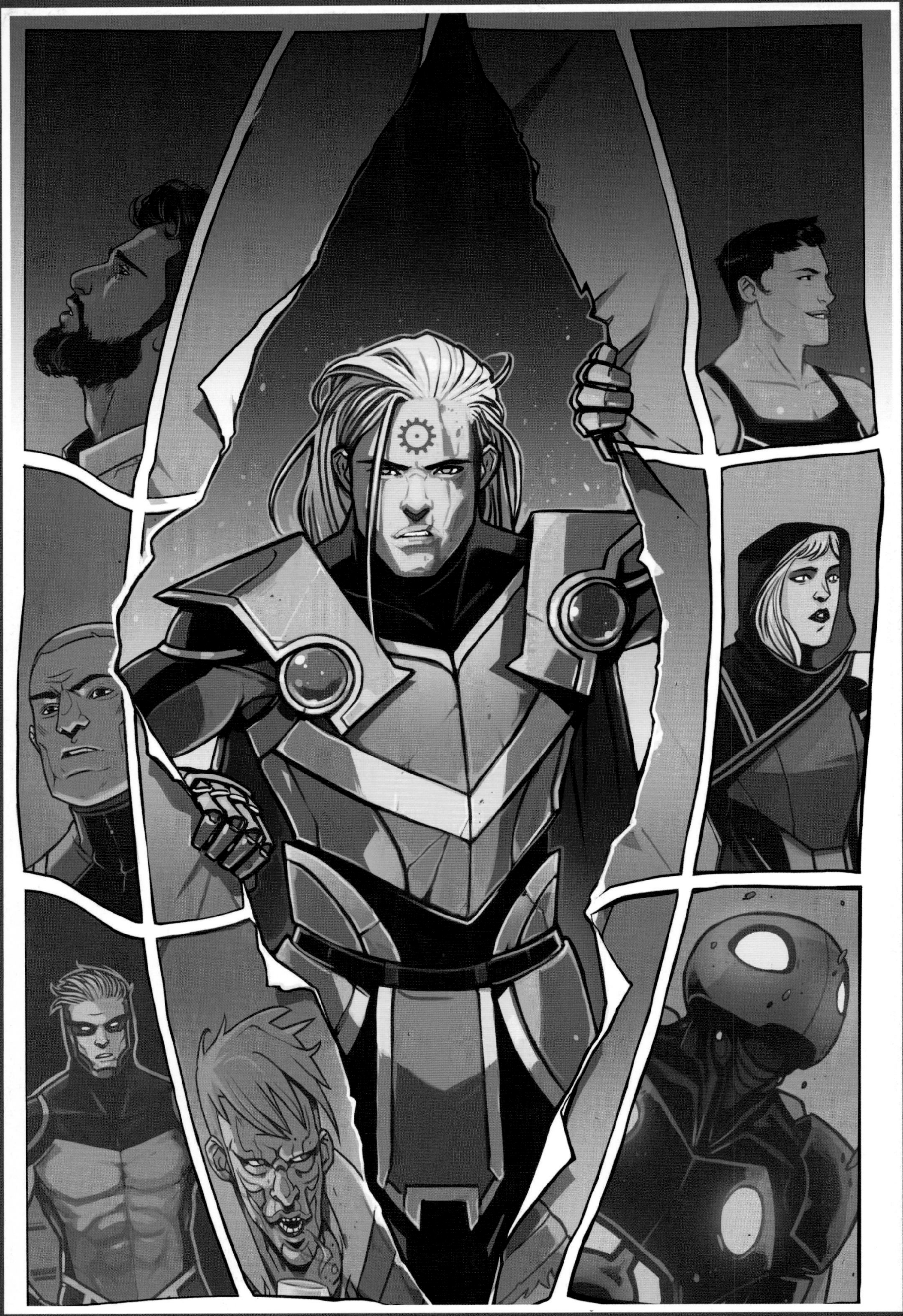

ISSUE FIVE VARIANT COVER BY CASPAR WIJNGAARD

CREATOR BIOS

Kieron Gillen is a writer, based in London. He is best known as the co-creator of books such as The Wicked + the Divine, DIE, Phonogram and Once & Future, and has written many books for Marvel comics. His favorite panel grid is the eight panel grid, but he's 9-panel-grid curious.

Caspar Wijngaard is a comic artist based in England. Co-creator of acclaimed Neon noir series LIMBO and the celebrated YA series Angelic. He's often found drawing Star Wars comics over at Marvel and foreverdreaming in an endless void of 9 panel grids.

Mary Safro is a Dublin-based comic artist from Latvia. She's mostly known for her cyberpunk series "Drugs & Wires". This book is both her debut and retirement as a colorist. You can blame the relentless 9-panel grids for that.

Hassan Otsmane-Elhaou has lettered comics like Red Sonja, Shanghai Red, and the one you've just read. He's also the editor behind Eisner Award-winning PanelxPanel magazine. Most of his time is spent deciding who'd win in a fight between a six-panel grid and a nine-panel grid.

PETER CANNON

THUNDERBOLT